People of the

NEW TESTAMENT

BOOK V

The Primary Holy Women,
Major Female Disciples and Relations
of Jesus, Minor Disciples & Others

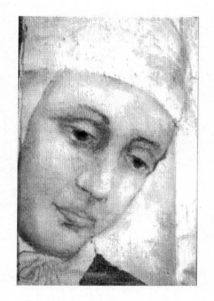

People of the
NEW TESTAMENT

BOOK V

The Primary Holy Women, Major Female Disciples and Relations of Jesus, Minor Disciples, & Others

From the Visions of
ANNE CATHERINE EMMERICH

Selected, Edited & Arranged
With Extensive New Translations from
the Original Notes of Clemens Brentano by
JAMES R. WETMORE

Volume 7 of 12
of the Series: *New Light on the*
Visions of Anne Catherine Emmerich

(With 21 Illustrations)

 Angelico Press

First published in the USA
by Angelico Press 2018
Revised Text, New Text, Translations,
and Layout © James R. Wetmore 2018

For information, address:
Angelico Press
169 Monitor St.
Brooklyn, NY 11222
angelicopress.com

ISBN 978-1-62138-373-4 (pbk)
ISBN 978-1-62138-374-1 (cloth)

Cover Image:
J. James Tissot (French, 1836–1902)
The Canaanite's Daughter (detail), Brooklyn Museum,
purchased by public subscription: 00.159.117
Reproduced by permission of the Brooklyn Museum
Cover Design: Michael Schrauzer

CONTENTS

Major Women Disciples and Relations of Jesus

Minor Women Disciples and Others

Women Mentioned During Jesus's Journey East

Preface

ANNE Catherine Emmerich was born on September 8, 1774, at Flamske, near Coesfeld, Germany. From early childhood she was blessed with the gift of spiritual sight and lived almost constantly in inner vision of scenes of the Old and New Testaments. As a child, her visions were mostly of pre-Christian events, but these grew less frequent with the passing years, and by the time she had become, at twenty-nine, an Augustinian nun at the Order's convent in Dülmen, Germany, her visions had become concerned primarily with the life of Jesus Christ, although they encompassed also the lives of many saints and other personages (some unknown as yet to history) as well as far-reaching insights into the creation, the fall, a mysterious mountain of the prophets, the spiritual hierarchies, paradise and purgatory, the heavenly Jerusalem, and much besides.

In the context of Anne Catherine's visions, and related conversations, much was said also of spiritual labors, described symbolically as work in the "nuptial house," the "inner chamber," the "garden," and the "vineyard." In this way many teachings on the inner life and prayer came forward, along with detailed accounts of healing work and journeys for "poor souls" in purgatory or in past epochs. Anne Catherine also showed considerable concern for the souls of those around her, especially her later amanuensis Clemens Brentano, in connection with his initial lack of faith.

Owing to difficult political circumstances, Anne Catherine's convent was disbanded on December 3, 1811, and one by one the nuns in residence were obliged to leave. Anne Catherine—already very ill—withdrew to a small room in a house in Dülmen. By November, 1812, her illness had grown so severe that she was permanently confined to bed. Shortly thereafter, on December 29, 1812, she received the stigmata, a manifesting of the wounds suffered by Christ on the cross, and the highest outward sign of inner union with him. Unable to assimilate any form of nourishment, for the rest of her life she was sustained almost exclusively by water and the eucharist.

As news spread that she bore the stigmata (which bled on Fridays), more and more people came to see her. For us, the most significant of these was Clemens Brentano, who first visited her on Thursday morning, September 24, 1818. He was so impressed by the radiance of her being that he decided to relocate nearby in order to record her visions. Anne Catherine had already had a presentiment that someone—whom she called "the pilgrim"— would one day come to preserve her revelations. The moment Clemens Brentano entered her room, she recognized him as this pilgrim.

Brentano, a novelist and Romantic poet then living in Berlin, was associated with leading members of the Romantic Movement in Germany. He settled his affairs and moved from Berlin to Dülmen early in 1819. Thereafter he visited Anne Catherine every morning, noting down briefly all she related to him. After writing out a full report at home, he returned later the same day to read it back to her. She would then often expand upon certain points, or, if necessary, correct details.

On July 29, 1820, Anne Catherine began to communicate visions concerning the day-by-day life of Jesus. These visions encompassed the better part of his ministry, and she was able to describe in extraordinary detail the places he visited, his miracles and healings, his teaching activity in the synagogues and elsewhere, and the people around him. She not only named and described many of these people with astonishing concreteness, but spoke also of their families, their occupations, and other intimate biographical details.

It seems clear that Anne Catherine was called to relate these day-by-day details of the life and ministry of Jesus, and that Clemens Brentano was called to record all she communicated of her visions. They worked together daily until her death on February 9, 1824, except for one period of six months, during which Brentano was away, and several shorter periods when, mainly due to illness, it was impossible for Anne Catherine to communicate her visions.

ENCOUNTERING the visions of Anne Catherine Emmerich can raise the question: how is it possible that this woman, who never left the German region in which she was born and had very little education, could describe in such detail not only the story of creation; heaven, hell, and purgatory; the fall of angels and humanity; the spiritual hierarchies and saints; the Promise and the Ark of the Covenant; the apocalypse; spiritual warfare; and the heavenly Jerusalem—but *also* the geography and topography of Palestine and the customs and habits of people living there at the time of Jesus Christ? To at least partially answer this, the researcher upon whose work the *chronological* aspects of this new edition is largely based, Dr. Robert Powell, undertook an exhaustive analysis of her work, gradually laying bare the historical reality underlying the life of Jesus (see "Chronology" below). But his work was not done in isolation, for others had earlier laid some groundwork.

For example the French priest Abbé Julien Gouyet of Paris, after reading an account of Anne Catherine's visions concerning the death of the Virgin Mary near Ephesus, traveled there and searched the region. On October 18, 1881, guided by various particulars in her account, he discovered the ruins of a small stone building on a mountain (Bulbul Dag, "Mount Nightingale") overlooking the Aegean Sea with a view across to the remains of the ancient city of Ephesus. Abbé Gouyet was convinced that this was the house described in Anne Catherine's visions as the dwelling of the Virgin Mary during the last years of her life. He was at first ridiculed, but several years later the ruins were independently rediscovered by two Lazarist missionaries who had undertaken a similar search on the basis of Anne Catherine's visions. They determined that the building had been a place of pilgrimage in earlier times for Christians descended from the church of Ephesus, the community referred to by St. John (Rev. 2:1–7). The building had been known in those days as Panaya Kapulu, the house of the Blessed Virgin, and was revered as the place where she had died. Traditionally, the date of her death, August 15, was the *very day* of the annual pilgrimage to Panaya Kapulu.

That Anne Catherine's visions provide spiritual nourishment had long been the experience of many spiritual seekers, but the discovery of Panaya Kapulu confirmed that her visions could also (at least in part) be corroborated along conventional lines of research.

Sources

THE visions of Anne Catherine Emmerich have been published in English translation in various editions since late in the nineteenth century. These editions focused primarily on the visions of the life of Jesus Christ and of Mary, with some material drawn from Old Testament times also. However the *original* notes of Clemens Brentano contained material on many other fascinating subjects. Much of this material has not been readily available before now, either in German or in English translation, a gap that this twelve-volume *New Light on the Visions Anne Catherine Emmerich* series is meant at least to begin filling.

Until now the only translations available of some of this latter material appeared in the two-volume biography of Anne Catherine by Rev. Carl E. Schmöger, first published in English in 1885. Rev. Schmöger, who was also instrumental in the selection and arrangement of the visions related to the life of Jesus Christ upon which later English translations were based, included in the biography a selection of the supplemental material mentioned above —but his selection was necessarily limited.

Clemens Brentano himself was only able to compile from his notes a few volumes for publication, and upon his death the notes passed to his brother Christian, who had been an interested participant in Clemens's work with Anne Catherine from the start (in fact, Christian had arranged his brother's first meeting with the visionary). Christian, however, proved unable to coordinate the notes any further. And so the first phase of this seemingly insurmountable task fell in due course to Rev. Schmöger.

Then, in the last decades of the twentieth century, the German publisher Kohlhammer commenced publishing, under the auspices of the *Frankfurter Brentano Ausgabe*, an intended complete edition of Brentano's works, projected to number as many as sixty volumes. Part of this project was the publication of facsimiles of the thirty-eight notebooks of Brentano's notes of the visions of Anne Catherine. (Brentano also noted down details of their conversations in other contexts, as well as his own experiences while attending her.) With the Kohlhammer edition, a wider public would finally gain access to the originals upon which later compilations and translations of the visions had been based. However, this noble project has not been completed, and at present there is no indication whether it will recommence. An additional impediment for researchers in dealing with the facsimiles is the fact that Brentano's notes were penned in a now archaic German script that only specialists can read.

Thus matters stood until Jozef De Raedemaeker, a dedicated Belgian researcher, undertook the enormous task of transcribing the full body of notes from the archaic script into modern German—making it available in printed and digital form in 2009. The combined 38 notebooks exceed 7,300 pages and include many hand-drawn illustrations as well as typographic conventions to identify the contributions of others present at Anne Catherine's bedside, who sometimes took notes or added comments, and sometimes drawings.

ANYONE who does even minimal research on the visions of Anne Catherine Emmerich as depicted in the works attributed to Brentano's notes will soon discover that there are conflicting opinions regarding their fidelity to the words of Anne Catherine herself. This would be a subject in itself, but some remarks may be offered here. First, Anne Catherine, who had little formal education, spoke in a Low-German dialect that even Brentano, at the outset, had some difficulty understanding. Secondly, the material that was eventually fit together into a connected account in the published versions often represents a collation of as many as a dozen or more passages gleaned from visions separated sometimes by months, or even years. This can be partially explained by the fact that the visions were often related to events in the ecclesiastical year, to feasts of saints, to individuals with specific needs or requests, or to the presence of relics.

And so a great deal of work had to be done to organize and knit together related segments of visions, and to then arrange them in a meaningful sequence. Then again, it was deemed necessary to refine the language sufficiently to render it in a more contemporary idiom. There is, then, a legitimate concern that so famous and gifted a literary figure as Clemens Brentano might, even if unintentionally, have introduced some of his own impressions, interpretations, and sensitivities into his renditions. And a similar concern could be raised concerning Rev. Schmöger's subsequent arrangements, as well as those of later editors and translators working at yet a further remove.

Much of the debate on this subject, however, took place without ready access to the original notes, a defect that has now been remedied. At certain points in his transcriptions De Raedemaeker addresses this issue by comparing fragments of the original notes with versions of these same fragments as they appear in Rev. Schmöger's edition, after he in turn had worked, in some instances, with Brentano's own compilations from his original notes—and in some cases there are non-trivial discrepancies. This is an area that requires further research.

Perhaps I myself may be permitted to chime in here, as there are not many who have entered into this vast field, and I can at least appeal to many years of engagement with the visions of Anne Catherine, *including* examining De Raedemaeker's transcriptions of all thirty-eight notebooks. While thus occupied, I inevitably began to identify for myself many of the original sources upon which Rev. Schmöger based his versions well over a century ago, and in such cases could assess the fidelity of the latter to the former. Although such details do not lie within the scope of this series, I can say that, with very rare exceptions—especially allowing for the frequent need to splice together disparate fragments—Rev. Schmöger's renderings remain remarkably true to the original, and any minimal divergences are for the most part quite trivial, insofar as I have been able to investigate.

During this process, however, I *was* struck by the fact that considerable material had been *omitted*. This may well have been owing to the enormity of the task, as also to pagination limits set by the publisher; or also, partly a measure of Rev. Schmöger's personal judgment and concerns. Perhaps some of the excluded material seemed unintelligible to him, or even scandalous. However that may be, in this current series as much as possible of this neglected material has been extracted, translated, and incorporated in the relevant volumes.

It needs to be said also, in response to assertions (made mostly without benefit of access to his actual notes) that Brentano misrepresented Anne Catherine, or, even worse, took advantage of his notes to compile an independent literary work that might embellish his reputation, that in fact, in his notes, Brentano *candidly* reports *exactly* what he heard Anne Catherine say, *no matter* how extraordinary, puzzling, or even apparently contradictory. He himself offers many instances where only later—sometimes years after Anne Catherine had died—he (often with the help of academic experts) finally began to understand previously incomprehensible passages in the visions. He steadfastly refused—according to his own account and that of others—to edit out "difficulties," feeling himself, rather, under a sacred obligation to preserve his record intact and unaltered for posterity. And when the notes passed to his brother Christian, the latter adhered to the same policy.

Even without the benefit of access to the original notes on the part of most researchers, and even in face of an undercurrent of scepticism as to the authenticity of the visions, it may be worthwhile, in drawing this matter to a close for our present purposes, to note that on October 3, 2004, Anne Catherine was beatified by Pope John Paul II, who remarked: "Her example opened the hearts of poor and rich alike, of simple and cultured persons, whom she instructed in loving dedication to Jesus Christ." And in the Vatican's biography of Anne Catherine we read: "Her words, which have reached innumerable people in many languages from her modest room in Dülmen through the writings of Clemens Brentano are an outstanding proclamation of the gospel in service to salvation right up to the present day."

Chronology

PERHAPS the most surprising feature of this new series on Anne Catherine Emmerich will be the inclusion of *historical dates*—and so a brief discussion of this feature is offered below.

As described earlier, Anne Catherine was so attuned to the life of Jesus Christ as a mystical-historical reality that her comprehensive visions encompassed even minute details of time and place—testable "coordinates" in fact. This degree of precision was made possible by the many temporal as well as geographical descriptions and references contained in the visions—as mentioned earlier in connection with the discovery of the house of the Blessed Virgin.

Many chronologies of the life of Jesus Christ have been put forward over the centuries, but the dates offered in this current series differ from previous efforts in that they derive from the application of modern chronological and astro-chronological science to the whole of Anne Catherine's visions—which latter constitute a vast body of data internally consistent as to time and place to an extraordinary degree, so that, taking the generally agreed upon time period of Jesus's life, results of a high degree of reliability can be determined.

Naturally, the overriding value of the visions lies in the additional insight they offer into the life of Jesus Christ, so that for some the dating may represent no more than a convenient framework for study and meditation. Such readers need not trouble themselves about the specific dates, although they may nonetheless find that the chronology offers a useful way to maintain their orientation within any given volume, as also when referring to events in volumes already read. Some, however, will wish to assess for themselves the method by which specific dates have been thought reliable enough to include here. They may read elsewhere[1] the story of the determination of the chronology of the life of Jesus Christ included in these volumes.

---

[1] *The Visions of Anne Catherine Emmerich*, Book III, Appendix I (Kettering, OH: Angelico Press, 2015), which is based on the work of Dr. Robert Powell.

The New Light on the Visions
of Anne Catherine Emmerich *Series*

THE present book is one of the twelve volumes of the "New Light on the Visions of Anne Catherine Emmerich" series published by Angelico Press. This series supplements two earlier Angelico publications: *The Visions of Anne Catherine Emmerich*, Books I–III (1,700 pages in large format, with 600 illustrations and forty-three maps); and the smaller-format, slightly abridged edition: *Life, Passion, Death, & Resurrection of Jesus Christ (A Chronicle from the Visions of Anne Catherine Emmerich)*, Books I–IV (1,770 pages with 150 illustrations and 43 maps). As described earlier, in 2009 Clemens Brentano's original notes of Anne Catherine's visions became readily available for reference. At that time the above texts were already nearing completion. With the appearance of these notes, however, the editor resolved to pause, and, to the extent possible, research this vast body of notes to ascertain what further light they might shed on what had by then been prepared for publication. While the better part of another decade was devoted to the task, much research, of course, remains to be done (see "Future Prospects" below). But at some point one must call a halt, and so, after the insertion of relevant new translations into the two sets mentioned above and their publication in 2015–2016, the present series was conceived as a means to present in various contexts such new material as has since then been selected and translated from the notes.

In general, the content of each volume of this series consists (1) of material selected by individual or theme from earlier translations—reviewed, supplemented, and revised where necessary, especially for consistency of usage; and (2) of newly selected and translated material germane to the content of that volume. With regard to both individuals and themes, the procedure was to extract every reference thus far located in the notes and in prior translations and weave them together into a connected account. The reader can thus find in one place almost all of what Anne Catherine had to say about any given individual or theme.

Virtually every individual in the biblical visions (approximately 250 in total) is referenced in the five *People of the New Testament* volumes (which include also some figures from earlier and later times). A separate volume, *The Life of the Virgin Mary*, is dedicated to Mary and her ancestry (including much on the Essenes); and another volume, *Scenes from the Lives of the Saints*, treats of fifty-nine saints. Separate volumes cover events prior to the appearance of the holy family: *First Beginnings* and *Mysteries of the Old Testament*. Two further volumes cover a multitude of separate themes: *Inner Life and Worlds of Soul & Spirit* and *Spiritual Works and Journeys*. A final volume represents a condensed, edited, rearranged, supplemented, and retypeset edition of Rev. Carl E. Schmöger's exhaustive biography of Anne Catherine, first published in English in 1885. For clarity of organization, much of this biography in its original form has been redistributed among other volumes of this series. What remains has also been enriched with newly-translated material. A list of all twelve volumes of this series appears at the conclusion of this preface.

Practical Considerations

IN view of the sometimes extensive wealth of material presented concerning certain individuals—especially major characters—a judicious essentializing of scenes has sometimes been resorted to. In some cases, especially those of closely related apostles and disciples (or others regularly treated together in the visions), rather than duplicating material, the expedient adopted was to disentangle scenes to the extent possible, so that the full story could be garnered gradually by reading the separate accounts of each. Nonetheless, since readers may jump around in their selection of individuals to study, some repetition was unavoidable in order to provide enough context to keep the separate accounts reasonably sequential and unified. Put another way, these volumes are conceived primarily as reference works to which one turns for particulars on specific persons or themes rather than as connected narratives to be read cover to cover. Of course, the volumes may be read in the latter fashion also, in which case the occasional repeated material will be more noticeable.

Another consideration was that some individuals play so great a role in the visions (e.g., John the Baptist, St. Joseph, Peter, Matthew, Judas, and the Virgin Mary) that it would be impractical to include every mention in a chronological itinerary. Emphasis in such cases has been placed primarily on more general and newly-translated material. Inquisitive readers can of course turn to the index of the large-format, three-volume *The Visions of Anne Catherine Emmerich* to expand their research on such individuals.

It must be well understood that all the editor could do was work with what Anne Catherine actually said. Some little-known (or even totally unknown) individuals may enjoy longer accounts in these volumes than other, very well known, figures from the gospels or later Christian tradition! There can be no question of assigning relative importance to any individual based solely upon how extensive Anne Catherine's visions of that person may have been. Likewise, stories may have gaps, or sometimes end abruptly. It is indeed unfortunate that (as Brentano repeatedly laments in his notes) so much was lost owing to Anne Catherine's considerable suffering, household distractions, and the many obligations laid upon her—all of which interfered with her visions and her capacity to recall them. And yet withal, how much we have to be grateful for!

To streamline as far as possible a complex text, these usages were established: The voice of the narrator (Rev. Schmöger) is put in italics. Direct citations from Brentano (and a few others) are put in quotes. Anne Catherine's text bears no quotation indicators *except* where references to her words are embedded in the two contexts just mentioned. Parentheses enclose supplemental material from Anne Catherine or Brentano; brackets enclose material from Rev. Schmöger or the present editor. Footnotes from the hand of Brentano are followed by CB; those consisting of further visionary content from Anne Catherine are—for clarity in this context—enclosed in quotation marks; all other unattributed footnotes have been supplied by the present editor, sometimes incorporating what seemed worth retaining from notes by others in earlier editions.[1]

---

[1] The most useful material of this sort has been integrated from notes to a version of *The Life of the Virgin Mary* provided by Rev. Sebastian Bullough, O.P., to whom we express our gratitude.

For convenience, especially in itineraries of individuals, dates are incorporated in what is otherwise purely Anne Catherine's visionary text. It must, however, be well understood that these dates are derivative, as mentioned in "Chronology" above, *not* from the hand of Anne Catherine. As another help, for many major figures, summaries are provided at the outset. These are often in the third person—as they represent a condensation by the editor—but are nonetheless derived directly from the visions.

In such a context as these visions represent, capitalization (a topic upon which there are many and various usages, and often passionate opinions) represented a particular challenge. In the end, after experimenting with progressively increasing degrees of simplification, it was determined—in order not to overly fatigue the reader of what essentially amounts to an extended narrative rather than devotional reading properly speaking—to implement a very spare policy indeed, reserving capitalization to the Deity, and to certain terms that in Anne Catherine's visions assume a unique significance, such as the Ark of the Covenant, and what she calls the Promise, or sometimes the Holy Thing, the Mystery or Sacrament (in this special sense), or even the Germ or Seed. Finally, in cases where more general considerations are followed by chronological extracts forming a connected itinerary, the break is signaled by a row of five typographic crosses.

Prospects for the Future

AS editor of this series I am only too aware of my limitations in the face of the awe-inspiring magnitude of the task. My initial inspiration was solely the *spiritual value* of Anne Catherine's visions as a means to help seekers find their way *back* to a faithful connection with Jesus Christ; or, in the case of so many in our time, find their way *for the first time* to a dawning awareness of what they may thus far have failed to see. Further, there are great, resonant depths in the visions, like choirs of symbolism. As time went on I could only go deeper, entering upon the work that has led now, finally, to completing this series. Along with spiritual benefits and guidance, it was and will ever remain also a thrilling journey of discovery. Now, with Brentano's original notes available thanks to the efforts of Jozef De Raedemaeker, there are further depths to explore, as alas—despite so many years of work—the rich sod has only been broken.

In the visions will be found fascinating indications and hints for archeologists, historians, linguists, theologians, students of comparative religion, chronologists, specialists in symbolism, and more. Over and above the *primary element* of spiritual inspiration, it is my hope that such specialists may in due course take up these visions (including the entire corpus of Brentano's notes) and press further forward. How one would love to see a foundation, a university, a religious sodality, or some private individual or group sponsor so important and propitious a project. If the largely solitary results presented here serve to advance such future research, if hearts and souls are moved and enriched by *The Anne Catherine Emmerich Series* as a whole, the effort will have achieved its primary purpose.

JAMES RICHARD WETMORE

Acknowledgments

IT is difficult to sift out elements from earlier translators of these visions, but our main debt of gratitude for much of the English text taken as a foundation in the current work is owed to Sir Michael Palairet. Incalculable thanks are owed to Jozef De Raedemaeker for his past and present work with the original handwritten notes of Clemens Brentano. Occasional assistance with translation was received from Mado Spiegler, James Morgante, and especially Harrie Salman. A special thanks goes to Robert Powell, who has been a companion at every stage of this journey owing to his dedication to Anne Catherine in every respect: researching, translating when necessary, and, preeminently, applying his skills to the task of establishing the chronology that has been incorporated in this edition (in which connection Fr. Helmut Fahsel should also be mentioned). Most line drawings in the volumes are taken from Brentano's notes; the occasional paintings included are from the hand of James J. Tissot, as are all but one of the cover illustrations.

The New Light on the Visions
of Anne Catherine Emmerich Series

People of the
New Testament
Book V
*The Primary Holy Women,
Major Female Disciples and Relations
of Jesus, Minor Disciples & Others*

Magdalene Before Her Conversion

xvi

The Repentant Magdalene

xvii

Martha

xviii

The Holy Women

An Overview Organized
by Geographic or Familial Association

THIS initial overview[1] will be followed by fuller accounts of each of the holy women here mentioned (and others), consisting of extracts from previously published editions and new translations of material that has come to light in the recently published original notes made by Clemens Brentano (and others) at the bedside of Anne Catherine Emmerich. Later sections in the book will deal in the same way with virtually every female figure who appears in the whole of Anne Catherine's visions (other than Mary and her ancestors),[2] including women from many centuries prior to the time of Jesus, as well as many centuries after, right up to her own time. A separate volume[3] includes what Anne Catherine was able to contribute to our knowledge of many saints (both women and men).

Jesus's Conversations with Silent Mary

LIKE the aged Essene Eliud of Nazareth,[4] the type of the mystic living in contemplative solitude, we find among the holy women Lazarus's middle sister, *Silent Mary.* She has her own quarters with an enclosed garden on the grounds of the Bethany estate of

---

[1] This overview draws extensively upon Fr. Helmut Fahsel's *Der Wandel Jesu in der Welt* (Basel: Ilionverlag, 1942). To his words, translated here from the German, is added on occasion new material drawn from the notes of Clemens Brentano, which became available in a readily accessible form (in German) in 2009 thanks to the devoted efforts of Jozef De Raedemaeker, as well as chronological indications drawn from the complete edition of the *Visions of Anne Catherine Emmerich*, recently published also by Angelico Press.

[2] See *The Life of the Virgin Mary.*

[3] See *Scenes from the Lives of the Saints.*

[4] See "Eliud the Essene," in *People of the New Testament III.*

1

Martha. Her family considers her mentally handicapped, but Jesus judges differently, telling Eliud, "She is not for this world, therefore is she now altogether secluded from it. But she has never committed a sin. If I should speak to her, she would perfectly comprehend the greatest mysteries."

Jesus has with her two long private and very profound conversations, in which she speaks ecstatically of the mysteries of the Trinity and of the Incarnation. Jesus interrupts her now and then with a prayer of gratitude to the heavenly Father, then blesses her and predicts her impending liberation from earthly life; this occurs in April, AD 30, in the presence of the Blessed Virgin and the other holy women.

The Three Closely-Related Marys

AMONG the holy women in Galilee we find first and foremost *three Marys*, all close relatives of Jesus:

The first, *Mary Heli*, is the daughter of Joachim and Anne, born nearly twenty years before Mary of Nazareth. She is not the child of promise, and is called Mary of Heli—by which she is distinguished from the other of the same name—because she is the daughter of Joachim (or Heliachim). Her husband, Cleophas, is a nephew of Joseph, who brought a son from a previous marriage with him into the marriage with Mary Heli. This son is Matthias, who is later elected by the disciples to take the place of Judas Iscariot in the circle of twelve. To her husband Cleophas, Mary Heli bears three sons—Sadoch (Zadok), James, and Heliachim (Joachim)—and one daughter, Mary Cleophas, who is therefore a niece of Mary of Nazareth (although older than her aunt). Sadoch, James, Heliachim, and Matthias are known as the "brothers of the Lord," although in fact they are cousins to Jesus. All four become disciples of John the Baptist, and after the death of John become disciples of Jesus. Later, after the death of Cleophas, Mary Heli marries a priest named Obed, to whom she bears a son, Jairus. She lives at Japha, a small place about one hour south of Nazareth. Mary Heli is the firstborn child of her parents, Anne and Joachim. Anne is about twenty-four years old when she gives birth to Mary Heli. Nineteen years and five months later, at the age of approximately forty-three, she conceives her long-awaited second child, Mary. She is present at the burial of Christ Jesus.

The second, *Mary Salome*, is a cousin of Mary of Nazareth and the wife of the fisherman Zebedee. Mary of Nazareth is the daughter of Anne and Joachim, and Mary Salome is the daughter of Sobe and Solomon—and Anne and Sobe are sisters, daughters of the Essenes Ismeria and Eliud.[1] Zebedee and Mary Salome have two sons, James and John, sometimes referred to as the sons of Zebedee. They became disciples of Jesus—John being the only one of the twelve present at the death and burial of Christ and who, together with Peter, is in the garden of the holy sepulcher on Easter Sunday morning.

Near the beginning of Jesus's ministry, Mary Salome lives in the house which previously had been home to the holy family in Nazareth. Later she lives near Capernaum. Mary Salome is named in the gospel as one of the four Marys directly beneath the cross, the others being the Virgin Mary, Mary Magdalene, and Mary Cleophas.

The third, *Mary Cleophas*, niece and childhood playmate of the Virgin, is the daughter of Mary Heli. Because of the age difference between Mary Heli and Mary of Nazareth—the second daughter, or child of promise—Mary Cleophas, although a niece of Mary, is about four years older than her. Mary Cleophas is wife, first, of Alpheus, whose children she bears: Judas Thaddeus (or just Thaddeus), Simon the Zealot, James the Less, and Susanna (or Susanna Alpheus). From his first marriage, Alpheus had brought his son Levi (latter called Matthew). Thaddeus, Simon, James the Less, and Matthew all later become one of the twelve apostles of Jesus. Later still, Mary Cleophas will marry Sabba, by whom she has a son, the disciple Joseph Barsabbas (or Joses Barsabbas). Mary Cleophas's third and final marriage is to the Greek Jonah, who comes with a son by a first marriage, the disciple Parmenas. With Jonah she bears one more son, Simon the Just.[2]

---

[1] There is a third daughter, Maraha, who is younger than Sobe and older than Anne.

[2] Mary Cleophas is distantly related to Peter through her third husband.

At the start of Jesus's teaching travels, Mary Cleophas settles in the neighborhood of Capernaum, close by the house of the Blessed Virgin. She recommends her sons to Jesus as disciples, and later she lives in Cana. On November 25, AD 30, Mary Cleophas, who is lying desperately ill with fever at the home of Peter in Bethsaida, is healed by Jesus. She is very active in the care of the sick and the poor at the time of the mountain sermons. Mary Cleophas stands also at the cross, and dies five years after the Ascension.

Three Other Women Relatives of Jesus

THE second group of three Galilean women who are close relatives of Jesus include *Mahara*, youngest sister of Anne (that is, an aunt of the Virgin), living in Sepphoris in the former home of Anne's parents, where she often lodges Jesus and his mother. Her two sons, Arastaria and Cocharia, are among the very first disciples of Jesus, being received on August 14, AD 29. Then there is *Susanna*, wife of Alpheus of Nazareth, daughter of Alpheus and Mary Cleophas, and thus sister of the apostles Thaddeus, Simon the Zealot, and James the Less (and stepsister of Matthew, Parmenas, and Simon the Just). Finally, there is *Anna Cleophas*, Cleophas's daughter by his first marriage, mother of Nathaniel. To differentiate him from the other two Nathaniels,[1] he is sometimes called the Little Cleophas, and Jesus is very fond of him.

The Five Holy Widows

TO the so-called five holy widows belong first and foremost the three mothers of the earliest disciples of Jesus: *Lea* and *Seba* of Nazareth, whose sons Kolaya and Eustachius, respectively, are received by Jesus on August 4, AD 29; and *Sobe*, daughter of the elder Sobe and cousin to the Blessed Virgin, who on many occasions lodged Jesus and his mother in Cana, and whose nephew is Nathaniel, the bridegroom at the wedding of Cana, who lives in Capernaum and, at about the same time as the other two, be-

---

[1] The early disciple Nathaniel Chased, and Nathaniel, the bridegroom of Cana (sometimes called by his baptismal name Amandor—derived from the word "Amen"—but not to be confused with Amandor, the son of Seraphia).

comes a disciple of Jesus. Then there is the wealthy widow *Maroni of Nain*, sister of James the Greater's wife and mother of Martialis—the youth of Nain whom Jesus raises from the dead—and who, after this miracle has taken place, lodges Jesus and the disciples both at her summer estate and her great house in Nain, and places a portion of her wealth at the disposal of the community, in which she then becomes one of the most active women. At her request and with the help of his own mother, Jesus then heals from a distance Maroni's friend the widow *Mary of Nain* from possession, after which she also enters the circle of the holy women.

The Jerusalem Women

DUE to her organizing talents and apostolic zeal, Lazarus's oldest sister *Martha* stands at the head of the Jerusalem women. At first, she is ever underway with her brother and the women assistants, establishing new hostels, supervising the established ones, and ensuring that all of them are regularly provided with household implements, fresh food, and blankets for the disciples and apostles.

Then we have *Seraphia* from Jerusalem, daughter of a brother of John the Baptist's father Zechariah (and thus a cousin to John the Baptist), in whose ancestral house near the Jerusalem fish-market Joachim and Anne had moved when they brought their little daughter to the Temple. Seraphia is related also to the old priest Simeon, and a friend of his sons. At the time of Jesus's teaching travels, she is married to Sirach, a member of the Temple council, and suffers much from his initial hostility toward Jesus. Following his conversion by Joseph of Arimathea and Nicodemus, Sirach becomes better disposed and allows his wife to follow Jesus and serve him and the disciples. She is a tall, beautiful, and courageous woman, and is the one who with a cloth wipes the brow of Jesus on his way to the cross. The cloth acquires thereby an image of the face of Jesus, and for this reason she is given the name *Veronica* (from *vera icon,* or "true image"). Her son Amandor is one of Jesus's earliest followers.

Third, there is *Susanna of Jerusalem*, the illegitimate daughter of Joseph's brother Cleophas. From her grandfather, a Persian nobleman, she has acquired wealth and has married the government official Matthias, relative of the later apostle Matthias. Born in Gophna, she lives in the Temple as a little girl, like the Virgin Mary. From the beginning she is part of Lazarus's circle in Bethany and accompanies Martha on her rounds, supporting her with generous offerings. Later, she is present at the burial of Jesus.

Fourth, the widow *Salome* (like Susanna, related to the holy family on Joseph's side) has lived for a long time with Martha in Bethany, is present at the burial of Jesus, and accompanies Magdalene, Mary Cleophas, and Johanna Chusa when they go to the sepulcher on the morning of the resurrection.

Fifth, *Mary Mark*, a relative of the old priest Simeon, lives with her son John Mark northeast of Jerusalem and often has Jesus stay at her house. The Virgin Mary stays with her before the crucifixion, and she stands facing the Virgin at the burial.

Sixth, *Johanna Chusa*, is a tall, pale, stern woman, but strong and energetic. She is a niece of the prophetess Anna of the Temple, and her son is acquainted with the twelve-year-old Jesus when the latter remains behind in Jerusalem. Later he is one of the secret disciples in Jerusalem. Johanna is often at the Bethany estate and collaborates with Martha on maintaining the hostels. Jesus often dines at her house with his disciples, and she is the one who, with Veronica and *Mary of Hebron* (Elizabeth's niece), travels to Machaerus with a few servants from Jutta to find and retrieve the Baptist's head. She is also one of the four holy women who bear witness to the Risen Christ in the garden of the holy sepulcher on Easter Sunday morning.

The Converted Sinners

Mary Magdalene, youngest sister of Lazarus, belongs to the intimate circle of Jesus and his mother, and heads the list of converted sinners as the "type" of all saintly sinners. At the age of seven she loses her parents, who have spoiled their youngest and extremely beautiful and precocious daughter. By the age of nine she already has admirers. As her talents and qualities grow and blossom, the rumors and astonishment surrounding her grow in equal measure. She has a very active social life, is well educated, and writes aphorisms about love on little parchment rolls, which she exchanges with her suitors. When she is eleven, she moves with her large retinue of maids and servants to the castle of Magdalum, which falls to her by lot at her parents' death. In her new lodgings she is soon entertaining officers from the garrisons of Magdalum and surroundings. Initially she associates with witty men, but over time the level of her intimate male and female friends sinks ever lower.

Magdalene receives the first ray of grace on the final day of Jesus's forty-day fast. She is moved and overcome by a sudden foreboding about her life and a longing for salvation. However the inner motivation does not last long. In January, AD 30, Martha convinces Magdalene to join her on a trip to Jezreel to see the new prophet from Nazareth. When they arrive, Jesus has already left, but Magdalene hears from eyewitnesses about the miracles he has just performed. One month later Magdalene is again in Jezreel at the instigation of her brother and her sister Martha, as well as of Veronica and Johanna Chusa, who had visited her. From the window of the inn she catches a glimpse of Jesus entering the town with his disciples and he blesses her with a glance. Shaken and overcome, she rushes into a leper-hostel and then returns to Magdalum with her siblings. But she soon reverts to her old ways. On July 19, AD 30, in the circle of his followers, Jesus tells them to pray for Magdalene, saying she will soon come and become an example for others. On November 8th, at the mountain sermon near Gabara, she experiences a second conversion, and on December 26th, her final conversion.

From then on she lives in the residence of her deceased sister Silent Mary in Bethany, repeatedly asks Jesus to help their dying brother Lazarus, anoints him several times at table (the last time being at the Last Supper), stands under the cross, accompanies the body to the burial, and is the first to experience the resurrected Christ at the sepulcher.

The *first* to have been converted by Jesus is *Dinah the Samaritan woman*, who is known to us through her lengthy conversation with Jesus at Jacob's well. The daughter of a mixed marriage (her mother Jewish and her father pagan), she was born on an estate not far from Damascus. Orphaned at an early age, she has five

7

husbands in a row, from whom she separates, partly out of grief, partly because she has found new lovers. From these marriages, she has three daughters and two sons, who all reside with their fathers when she must leave Damascus. At the time of the meeting at Jacob's well she is living out of wedlock with a relative of one of her husbands, a rich Sichem merchant. The people of Sichem know nothing about the illegitimacy of this union and appreciate Dinah for her charming and witty ways. Following her conversion, Jesus introduces Dinah to his mother, and she becomes one of the most active helpers in the Christian community. Along with Magdalene, Mary Cleophas, Veronica, and Mara, she is among the most beautiful women of the community, although the Virgin outshines them all.

About a month after Dinah's conversion there comes to Ainon a wealthy woman from Suphan in the land of the Moabites, *Mara the Suphanite*. Her Jewish husband lives in Damascus and has thrown her out after she has had four consecutive lovers, from whom she bears three children. She has lived in Ainon for a good while, full of contrition. She behaves well and listens to the Baptist's preaching against adultery, which leaves her shaken. However she is often possessed by a demon, and this happens again upon the arrival into town of Jesus, in whom she has placed her last hope. Jesus frees her from the demonic influence, blesses her illegitimate children, places the children's hands in that of their healed and fully-converted mother, and is rewarded with many gifts at a banquet in his honor in the festive house. Upon his return to Ainon, Jesus helps Mara reconcile with her husband. Dinah and Veronica accept her kindly into the circle of the Helping Women.

On October 25, AD 30, the rich pagan widow *Lais* from Nain comes to hear Jesus teach on the preaching mountain in Meroz, where she asks for his help with her two daughters, Athalia and Sabia—both conceived out of wedlock—who are at her home, possessed by a demon. Jesus hears her tearful prayer and immediately heals her daughters from a distance. All three women join the circle of the helping women and accompany the mother of Jesus when she goes and teaches among the pagan caravans, mid-November of the same year.

Other Women Converts

THAT same month, October AD 30, while making her rounds visiting the sick, the Blessed Virgin makes the acquaintance of *Enue*, the pagan widow of a Caesarea Philippi Jew, and does much to strengthen her faith. Enue suffers from an issue of blood. On December 1, AD 30, while in a crowd, she touches the hem of Jesus's tunic and is immediately healed (Matt. 9:20). Two days later, Enue's sister-in-law *Lea*, the wife of a Pharisee (Paneas) very hostile to Jesus,[1] sings the Lord's praises to Mary during a sermon (Luke 11:27), and on March 6, AD 31, Jesus is a guest in the house of Enue's pagan uncle in Caesarea-Philippi; at table, Enue's grateful daughter anoints Jesus in the presence of her well-pleased mother.

Similarly to Lais of Nain, there appears in mid-February, AD 31, the widowed pagan owner of a factory in Ornithopolis, who in the gospel (Matt. 15:22 and Mark 7:26) is designated as the woman from Canaan and Syrophoenicia—or *the Syrophoenician woman*. She encounters Jesus in the city of Dan and, in tears, resolutely asks for the healing of her possessed daughter. The Lord is touched by her faith, and not only heals the daughter at a distance but also heals the mother of a spinal deformation; and on the following day he heals her deaf-mute relative. The grateful and generous Syrophoenician woman now puts herself at the service of Jesus's interests among the diaspora Jews in Syrophoenicia. Each time he visits Ornithopolis (twice a year) she organizes a banquet in his honor. During one such banquet, her daughter donates to Jesus all her jewels and artworks, which precious objects Jesus immediately redeems for the benefit of the poor in the diaspora communities.

By the end of the second year of Jesus's teaching, the holy women assisting the community number approximately thirty-seven. By the end of his wanderings, counting all the maids and caretakers in the hostels, the number has mounted to seventy.

---

[1] This Lea is to be distinguished from the holy woman of the same name mentioned above in the section "The Five Holy Widows."

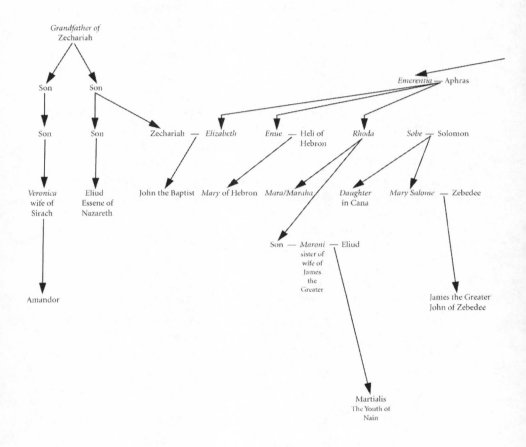

Close Relations of Jesus

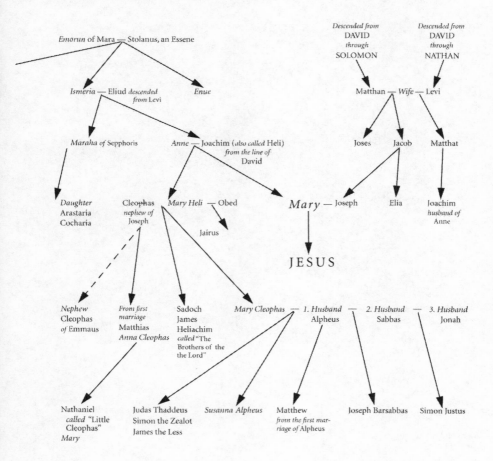

Emorun of Mara — Stolanus, an Essene

Descended from
DAVID
through
SOLOMON

Descended from
DAVID
through
NATHAN

Ismeria — Eliud *descended from Levi*

Enue

Matthan — Wife — Levi

Maraha *of* Sepphoris

Anne — Joachim (*also called* Heli) *from the line of* David

Joses   Jacob   Matthat

Daughter
Arastaria
Cocharia

Cleophas
nephew of Joseph

Mary Heli — Obed

Mary — Joseph

Elia

Joachim *husband of* Anne

Jairus

JESUS

Nephew
Cleophas
of Emmaus

From first marriage
Matthias
Anna Cleophas

Sadoch
James
Heliachim
called "The Brothers of the Lord"

Mary Cleophas — 1. Husband Alpheus — 2. Husband Sabbas — 3. Husband Jonah

Nathaniel
called "Little Cleophas"
Mary

Judas Thaddeus
Simon the Zealot
James the Less

Susanna Alpheus

Matthew
from the first marriage of Alpheus

Joseph Barsabbas

Simon Justus

Some of the Holy Women

The Primary Holy Women

Mary Heli

THE story of the Virgin Mary's elder sister Mary Heli finds its proper place within the greater story of their parents Anne and Joachim, itself recounted in the larger context of the ancestors of Mary,[1] to which section the reader is referred. Some extracts only are offered here in expanding what was said in the preceding overview regarding "The Three Closely-Related Marys."

The first child born to Anne in her father's house was a daughter, Mary Heli, but she was not the child of promise. The signs that had been predicted were not present at her birth, which was attended by some trouble. I saw that Anne, when with child, was distressed about her servants. One of her maidservants had been led astray by a relation of Joachim. Anne, in great dismay at this infringement of the strict discipline of her house, reproached her somewhat severely for her fault, and the maidservant took her misfortune so to heart that she was delivered prematurely of a stillborn child. Anne was inconsolable over this, fearing that it was her fault, with the result that her child was also born too soon. Her daughter, however, did not die. Since this child had not the signs of the Promise and was born too early, Anne looked upon this as a punishment of God, and was greatly distressed at what she believed to be her own sin. She had, however, great joy in her newborn little daughter, who was called Mary. She was a dear, good, gentle child, and I always saw her growing up rather strong and fat. Her parents were very fond of her, but they felt some uneasiness and distress because they realized that she was not the expected Holy Fruit of their union. They therefore did penance and lived in continence for a long time.

---

[1] See *The Life of the Virgin Mary.*

Afterwards Anne remained barren, which she looked upon as the result of her having sinned, and so redoubled all her good works.[1] I saw her often by herself in earnest prayer; I saw too how they often lived apart from each other, gave alms, and sent sacrifices to the Temple.

Anne and Joachim had lived with Anne's father Eliud for some seven years, as I could see by the age of their first child (Mary Heli), when they decided to separate from their parents and settle in a house with land in the neighborhood of Nazareth that had come to them from Joachim's parents. There they intended in seclusion to begin their married life anew, and to bring down God's blessing on their union by a way of life more pleasing to Him. I saw this decision being taken in the family, and I saw Anne's parents making the arrangements for their children's new home.

When everything was ready, the menservants and maidservants joined the procession and drove the flocks and herds and the beasts of burden before them to the new home, which was some five or six hours' journey distant. I think it had belonged to Joachim's parents. After Anne and Joachim had taken leave of all

---

[1] Anne Catherine says many profound and wonderful words about the procreation of people of both high and lowly descent. In this connection she appeals to a place in a gospel that says that the son of the servant girl shall not be among the inheritors, and that speaks of the children of free people. She says she had always known that this does not so much relate to the servant girl, but to the flesh, to servile submission to lust. She expresses herself with some difficulty and vagueness, but she seems to have a deep insight into the secret of the matrimonial laws of the Jews and of other nations. She takes as an example Mary Heli, the eldest daughter of Anne, and says that her parents Joachim and Anne did not procreate Mary Heli in accordance to these laws—that in this procreation their own flesh, their own slavery [to desire] was involved. She connects with these laws the duty of abstinence, praying, fasting, giving alms, marriage as a practice of penance, and yearning to serve God, having no other purpose than to augment the kingdom of God. Anne and Joachim believed they had committed a sin when they procreated their oldest daughter. CB

The note most likely refers to Galatians 4:22–23: "For it is written that Abraham had two sons, one by the slave woman [Hagar] and the other by the free woman [Sarah]. His son by the slave woman was born according to the flesh, but his son by the free woman was born as the result of a divine promise."

friends and servants, with thanks and admonitions, they left their former home with much emotion and with good resolutions. Anne's mother was no longer alive, but I saw that the parents accompanied the couple to their new home. Perhaps Eliud had married again, or perhaps it was only Joachim's parents who were there. Mary Heli, Anne's elder daughter, who was about six or seven years old, was also of the party.

When the travelers arrived in the house they found everything already in order and in its place, for the old people had sent the things on ahead and had them arranged. The menservants and maidservants had unpacked and settled all the things just as beautifully and neatly as when they were packed up, for they were so helpful and worked so quietly and intelligently by themselves that one did not have to be giving them orders all the time about every single thing, as one must do today. Thus everything was soon settled and quiet, and the parents, having brought their children into their new home, blessed and embraced them in farewell and set off on their journey home accompanied by their little grand-daughter (Mary Heli), who went back with them.

I now saw the holy couple beginning an entirely new life here. It was their intention to offer to God all that was past, and to behave as though their marriage had only then taken place, endeavoring to live in a manner pleasing to God, and thus to bring down upon them His Blessing, which they so earnestly desired beyond all else.

For nineteen years after the birth of their first child they lived thus devoutly before God in constant yearning for the gift of fruitfulness and with an increasing distress. I saw ill-disposed neighbors coming to them and speaking ill of them, saying that they must be bad people since no children were born to them, that the little girl with Anne's parents was not really her daughter but had been adopted by her because of her barrenness, otherwise she would have had her at home, and so forth. Each time they heard such words, the distress of the good couple was renewed.

Mary Cleophas

MARY CLEOPHAS was the daughter of the Virgin Mary's older sister (Mary Heli).[1] Her father was named Cleophas, and her (first) husband, Alpheus. They had three sons: James the Less, Simon, and Judas Thaddeus. These sons were not childhood friends of Jesus, because they lived too far distant. They did know him though, having seen him on occasions when their parents went to visit. The early playmates of Jesus from Nazareth for the most part fell away from him.

As has been said, when of age, Mary Heli married Cleophas, and from this union bore Mary Cleophas, who when of age married Alpheus. Alpheus brought to the marriage his son Matthew (Levi) the tax collector, and with Mary Cleophas fathered two daughters, Susanna Alpheus and Mary Alpheus, as well as the three sons mentioned above, all of whom went on to become part of the circle of the twelve apostles of Jesus. When widowed, Mary Cleophas married Sabbas, to whom she bore another son, Joseph (or Joses) Barsabbas, who later became a major disciple; however, unlike his four brothers, not one of the twelve.[2] Her third husband was a Greek, Jonah, who brought with him a son, Parmenas, from an earlier marriage. Parmenas also became a disciple of Jesus. To Jonah, Mary Cleophas bore a son, Simeon Justus, who was about ten years old at the time of Jesus's resurrection.[3]

At the start of Jesus's Ministry, Mary Cleophas settled in the neighborhood of Capernaum close to the house of the Blessed

---

[1] Because of the age difference between Mary Heli and the Virgin Mary (the second daughter), Mary Cleophas, although a niece of Mary, was about four years older than her. She was the playmate of the young Mary.

[2] However, at the time a replacement for Judas was decided, the two candidates considered where Matthias and Joseph Barsabbas. The former was chosen.

[3] Simeon Justus, after the death of James the Lesser, became the second bishop of Jerusalem.

Virgin. Later she lived in Cana. On November 25, AD 30, Mary Cleophas, who lay desperately ill with fever at the home of Peter in Bethsaida, was healed by Christ Jesus. She died five years after Christ's ascension.[1]

On another occasion, Anne Catherine learned that with her husband Alpheus, Mary Cleophas bore, first of all, Judas Thaddeus (who was slightly older than Jesus), Simon, and then a daughter named Mary (not the step-daughter of the same name).[2] The Mary Alpheus born of Mary Cleophas's marriage with Alpheus married a twenty-four-year-old temple servant named David, from the line of Levi, whose task was to purify the vessels used in the blood sacrifices. They lived together in Jerusalem in a house attached to the Temple. David was only permitted to be together with his wife for stretches of eight days, at certain times, during which his duties were taken over by another servant. And before he returned to his service, he had to submit to purifications. He was a very pious Jew, but withal a strict observer of the law. He was somewhat provoked by the disorderliness of the travels of Jesus and his disciples. He was acquainted with Nicodemus,

---

[1] On another occasion Anne Catherine said, regarding the death of Mary Cleophas: "After the death of Jesus, Mary Cleophas spent an extended period living together with the other holy women in Jerusalem, but after the passage of perhaps five years she died during a persecution as she was wandering through the wilderness, in a quarry near Rama or Arimathea. She was later buried by her friends in Jerusalem. I also saw much regarding the later dispersal of her bones, but most of this I have forgotten. As a child she was somewhat thick-set and heavy, but later grew to be graceful and delicate. Her hair was black, and her complexion browner than that of the Virgin Mary."

[2] The matter is rather confusing. From Brentano's notes, it appears that at a certain point Anne Catherine came to understand that when Mary Cleophas married Alpheus, the latter brought into the marriage not only his son Levi (the later apostle Matthew), but also a daughter, Mary, who is thus called Mary Alpheus. However, according to other notes we learn that from the marriage of Mary Cleophas and Alpheus, among the other children born to them, the later apostles Judas Thaddeus, Simon the Zealot, and James the Less—as well as Susanna Alpheus—was another Mary, who would also be called Mary Alpheus, after her father, so that in the combined family there were now step-sisters both with the same name (at least, as we come to know them in the context of Anne Catherine's visions).

who in due course placated David's reservations and convinced him to join the community, a step that his wife Mary had taken already. I had seen this Mary, and her step-sister Mary (Matthew's sister), often among the women, but only on this occasion did I finally understand who they were. The Mary who was the wife of David I saw often in service to the Blessed Virgin during the time of her tribulations.

Mary Cleophas was a handsome, quite distinguished-looking woman. She spoke with Jesus that morning of her five sons, and entreated him to take them into his own service. One, Simon, was a clerk, or a kind of magistrate; two were fishermen, James the Less and Judas Thaddeus. These three together were the sons of her first marriage. Alpheus, her first husband, was a widower with one son when she married him. This stepson was named Matthew. She wept bitterly when she spoke of him, for he was a publican. Joseph Barsabbas, who also was at the fishery, was her son by her second husband Sabbas; and by her third marriage with the fisherman Jonas,[1] she had another son, the young Simeon, still a boy. Jesus consoled her, promising that all her sons would one day follow him. Of Matthew, whom he had already seen when on his way to Sidon, he spoke words of comfort, foretelling that he would one day be one of his best disciples.

Next morning Jesus again taught in the synagogue before an immense crowd. Meanwhile Mary Cleophas had become so sick that the Blessed Virgin sent to Jesus to implore his help. Jesus then went to Peter's near the city where Mary, the widow of Nain, and the sons and brothers of the sick woman were. The sorrow of little Simeon, then about eight years old, was quite remarkable. He was the youngest son of Mary Cleophas by her third husband, Jonas, who was the young brother of Peter's father-in-law, who had been associated with him in the fishery, and who had died about half a year previously.

When the Blessed Virgin and Mary Cleophas came to Jesus, he stretched out his hand to his mother, his manner to her being affectionate, though very earnest and grave. Mary was anxious

---

[1] As already mentioned, Jonas also brought his son Parmenas to this marriage.

about him. She begged him not to go to Nazareth, for the feeling against him there was very bitter. The Pharisees belonging to Nazareth, who had heard him in the synagogue of Kimki, had again roused indignation against him. Jesus replied to his mother's entreaties that he would await where he was the multitude that were to go with him to the baptism of John, and then pass through Nazareth. Jesus conversed much with his mother on this day, for she came to him two or three times. He told her that he would go up to Jerusalem four times for Passover, but that the last time would be one of great affliction for her. He revealed to her many other mysteries, but I have forgotten them.

The Two Marys Watch the Tomb

19

Mary Salome

MARY SALOME was a cousin of Mary of Nazareth (the Virgin Mary) and the wife of the fisherman Zebedee: Mary of Nazareth was the daughter of Anne and Joachim, and Mary Salome was the daughter of Sobe and Solomon—and Anne and Sobe[1] were sisters, daughters of the Essenes Ismeria and Eliud. (There was a third daughter, Maraha, who was younger than the other two). Mary Salome, Anne's niece, was about the same age as Anne's eldest daughter, Mary Heli. She was, then, the daughter of the aunt of the Mother of God.

Zebedee and Mary Salome had two sons, James and John, sometimes referred to as the "sons of Zebedee." In their early years James and John did not know Jesus personally, but they later became disciples of Jesus—John being the only one of the twelve who was present at the death and burial of Christ, and who, together with Peter, was in the garden of the holy sepulcher on Easter Sunday morning.[2]

Near the beginning of Jesus's ministry, Mary Salome lived in the house which previously had been the home of the holy family in Nazareth. Later she lived near Capernaum. Mary Salome is named in the Gospel of Matthew as one of the holy women at the foot of the cross. She was one of the four Marys directly beneath the cross, the others being the Virgin Mary, Mary Magdalene, and Mary Cleophas.[3] She is also referred to in the Gospel of Matthew

---

[1] This sister of Anne, Sobe, lived originally in Bethlehem and later with Anne in her residence.

[2] Peter, James, and John were the three disciples who witnessed the Transfiguration of Jesus on Mount Tabor in the night April 3/4 of the year AD 31. They were also present with Jesus in the garden of Gethsemane in the night April 2/3 of the year AD 33 after the Last Supper. These three—Peter, James, and John—represent faith, hope, and love.

[3] Elsewhere in Brentano's notes, we read: "In vision on Easter night, Saturday/Sunday, March 29/30, 1823, Anne Catherine referred to five holy women

as requesting of Jesus, "Command that these two sons of mine [James and John] may sit, one at your right hand and one at your left, in your kingdom." (Matt. 20:20–28)

✝ ✝ ✝ ✝ ✝

ON Wednesday, June 29, AD 29, Jesus was in Cana, where he visited his widowed cousin Mary of Cana, the daughter of Sobe and the sister of Mary Salome. (Mary of Cana was also the aunt of the bridegroom Nathaniel who, six months hence, married the daughter of the wealthy Israel of Cana.)

On Tuesday, September 20, AD 29, Anne Catherine reports seeing Mary and four holy women leaving the house and wending their way through a field near Tiberias. They had with them two servants from the fishery. One went on ahead, the other followed, both laden with baggage which they carried on a pole across the shoulder, a pack in front and another behind. The four women were Johanna Chusa, Mary Cleophas, Mary Salome, and one of the three widows. They were going to Bethany by the usual route, which ran by Shechem to the right. The following night, Wednesday, September 21, AD 29, Jesus went to Lazarus's, where he saw the Blessed Virgin, Johanna Chusa, Mary Cleophas, the widow Lea, and Mary Salome passing the night at an inn between the Desert Gibea and the Desert Ephron, about five hours from Bethany. At about half-past one the following day, Thursday, September 22, AD 29, the Blessed Virgin arrived in Bethany with Johanna Chusa, Lea, Mary Salome, and Mary Cleophas. The servant had in advance announced their approach.

After the turn of the year, on Thursday, January 18, AD 31, Martha, Mary Magdalene, and the widow Mary Salome, who was living in Bethany as a guest of Martha, came to meet Jesus on his way to Bethany. That evening Jesus and his friends and disciples shared a meal in Bethany. After everyone had gone to bed, Jesus went alone to pray on the Mount of Olives.

Two months later, on Friday, March 23, AD 31, as Jesus and the

present at the resurrection (including Mary Salome), rather than the four usually mentioned as having been there."

disciples were approaching Ephron, they were met on the way by Mary Magdalene and the widow (Mary) Salome, who had come together from Bethany to greet Jesus. After resting and talking with the two women, Jesus and the four disciples continued on their way.

Another two months later, on Saturday, May 17, AD 32, accompanied by Peter, James, and John, Jesus went to Bethabara, where he was joined by Matthew and another apostle. A large crowd had gathered. Jesus healed a great many people. It was here that Jesus spoke of marriage, blessed the children brought to him (Matthew 19:10–15), and advised the rich youth (Matthew 19:16–26). This last incident was followed by the exchange of words between Peter and Jesus recorded in Matthew 19:27–30. Then, toward evening, Jesus went to dine in a house where about ten of the holy women were gathered. These included Martha, her maidservant Marcella, Mary Magdalene, Mary Salome, Mary Cleophas, Veronica, and Mary Mark of Jerusalem. Jesus continued to teach. That evening, Jesus and all those gathered together in Bethany celebrated the sabbath in the great hall of the castle. He spoke much about the paschal lamb and about his future suffering. Of the holy women, Veronica, Martha, Magdalene, and Mary Salome then went on to Jerusalem. I saw Mary Salome with her sons, John and James the Greater, coming to Jesus and requesting that they should be allowed to sit, one at his right and the other at his left.

Yet another two months later, toward the evening of Tuesday, July 22, AD 32, Jesus and the apostles, who were journeying toward Bethany, reached the inn of a little place near Bahurim. Here Jesus taught concerning the laborers in the vineyard (Matthew 20:1–16). Mary Salome, the mother of James and John, approached him (again) to request that her two sons be allowed to take a place beside him in his kingdom (Matthew 20:20–21). Two days later, Thursday, July 24, AD 32, from this little place near Bahurim, Pharisees reported back to Jerusalem concerning Jesus. Jesus still taught upon the laborers in the vineyard, and when the mother of James and John heard him speak of the near fulfillment of his mission, she thought it only proper that his own relatives should have honorable posts in his kingdom. She consequently approached him (yet again) with a petition to that effect, but he sternly rebuked her.

The following day, Friday, July 25, AD 32, Jesus and the apostles made their way to Bethany. As he walked, Jesus taught. Mary Salome went on ahead, arriving in Bethany toward evening. She went first to Martha to tell her that Jesus was approaching. Mary Magdalene went with Mary Salome to greet him, but she returned without having spoken to him.

Some nine months later, on the evening of Holy Thursday, April 2, AD 33, there was little bustle in Jerusalem. The Jews were in their homes busied with preparations for the feast. The lodgings for the Passover guests were not in the neighborhood of the Mount of Olives. As I went to and fro on the road I saw here and there friends and disciples of Jesus walking together and conversing. They appeared to be uneasy and in expectation of something. The mother of the Lord, with Magdalene, Martha, Mary Cleophas, Mary Salome, and Salome, had gone from the cenacle to the house of Mary Mark. Alarmed at the reports that she had heard, Mary and her friends went on toward the city to get some news of Jesus. Here they were met by Lazarus, Nicodemus, Joseph of Arimathea, and some relatives from Hebron, who sought to comfort Mary in her great anxiety.

At the time of Jesus's arrest, when a shouting band hurried from Ophel by torchlight to meet the approaching procession, the disciples lurking around dispersed in all directions. I saw that the Blessed Virgin, in her trouble and anguish, with Martha, Magdalene, Mary Cleophas, Mary Salome, Mary Mark, Susanna, Johanna Chusa, Veronica, and Salome, again directed her steps to the valley of Jehosaphat. They were to the south of Gethsemane, opposite that part of the Mount of Olives where was another grotto in which Jesus had formerly been accustomed to pray.

Later, after the crucifixion, the men laid the sacred body of Christ Jesus on the leathern litter, placed over it a brown cover, and ran two poles along the sides. I thought right away of the Ark of the Covenant. Nicodemus and Joseph carried the front ends on their shoulders; Abenadar and John, the others. There followed the Blessed Virgin, her elder sister Mary Heli, Magdalene, and Mary Cleophas. Then the group of women that had been seated at some distance: Veronica, Johanna Chusa, Mary Mark, Mary Salome, Salome of Jerusalem, Susanna, and Anna, a niece of Joseph. The other women, namely, Maroni of Nain, Dinah the Samaritan, and Mara the Suphanite. were at the time with Martha and Lazarus in Bethany.

On the eve of the resurrection, the table at which the holy women were standing had an undersupport with crossed feet, something like a dresser, and was covered with a cloth that hung down to the floor. I saw lying on it bunches of all kinds of herbs mixed and put in order, little flasks of ointment and nard water, and several flowers growing in pots, among which I remember one, a striped iris, or lily. The women packed them all in linen cloths. During Mary's absence, Magdalene, Mary Cleophas, Johanna Chusa, and Mary Salome went to the city to buy all these things. They wanted to go early next morning to scatter them over the body of Jesus in its winding sheet and pour upon it the perfumed water. I saw a part of it brought by the disciples from the dealer and left at the house without their going in to speak to the women.

Martha

MARTHA was one of fifteen children, of whom six died young. Of the nine that survived, only four were living at the time of Christ's teaching. These four were: Lazarus; Martha, about two years younger; Mary, looked upon as simple-minded (whom we shall call Silent Mary), two years younger than Martha; and Mary Magdalene, five years younger than Silent Mary. The latter is not named in scripture, nor reckoned among the Lazarus family; but she is known to God.[1]

After the death of their father, lots were cast as to how the inheritance should be apportioned. The castle at Magdala and other properties in that area of the Sea of Galilee fell to Magdalene; the castle at Bethany to Martha and Silent Mary; and the property on Mount Zion as well as a large number of properties in Southern Galilee and the castle near Herodium fell to Lazarus. However, Martha made the main part of the castle at Bethany available to her brother, who preferred to stay there. Here in Bethany, and also in Lazarus's house on Mount Zion, Jesus was frequently a guest, and often met with Lazarus's close friends.

Due to her organizing talents and apostolic zeal, Martha stands at the head of the Jerusalem women. She applied her gift with apostolic fervor as a true servant of the community of disciples and the community of holy women. She lived simply and sought

---

[1] On Thursday, September 8, AD 29, while walking with the aged Essene Eliud, Jesus said of this family: "Martha is good and pious. She will, with her brother, follow me." Of Mary the Silent, he said: "She is possessed of great mind and understanding; but, for the good of her soul, they have been withdrawn from her. She is not for this world, therefore is she now altogether secluded from it. But she has never committed sin. If I should speak to her, she would perfectly comprehend the greatest mysteries. She will not live much longer. After her death, Lazarus and his sister Martha will follow me and devote all that they possess to the use of the community. The youngest sister Mary has strayed from the right path, but she will return and rise to higher sanctity than Martha."

always to do good works. Initially together with her brother, and then increasingly with the help of some of the holy women, she was constantly occupied with caring for the needs of Jesus and the community of the disciples and holy women—establishing new hostels, supervising the established ones, and ensuring that all of them are regularly provided with household implements, fresh food, and blankets. Then we have Seraphia from Jerusalem, daughter of a brother of John the Baptist's father Zechariah. Third, there is Susanna of Jerusalem, the illegitimate daughter of Joseph's brother Cleophas. From the beginning she is part of Lazarus's circle in Bethany and accompanies Martha on her rounds, supporting her with generous offerings. Fourth, the widow Salome (like Susanna, related to the holy family on Joseph's side) has lived for a long time with Martha in Bethany, is present at the burial of Jesus, and accompanies Magdalene, Mary Cleophas, and Johanna Chusa when they go to the sepulcher on the morning of the resurrection. Fifth, Mary Mark, a relative of the old priest Simeon, lives with her son John Mark northeast of Jerusalem and often has Jesus stay at her house. Sixth, Johanna Chusa, is a tall, pale, stern woman, but strong and energetic. She is a niece of the prophetess Anna of the Temple. Johanna is often at the Bethany estate and collaborates with Martha on maintaining the hostels.

About three years after Christ's resurrection, Martha and her brother Lazarus and her sister Magdalene were captured by the Jews and set adrift on the Mediterranean Sea together with four others in a small boat. Through providence they landed in the south of France, where she began missionary activity. Whereas Lazarus remained as bishop of Marseilles, and her sister Mary Magdalene retired to lead the life of a hermit in a cave at Saint-Baume, east of Marseilles, Martha went with her maidservant Marcella north of Marseilles and founded a community there. After witnessing Martha raise someone who had died of drowning, many people converted to Christianity. So close was her bond with her younger sister, Mary Magdalene, that Martha, although in a different region of the south of France, died about one week after her death. According to tradition, it was at the town of Tarascon, Provence, that she passed away.

On another occasion Anne Catherine says further: About three

years after Pentecost, persecution of Christians by the Jews intensified, and while Mary Magdalene was visiting her brother and sister in Bethany, the three were arrested. On this occasion Lazarus,
Martha, and Mary Magdalene were taken into custody, as well as
the sisters' maidservants Marcella and Sarah and two other people
who were visiting Lazarus at the time: one of the seventy-two disciples, named Maximin, and the man born blind who was healed
by Jesus, Celidonius, sometimes known as Sidonius. These seven
were arrested and taken to the Mediterranean coast (somewhere
close to present-day Tel-Aviv), where they were put into a little
boat, towed far out to the sea, and cut loose. The intention was
that they should perish, but this did not happen. Through divine
providence the little boat made it across the Mediterranean, the
family, servants, and companions coming ashore at a place in the
south of France now called Saintes-Maries-de-la-Mer.

Having been raised from the dead, Lazarus possessed an extraordinary power, as did Mary Magdalene, and Martha too, after
having spent so much time in the presence of Jesus. When Lazarus spoke, it was a powerful experience for all who heard. While
Sarah stayed behind in Saintes-Maries-de-la-Mer, the rest of the
group went to the town of Massilia (or Marsilia, present-day
Marseilles), further eastward along the coast. There they lived,
and because of Lazarus's presence and the power of his speech, a
whole community was soon converted to the new religion of
Jesus Christ, the messiah, who had died and risen from the dead.
Lazarus baptized them and became the bishop of this first community of Christians in Europe. Lazarus remained as bishop of
Marseilles, Magdalene retired to lead the life of a hermit in a cave
at Saint-Baume, east of Marseilles, and Martha traveled with her
maidservant Marcella north of Marseilles and founded a community there, as further described below.

*Anne Catherine saw some details regarding Martha's time in France,
of which what remains is here given:*

I saw holy Martha. She had left Marsilia (Marseilles) with Marcella, a second maiden, and a group of women who accompanied
her to a remote region where a number of pagan women were
living in huts built among nearly inaccessible cliff caves. They had
been kidnapped and enslaved by an enemy of their people, and

then taken to this wild place, where they were kept under guard. Martha and her companions settled close by these captive women. They began by erecting small huts set close together, but later built a cloister and a church. The latter consisted at first only of four walls over which they stretched a wattled roof of twigs and sod. As time went by, the edifice was enlarged and strengthened. They set about to convert the enslaved women, some of whom then joined their company. But others proved the cause of much suffering by betraying them to local inhabitants who in turn persecuted them.

Not far distant was a city called, it seemed to me, Aquen (Aquae, now Aix), where there must have been hot springs, for I saw much steam wafting about. There, on the bank of a broad river, I saw Martha slay a monster that had frequented its waters and done much harm. It would capsize boats, and sometimes came on land to feast on both men and beasts. The evil creature was like an enormous swine with a massive head, short legs like those of a turtle, nether parts like a fish, and short, leathery wings with claws at their end. Martha had come upon this monster along the wooded shore just as it was consuming a man. Many others were with her at the time. Invoking the Name of God, she strangled it with a strap she wrapped around its throat, as those standing by finished the job with stones and spears.

Martha often preached the gospel to the folk of the region, sometimes in open fields, sometimes on the riverbank. For this purpose she, along with her companions, would raise up a platform of stones laid stepwise so that a hollow was left within rather like a vault, over which was placed a broad stone upon which she would stand. Truly, she excelled even masons at this work, so extraordinarily active and well-organized was she.

Once, as I beheld her teaching from such a stone structure along the river, from the further bank I saw a young man who wished to swim across, that he might listen to her words. But the water swept him away and he drowned. Immediately thereafter I saw how the local people slandered Martha on account of the youth's death, and accused her also of having converted the enslaved women to her own faith. Next day the corpse of the drowned youth was discovered by his father, who in the presence of many onlookers laid it before Martha, announcing that if she could raise his son from the dead, he would confess her God. In the Name of Jesus, Martha commanded the youth to revive, and after he was raised, both he and the father converted to Christ—though others yet persecuted her as a sorceress. At the time one of her companions from Palestine—I believe it was the disciple Maximin—was in the area and came to baptize the new converts and serve the Lord's Supper. Martha labored much, teaching and converting many. At this time, Magdalene was living to the west in a remote cave, engaged in a great work of expiation. Lazarus was still in Marsilia. I saw that Martha died a short time after Magdalene.

On another occasion, having beheld several events in Martha's life, Anne Catherine provided more details regarding the location of her community in France, in connection with the abode of the later couple called Datula and Pontianus:[1]

The castle of Pontianus was on an island in the Rhone about seven leagues from Avignon and Nîmes, near a little village later known as St. Gabriel's. It owed its origin to a miracle by which a man had been saved during a storm on the lake. Tarascon and Martha's Solitude [or monastery] were not far off, being situated on a mountain lying between the Rhone and a lake.[2] (In this connection she mentions the town of Arelat [Arles] as well as Martha's cloistered community of women.) The earlier religious communities of Martha and Thekla[3] were more regulated—having a specific rule—than Datula's later community, which was more of the nature of fugitive women living a withdrawn, common life in cave and forest. There was a most vivid memory during Datula's lifetime of the presence in their region at one time, among the early, secluded Christians, of Lazarus, Magdalene, and Martha. Chris-

---

[1] See "Datula and Pontianus" in *Scenes from the Lives of the Saints.*

[2] Anne Catherine notes that earlier, at the time of Martha, the region was quite wild, more so than at the time of Datula and Pontianus: it was mostly dense forest with here and there a fortified castle, or fortress. In those days there were also more islands at the mouth of the Rhone than later on, and she recalled a bridge built over the river, on which trees grew. There is reference in the notes to a map, which however has not been discovered.

[3] Disciple and companion of Paul. See "Thekla" in *Scenes from the Lives of the Saints.*

tians would gather at Magdalene's cave, and also places where Martha had been active, to hold mass—as also, I believe, at their graves. It is beyond credibility to me that any doubt can remain that Lazarus, Magdalene, and Martha died there.

We find in Brentano's notes that Anne Catherine said further, regarding the location of Martha's monastery (in connection with a hand-drawn map that has unfortunately gone missing):

The monastery was situated in the mountains between Arelat and Tarascon, and east of a small river flowing between a small lake and a larger, hook-shaped body of water communicating with the sea. Here Martha had gathered together many pious women. She also traveled to Avignon, where she taught, and healed a drunken youth.

On this occasion Anne Catherine quite precisely pointed out on the map the town of Marsilia where, as she said, Martha [and the others] had made landfall [after their miraculous journey from the Holy Land]. She added also that there was at that time in the wilderness around Tarascon a dragon wreaking havoc among the people, which Martha slew by making the sign of the cross.[1]

AS *with other major figures, we refer the reader to the full text of* The Visions of Anne Catherine Emmerich *for complete details on Martha. The few chronological references offered below are meant only to emphasize a few salient points.*

On Wednesday, September 21, AD 29, Jesus arrived in Bethany by night. Lazarus had been perhaps for some days at his house in Jerusalem on the west side of Mount Zion, the same side as Mount Golgotha. But he must have heard from the disciples of Jesus's intended visit to Bethany, for he had come thither in time

---

[1] See above, where this event is apparently described, though here the creature is described as a monster, and his death attributed to both the invocation of the Name of God, and other actions on the part of Martha and others present. Anne Catherine goes on to say: "Magdalene also slew at her hermitage a dragon obstructing the entrance to her cave. She took hold of it and cast it down." In truth, Anne Catherine saw this as some sort of demonic apparition. See also "Dragons" in *Inner Life and Worlds of Soul & Spirit*.

to receive him. The castle in Bethany belonged in reality to Martha; but Lazarus loved to be there, so he and his sister kept house together. They were expecting Jesus, and a repast was in readiness. Martha dwelt in a house on the other side of the courtyard. There were guests assembled in both houses. With Martha were Seraphia (Veronica), Mary Mark, and some others. Jesus went, accompanied by Lazarus, to the abode of the women, and Martha took him to her sister Silent Mary, with whom he wished to speak. A wall separated the large courtyard from a smaller one, which latter, however, was still quite spacious. In it was an enclosed garden adjoining Mary's dwelling. They passed through a gate, and Jesus remained in the little garden while Martha went to call her silent sister and bade her come down into the garden, for there someone was waiting to speak to her. Silent Mary was very obedient. Without a word she threw her veil around her and followed her sister into the garden. Then Martha retired. After his interview with Silent Mary, Jesus went back to Lazarus and Martha and said to them something like the following: "She is not without understanding, but her soul is not of this world. She sees not this world, and this world comprehends her not. She is happy. She knows no sin."

In January, AD 30, Martha convinced Magdalene to join her on a trip to Jezreel to see the new prophet from Nazareth. Although Jesus had already left by the time they arrived on the tenth day of the month, Magdalene heard from eyewitnesses about the miracles he had just performed. One month later, on February 9, Magdalene was again in Jezreel at the instigation of her brother Lazarus and her sister Martha, as well as of Veronica and Johanna Chusa, who had been visiting with her. From the window of the inn where she was staying she caught a glimpse of Jesus entering the town with his disciples, and he blessed her with a glance. Shaken and overcome, she rushed into a leper-hostel and then returned to Magdala with her siblings. But she soon reverted to her old ways. On July 19, AD 30, in the circle of his followers, Jesus told them to pray for Magdalene, saying she would soon come and become an example for others. Then one day Martha received guidance to go to Magdalene because she knew that Jesus was going to be teaching in the area of Magdala, in a place called Gabara—northwest of Tiberias—not far from the Sea of Galilee. Martha managed to persuade her sister to come and hear Jesus preach on a hill near Gabara on November 8, AD 30.[1] Seven weeks after the encounter with Jesus at Gabara, on December 26, AD 30, Martha again managed to persuade Magdalene to come and hear Jesus speak, this time in a place called Azanoth, a few miles northwest of Gabara. On this occasion Jesus cast out all seven demons, as described in great detail by Anne Catherine, and as is referred to briefly also in the gospel: "Mary, called Magdalene, from whom seven demons had gone out" (Luke 8:2).

On Sunday, July 23, AD 30, as Jesus explained his intention to teach throughout the land, Lazarus and some of the holy women made plans how best to help Jesus in his mission. Then the holy women themselves consulted together as to what district each should see to and what share each should take in the new establishments, to supply furniture, covers, clothes, sandals, etc., to provide for washing and repairing, and to attend to the furnishing of bread and other necessaries. All this took place before and during the meal. Martha was in her element.

On Thursday, August 31, AD 30, all the friends and disciples ate and slept with Jesus in one of the newly erected inns. They found ready for them, thanks to the forethought of Lazarus and the holy women, table furniture, covers, carpets, beds, screens, and even sandals and other articles of clothing. Martha had near the desert of Jericho a house full of women whom she kept busy preparing all these things. She had gathered together many poor widows and penniless girls, who were striving to lead a good life. There they lived and worked together. All was carried on quietly and unknown to the public. It was no little thing to provide for so many inns and so many people and to superintend them constantly—above all, to send messengers around to them, or give them personal attention.

In the year AD 44, as the Blessed Virgin felt her end approaching, in accordance with the directions of her divine Son, she

---

[1] To further encourage Magdalene to hear Jesus preach at the mountain, Martha told her that Dinah the Samaritan woman and Mara the Suphanite invited her there also.

called the apostles to her by prayer. She was now in her sixty-third year. At the time of Christ's birth she was in her fifteenth. Before his ascension, Jesus had made known to his most holy mother what she should say at the end of her earthly career to the apostles and some of the disciples who should be with her. He told her also that she should bless them, and that it would conduce very much to their welfare and eternal salvation. He entrusted to her also certain spiritual labors for the general good, which being accomplished, her longing after heaven was to be realized. Jesus had at the same time made known to Magdalene that she was to live concealed in the wilderness, and that Martha was to establish a community of women. He added that he himself would always be with them.

Jesus with Magdalene and Martha

Mary Magdalene

MARY MAGDALENE, the youngest sister of Lazarus, belonged to the intimate circle of Jesus and his mother, and heads the list of converted sinners as the "type" of all saintly sinners. She grew up at the family castle in Bethany, just northeast of Jerusalem. This is also where Lazarus was later raised from the dead by Jesus. Magdalene was the youngest of four children and was very beautiful.[1] She was about nine years younger than Lazarus and approximately seven years younger than Martha. The third sister, who in modern terminology would be called handicapped or impaired, was referred to as Silent Mary. She did not speak, but had profound inner visions. She was about five years older than Magdalene. However, she died at a relatively early age on April 8, AD 30, about six months after the ministry of Christ began on September 23, AD 29, the day of the baptism in the Jordan. As described in the section on Lazarus, the family was quite wealthy.

At the age of seven Magdalene lost her parents,[2] who had spoilt their extremely beautiful and precocious youngest daughter. She was tall and well-developed like a girl of more advanced age. She was full of frivolity and seductive art. She had had no great love for her parents even from her earliest age, on account of their severe fasts. Even as a child she was vain beyond expression, given to petty thefts, proud, self-willed, and a lover of pleasure. She was never faithful, but clung to whatever flattered her the most. She was, therefore, extravagant in her pity when her sensitive compassion was aroused, and kind and condescending

---

[1] Elsewhere Anne Catherine says: "the parents of Lazarus had in all fifteen children, of whom six died young. Of the nine that survived, only four were living at the time of Christ's teaching." Again, she says, as a variant: "of the remaining nine, only four came to know Christ."

[2] For a fuller account of Magdalene's parents, the properties inherited by their children, etc., see "Martha" and "Silent Mary" in this volume and "Lazarus and His Friends" in *People of the New Testament II*.

to all that appealed to her senses by some external show. Her mother had had some share in Magdalene's faulty education, and that sympathetic softness the child had inherited from her. Magdalene was spoiled by her mother and her nurse. They showed her off everywhere, caused her cleverness and pretty little ways to be admired, and sat much with her dressed up at the window. That window-sitting was the chief cause of her ruin. I saw her at the window and on the terraces of the house upon a magnificent seat of carpets and cushions, where she could be seen in all her splendor from the street. She used to steal sweetmeats and take them to other children in the garden of the castle. By the age of nine she already had lovers.

With her developing talents and beauty increased also the talk and admiration they excited. She had crowds of companions. She was taught, and she wrote love verses on little rolls of parchment. I saw her while so engaged counting on her fingers. She sent these verses around, and exchanged them with her lovers. Her fame spread on all sides, and she was exceedingly admired. But I never saw that she either really loved or was loved. It was all, on her part at least, vanity, frivolity, self-adoration, and confidence in her own beauty. I saw her a scandal to her brother and sisters, whom she despised and of whom she was ashamed on account of their simple life.

When the patrimony was divided, the castle of Magdalum fell by lot to Magdalene.[1] It was a very beautiful building. Magdalene had often gone there with her family when she was a very young child, and she had always entertained a special preference for it. She was only about eleven years old when, with a large household

---

[1] "After the death of their father, lots were cast as to how the inheritance should be apportioned. The castle at Magdalum and other properties in that area of the Sea of Galilee fell to Magdalene; the castle at Bethany to Martha and Silent Mary; and the property on Mount Zion as well as a large number of properties in Southern Galilee and the castle near Herodium fell to Lazarus. However, Martha made the main part of the castle at Bethany available to her brother, who preferred to stay there. Here in Bethany, and also in Lazarus's house on Mount Zion, Jesus was frequently a guest, and often met with Lazarus's close friends."

of servants, men and maids, she retired thither and set up a splendid establishment for herself. In her new lodgings she was soon entertaining officers from the garrisons of Magdalum and surroundings. Initially she associated with witty men, but gradually the character of her intimate male and female friends sank lower.[1]

Mary Magdalene was taller and more beautiful than the other holy women, including even the beautiful Dinah the Samaritan.[2] She was robust, yet graceful. She had very beautiful, tapering fingers, a small, delicate foot, and a wealth of beautiful long hair; and there was something imposing in all her movements. Being wealthy and beautiful, she enjoyed life and, correspondingly, lived sumptuously.[3] This was a source of great concern for her brother Lazarus and sister Martha, both of whom had in the meantime

[1] Elsewhere Anne Catherine says: "At the time she was converted by an instruction of Jesus, Magdalene was in her twenty-fifth year, having spent the preceding fourteen or so years leading a dissolute life in Magdalum. During the latter period she fell into a low state, sick, scorned, without means and careworn. Her fashionable coterie abandoned her. Her indulgent carousing had left her destitute. For a while she lived more simply and quietly, gradually regaining her health and beauty, after which she resumed her former lifestyle. At this time she kept company with two beautiful servant women. One of these was a bad sort, who abandoned Magdalene when she was converted. The other was as fair as a lily. Lazarus would release no further funds to her. To make money she had to offer herself (to men who wanted to enjoy her company). But since she was no longer sought after, she had to seek out and lure them herself; even common men would do, so long as they were attired with a minimum of elegance."

[2] Here Anne Catherine adds, however: "The Virgin Mary was the most beautiful of all. Although the beauty of her form was not unmatched by others, and in some respects Magdalene's beauty was even more striking, Mary stands out among them all, more especially through an indescribable silent blessing that emanated from her, and through her simplicity, meekness, youthfulness, earnestness, and purity."

[3] Elsewhere Anne Catherine says: "When I see the saints in a general way, without reference to my recognizing them, they appear to be in hierarchies and choirs, clothed according to their rank in the costume of the Church Triumphant, and not in that of the time in which they lived. Popes, bishops, kings, all the anointed; the martyrs, the virgins, etc., are in heavenly garments surrounded by glory. The sexes are not separated. The virgins have an entirely distinct, mystical rank. They were either voluntary virgins, or chaste married

become disciples of Jesus of Nazareth. Lazarus and Martha were praying for guidance as to how to go about introducing their sister to Jesus.[1]

Magdalum

MAGDALUM was a fortified place, consisting of several castles, public buildings, and large squares of groves and gardens. It was eight hours east of Nazareth, about three from Capernaum, one and a half from Bethsaida toward the south, and about a mile from the Sea of Galilee. It was built on a slope of the mountain and extended down into the valley that stretches off toward the lake and around its shores. One of those castles belonged to Herod. He possessed a still larger one in the fertile region of Galilee. Some of his soldiers were stationed in Magdalum, and they contributed their share to the general demoralization. The officers were on intimate terms with Magdalene. There were, besides the troops, about two hundred people in Magdalum, chiefly officials, master builders, and servants. There was no synagogue in the place; the people went to the one at Bethsaida. The castle of Magdalum was the highest and most magnificent of all; from its roof one could see across the Sea of Galilee to the opposite shore. Five roads led to Magdalum, and on every one at one half-hour's distance from the well-fortified place stood a tower built over an arch. It was like a watchtower whence could be seen far into the distance. These towers had no connection with one another; they rose out of a country covered with gardens, fields, and meadows. Magdalene had menservants and maids, fields and herds, but a very disorderly household; all went to rack and ruin.

Through the wild ravine at the head of which Magdalum lay far up on the height flowed a little stream to the sea. Around its banks was a quantity of game, for from the three deserts contiguous to

women, or martyrs to whom the executioners offered violence. I see Magdalene in a high rank, but not among the virgins. She was tall, beautiful, and so attractive that, had she not been converted to Jesus, she would have become a female monster. She gained a great victory!"

[1] See "James the Greater" in *People of the New Testament I* for a description of James's early interest in bringing Magdalene to listen to Jesus.

the valley the wild beasts came down to drink. Herod used to hunt here. He had also near his castle in the country of Galilee a park filled with game. The country of Galilee began between Tiberias and Tarichea, about four hours' distance from Capernaum; it extended from the sea three hours inland and to the south around Tarichea to the mouth of the Jordan. The rising valley with the baths near Bethulia, artificially formed from a brook nearby, lay contiguous to this region, and was watered by streams flowing to the sea. This brook formed in its course several artificial lakes and waterfalls in different parts of the beautiful district which consisted entirely of gardens, villas, castles, parks, walks, orchards, and vineyards. The whole year round found it teeming with blossoms and fruits. The rich ones of the land, and especially of Jerusalem, had here their villas and gardens. Every portion was under cultivation, or laid off in pleasure grounds, groves, and verdant labyrinths, and adorned with walks winding around pyramidal hillocks. There were no large villages in this part of the country. The permanent residents were mostly gardeners and custodians of the property, also shepherds whose herds consisted of fine sheep and goats. There were besides all kinds of rare animals and birds under their care. No street ran through Magdalum, but two roads from the sea and from the Jordan met here.

Introductory Itinerary

MAGDALENE received the first ray of grace on the final day of Jesus's forty-day fast,[1] as he was being ministered to by the angels. She was wonderfully agitated. At the time she was busied with finery for some amusement. Suddenly anxiety about her life seized upon her, and a longing rose in her soul to be freed from the chains that bound her. She cast the finery from her hands, but was laughed at by those around her.[2] However this inner motiva-

---

[1] The forty-day fast took place between October 11 and November 30, AD 29.

[2] Regarding this event, Jesus later consoled Lazarus on the subject of Magdalene, of whom he said that already there had fallen upon her soul a spark of salvation, which would entirely consume her. This conversation took place on Tuesday, January 24, AD 30.

tion did not last long. In January, AD 30, Martha convinced Magdalene to join her on a trip to Jezreel to see the new prophet from Nazareth. Although Jesus had already left by the time they arrived on the tenth day of the month, Magdalene heard from eyewitnesses about the miracles he had just performed. One month later, on February 9, Magdalene was again in Jezreel at the instigation of her brother Lazarus and her sister Martha, as well as of Veronica and Johanna Chusa, who had been visiting with her. From the window of the inn where she was staying she caught a glimpse of Jesus entering the town with his disciples, and he blessed her with a glance. Shaken and overcome, she rushed into a leper-hostel and then returned to Magdalum with her siblings. But she soon reverted to her old ways. On July 19, AD 30, in the circle of his followers, Jesus told them to pray for Magdalene, saying she would soon come and become an example for others.

Then one day Martha received guidance to go to Magdalene because she knew that Jesus was going to be teaching in the area of Magdalum, in a place called Gabara—northwest of Tiberius— not far from the Sea of Galilee. Martha managed to persuade her sister to come and hear Jesus preach on a hill near Gabara on November 8, AD 30.[1] Magdalene came dressed in her finest clothes with an attitude of curiosity to see the new prophet, but not with any sense of belief. She brought with her some friends who enjoyed living the life of luxury. Around ten o'clock Jesus arrived at the mountain, where there was a teacher's chair. He delivered a powerful discourse, culminating with the words: "Come! Come to me, all who are weary and laden with guilt! Do penance, believe, and share the kingdom with me!" At these words, Mary Magdalene was deeply moved inwardly. Jesus, perceiving her agitation, addressed his hearers with some words of consolation—words actually meant for Mary Magdalene—and she was converted. That evening, a Pharisee named Simon Zabulon invited Jesus to a banquet. During the meal, Mary Magdalene

---

[1] To further encourage Magdalene to hear Jesus preach at the mountain, Martha told her that Dinah the Samaritan woman and Mara the Suphanite had invited her there also.

entered the room carrying a flask of ointment, with which she anointed Jesus's head.[1]

However, while Jesus was speaking, Magdalene had an extraordinary experience. She became riveted by everything Jesus said, to the point that—and this is an event that is difficult for us to understand—Jesus cast a demon out from Mary Magdalene. In modern parlance we might call it some kind of obsession, but in those days it was said that the person was possessed by a demon. The following words spoken by Christ apply to her: "When the unclean spirit has gone out of a man, he passes through waterless places seeking rest; and finding none, he says: 'I will return to my house from which I came.' And when he comes he finds it swept and put in order. Then he goes and brings seven other spirits more evil than himself, and they enter and dwell there; and the last state becomes worse than the first." (Luke 11:24)

In fact, this is exactly what happened. Magdalene was soon again in her old track. She received the visits of men who spoke in the usual disparaging way of Jesus, his journeys, his doctrine, and of all who followed him. They ridiculed what they heard of Magdalene's visit to Gabara, and looked upon it as a very unlikely story. As for the rest, they declared that they found Magdalene more beautiful and charming than ever. It was by such speeches that Magdalene allowed herself to be infatuated, and her good impressions dissipated. She soon sank deeper than before, and her relapse into sin gave the devil greater power over her. He attacked her more vigorously when he saw that he might possibly lose her. She became possessed, and often fell into cramps and convulsions. Martha and Lazarus, who witnessed this, were of course now deeply concerned and kept praying for guidance as to what to do. This new condition lasted for almost exactly seven weeks.[2]

---

[1] This scene and the ensuing dispute with Simon Zabulon is described in Luke 7:36–50. In the gospels the woman who anoints Jesus is not in every instance identified as Mary Magdalene, but in this connection, on another occasion Anne Catherine says: "I had a great vision of Mary Magdalene. I have always seen the sinful woman who thrice anoints Jesus as the sister of Lazarus and Martha—that is, Mary Magdalene."

[2] Again and again we find this period of seven weeks in the life of Christ Jesus. For instance, Pentecost came seven weeks after the resurrection.

And so, seven weeks after the encounter with Jesus at Gabara on December 26, AD 30, Martha again managed to persuade Magdalene to come and hear Jesus speak, this time in a place called Azanoth, a few miles northwest of Gabara. On this occasion Jesus cast out all seven demons, as described in great detail by Anne Catherine, and as is referred to briefly also in the gospel: "Mary, called Magdalene, from whom seven demons had gone out." (Luke 8:2) This was of course an event of great importance in the life of Mary Magdalene. Something truly extraordinary had taken place through which she was able more and more to find her true calling.[1]

After he had cast out the demons, Jesus advised Magdalene to abide in the company of the Virgin Mary. Just as Jesus himself had a circle of disciples, who were all men—remembering that it was a patriarchal culture—so the Virgin Mary had a circle of women around her, which Anne Catherine refers to as the "holy women." Magdalene joined this circle of holy women and played an important role therein. This was all preparation for the great event, later, when she was the one who, on the morning of the resurrection, came to the empty tomb. There, in the garden of the holy sepulcher, she turned around and saw someone

---

[1] In summary, as was said above, on February 9, AD 30, from the window of the inn Magdalene caught a glimpse of Jesus entering the town with his disciples and he blessed her with a glance. She was shaken and overcome, but she soon reverted to her old ways. On July 19, AD 30, in the circle of his followers, Jesus told them to pray for Magdalene, saying she would soon come and become an example for others. Then, on November 8, at the mountain sermon near Gabara, she experienced a second conversion, and on December 26th, her final conversion. After Magdalene's final conversion she joined the circle of holy women around the Virgin Mary. Her brother Lazarus saw to Magdalene's request that her castle at Magdalum and her properties in that region be sold, and that the money thus raised be put at the disposal of the Lord for the payment of alms. From then on she lived in the residence of her deceased sister Silent Mary in Bethany, and (as we shall see) repeatedly asked Jesus to help their dying brother Lazarus, anointed Jesus several times at table (the last time being at the Last Supper), stood under the cross, accompanied the body to the burial, and was the first to experience the resurrected Christ at the sepulcher.

whom she thought to be the gardener—until she heard him speak. Then she knew: this is the Risen One; he has risen from the dead. Christ then spoke with her and said that she should go to the disciples and tell them that he would be ascending to the Father. He gave her the task of being a messenger. One of the Greek words for messenger is "apostle." Because it was Mary Magdalene who brought the news of the resurrection to the apostles, particularly to Peter and John, she is called the "apostle to the apostles."

JESUS was in Bethany on Wednesday, September 21, AD 29. Silent Mary, the simple sister of Lazarus, did not make her appearance. Before others she never uttered a word; but when alone in her room or the garden, she talked aloud to herself and to all the objects around her, as if they had life. She was very pious, though she never appeared in the school. She prayed in her own chamber. I think she had visions and conversed with apparitions. Her love for her brother and sisters was unspeakable, especially for Magdalene. From her earliest years she had been what she now was. No word had as yet been spoken in Jesus's presence in reference to Magdalene, who was then living at Magdalum in the height of her grandeur.

On Friday, October 21, AD 29, Jesus was again in Bethany, where he had a conversation with Silent Mary, whom he blessed. "The Son," she said, "would go to the servants in the subterranean prisons also. He would console them and set them free, because he had purchased their redemption. He would return with them to his Father. But at his second advent, when he would come again to judge, all those that had abused the satisfaction he had made and who would not turn from their evil ways, should be cast into the fire." She then spoke of Lazarus's death and resurrection: "He goes forth from this world," she said, "and gazes upon the things of the other life. His friends weep around him as if he were never to return. But the Son calls him back to earth, and he labors in the vineyard." Of Magdalene too she spoke: "The maiden is in the frightful desert where once were the children of Israel. She wanders in accursed places where all is dark, where never human foot has trod. But she will come forth, and in another desert make amends for the past."

After the turn of the year, on Thursday, February 9, AD 30, Jesus taught in Jezreel (where one month before he had publicly healed the sick) and performed many miracles before a great concourse of people. All the disciples from Galilee were here assembled to meet him. Lazarus, Martha, Veronica, and Johanna Chusa, who had come before from Jerusalem, had visited Magdalene at her castle of Magdalum to persuade her to go with them to Jezreel in order to see, if not to hear, the wise, the admirable, the most eloquent, and most beautiful Jesus, of whom the whole country was full. Magdalene had yielded to the persuasions of the women and, surrounded by much vain display, accompanied them thither. As she stood at the window of an inn gazing down into the street, Jesus and his disciples came walking by. He looked at her gravely as he passed with a glance that pierced her soul. An unusual feeling of confusion came over her. Violently agitated, she rushed from the inn and, impelled by an overpowering sense of her own misery, hid in a house wherein lepers and women afflicted with an issue of blood found a refuge. It was a kind of hospital under the superintendence of a Pharisee.

The people of the inn from which Magdalene had fled, knowing the life she was leading, cried out: "That's the right place for her, among lepers and people tormented with flows of blood!" But Magdalene had fled to the house of the leprous through that feeling of intense humiliation roused in her soul by the glance of Jesus, for she had made her way into that respectable position among the other women through a motive of pride, not wishing to stand in the crowd of poor, common people. Accompanied by Lazarus, she returned to Magdalum with Martha and the other women. The next sabbath was there celebrated by them, for Magdalum could boast a synagogue.

The following Sunday, February 12, AD 30, messengers came from Sidon begging Jesus to return with them, but he put them off kindly until a future day. The crowd became so great that at the close of the sabbath Jesus left Capernaum with some of his disciples, and escaped into a mountainous district about an hour to the north of the city. It was situated between the lake and the mouth of the Jordan, and was full of ravines. In the evening Jesus went to his mother's house between Bethsaida and Capernaum, whither had come Lazarus with Martha and the other women from Jerusalem. They were on their way from Magdalum and had called to take leave of Mary before returning to Jerusalem. He said that Martha was too anxious, that Magdalene had been very deeply affected, yet she would, notwithstanding, relapse once more into her old ways. She had not yet laid aside her fine attire, for, as she declared, one in her position could not dress so plainly as the other women, etc.

On Wednesday, July 19, AD 30, I saw Jesus conversing with Mary alone. She was weeping at the thought of his exposing himself to danger by going to Jerusalem. He comforted her, telling her that she must not be anxious, that he would accomplish his mission, and that the sorrowful days had not yet come. Some mention was made of Magdalene also. Jesus again told them to pray for her and think of her kindly, for she would soon be converted and become so good as to be an example for many.

On Sunday, July 23, AD 30, Jesus explained his intention to teach throughout the land, and Lazarus and the women made plans how best to help Jesus in his mission. Later, after an instruction, some of the men withdrew and Jesus went with others into the hall and walked up and down. Martha, who was passing to and fro, approached him and had a long talk about her sister Magdalene. She related what she had heard of her from Veronica, and her own consequent anxiety. While Jesus was walking up and down the hall with the men, the women sat playing a kind of lottery for the benefit of their new undertaking. During the game the holy women lost a very precious pearl that had fallen down among them. All moved back and looked for it most carefully. When at last they found it and were expressing their joy, Jesus came over to them and related the parable of the lost drachma and the joy of the owner upon finding it again. From their pearl, lost, carefully sought, and joyfully found, he drew a new similitude to Magdalene. He called her a pearl more precious than many others that, from the lottery table of holy love, had fallen and were going to destruction. "With what joy," he exclaimed, "will ye find again the precious pearl!" (Luke 15:8–10)

Then the women, deeply moved, asked: "Ah, Lord! Will that pearl be found again?" and Jesus answered: "Seek ye more earnestly than the woman in the parable sought the lost drachma, or the shepherd his stray sheep."

Profoundly touched at this answer, all promised to seek after Magdalene more diligently than after their lost pearl, and assured him that their joy upon finding her would far exceed what they now felt. Some of the women begged the Lord to receive among his disciples the young man of Samaria who, after Passover, had besought this favor of him on the road to that city. They praised his great wisdom and virtue. I think he was related to one of them. But Jesus replied that he could not count upon him, as he was blinded by love of riches.

On Wednesday, October 25, AD 30, during the healing of the sick, Manahem, the blind disciple of Coreae, who had been restored to sight and whom Jesus had sent with a message to Lazarus, returned from Bethany with the two nephews of Joseph of Arimathea. The holy women had sent by them money and gifts of various kinds to Jesus. Veronica and Johanna Chusa had also visited Mary. On their return journey they called to see Magda-lene, whom they found very much changed. She was depressed in spirits, her folly apparently undergoing a struggle with her good inclinations.

Magdalene's First Conversion

ON Tuesday, November 7, AD 30, while in Gischala, Jesus had sent some of the disciples around to the neighboring places to say that he would deliver a great instruction on the mountain beyond Gabara. There came in consequence, from a circuit of several hours, large crowds of people, who encamped around the mountain. On the summit was an enclosed space in which was a teacher's chair long out of use. Peter, Andrew, James, John, Nathaniel Chased, and all the rest of the disciples had come, besides most of John's disciples and the sons of the Blessed Virgin's eldest sister. There were altogether about sixty disciples, friends, and relatives of Jesus here assembled. The more intimate of the disciples were greeted by Jesus with clasping of both hands and pressing cheek to cheek.

Magdalene also wended her way to the mount of instruction near Gabara. Martha and Anna Cleophas had left Damna, where the holy women had an inn, and gone to Magdalum with the view of persuading Magdalene to attend the sermon that Jesus was about to deliver on the mountain beyond Gabara. Veronica, Johanna Chusa, Dinah, and the Suphanite had meanwhile remained at Damna, distant three hours from Capernaum and over one hour from Magdalum. Magdalene received her sister in a manner rather kind and showed her into an apartment not far from her room of state, but into this latter she did not take her.

There was in Magdalene a mixture of true and false shame. She was partly ashamed of her simple, pious, and plainly dressed sister who went around with Jesus's followers so despised by her visitors and associates, and she was partly ashamed of herself before Martha. It was this feeling that prevented her taking the latter into the apartments that were the scenes of her follies and vices.

Magdalene was somewhat broken in spirit, but she lacked the courage to disengage herself from her surroundings. She looked pale and languid. The man with whom she lived, on account of his low and vulgar sentiments, was utterly distasteful to her.

Martha treated her very prudently and affectionately. She said to her: "Dinah and Mara the Suphanite, whom you know, two amiable and clever women, invite you to be present with them at the instruction that Jesus is going to give on the mountain. It is so near, and they are so anxious for your company. You need not be ashamed of them before the people, for they are respectable, they dress with taste, and they have distinguished manners. You will behold a very wonderful spectacle: the crowds of people, the marvelous eloquence of the prophet, the sick, the cures that he effects, the hardihood with which he addresses the Pharisees! Veronica, Mary Chusa, and Jesus's mother, who wishes you so well—we all are convinced that you will thank us for the invitation. I think it will cheer you up a little. You appear to be quite forlorn here, you have no one around you who can appreciate your heart and your talents. Oh, if you would only pass some time with us in Bethany! We hear so many wonderful things, and we have so much good to do, and you have always been so full of compassion and kindness. You must at least come to Damna with me tomorrow morning. There you will find all the women of our party at the inn. You can have a private apartment and meet only those that you know," etc.

In this strain Martha spoke to her sister, carefully avoiding anything that might wound her. Magdalene's sadness predisposed her to listen favorably to Martha's proposals. She did indeed raise a few difficulties, but at last yielded and promised Martha to accompany her to Damna. She took a repast with her and went several times during the evening from her own apartments to see her. Martha and Anna Cleophas prayed together that night that God would render the coming journey fruitful in good for Magdalene.

A few days previously, James the Greater, impelled by a feeling of intense compassion for Magdalene, had come to invite her to the preaching soon to take place at Gabara. She had received him at a neighboring house. James was in appearance very imposing. His speech was grave and full of wisdom, though at the same time most pleasing. He made a most favorable impression upon Magdalene, and she received him graciously whenever he was in that part of the country. James did not address to her words of reproof; on the contrary, his manner toward her was marked by esteem and kindliness, and he invited her to be present at least once at Jesus's preaching. It would be impossible, he said, to see or hear one superior to him. She had no need to trouble herself about the other auditors, and she might appear among them in her ordinary dress. Magdalene had received his invitation favorably, but she was still undecided as to whether she should or should not accept it, when Martha and Anna Cleophas arrived.

On the eve of the day appointed for the instruction, Magdalene, with Martha and Anna Cleophas, started from Magdalum to join the holy women at Damna. Magdalene rode on an ass, for she was not accustomed to walking. She was dressed elegantly, though not to such excess nor so extravagantly as at a later period when she was converted for the second time. She took a private apartment in the inn and spoke only with Dinah and the Suphanite, who visited her by turns. I saw them together, an affable and well-bred confidence marking their conversation. There was, however, on the part of the converted sinners, a shade of embarrassment similar to what might be experienced on a military

47

officer's meeting a former comrade who had become a priest. This feeling soon gave way to tears and womanly expressions of mutual sympathy, and they went together to the inn at the foot of the mountain. The other holy women did not go to the instruction, in order not to annoy Magdalene by their presence. They had come to Damna with the intention of prevailing upon Jesus to remain there and not go to Capernaum, where Pharisees from various localities were again assembled.

Magdalene and her companions reached the mountain in good time, and found crowds of people already encamped around it. The sick of all kinds were, according to the nature of their maladies, ranged together in different places under light canopies and arbors. High upon the mountain were the disciples, kindly ranging the people in order and rendering them every assistance. Around the teacher's chair was a low, semicircular wall, and over it an awning. The audience had here and there similar awnings erected. At a short distance from the teacher's chair, Magdalene and the other women had found a comfortable seat upon a little eminence.

Around ten o'clock the following day, Jesus arrived at the mountain, where he delivered a powerful discourse. When he had vehemently urged the guilty to penance, when he had severely pronounced judgment upon the obdurate, he became once more all love, invited all sinners to come to him, and even shed over them tears of compassion. Then he implored his Father to touch their hearts that some, a few, yes, even one, though burdened with all kinds of guilt, might return to him. Could he gain but one soul, he would share all with it, he would give all that he possessed, yes, he would even sacrifice his life to purchase it. He stretched out his arms toward them, exclaiming: "Come! Come to me, ye who are weary and laden with guilt! Come to me, ye sinners! Do penance, believe, and share the kingdom with me!" Then, turning to the Pharisees—to his enemies—he opened his arms to them also, beseeching all, at least one of them, to come to him.

Magdalene had taken her seat among the other women with the self-confident air of a lady of the world, but her manner was assumed. She was inwardly confused and a prey to interior struggle. At first she gazed around upon the crowd, but when Jesus appeared and began to speak, her eyes and soul were riveted upon him alone. His exhortations to penance, his lively pictures of vice, his threats of chastisement, affected her powerfully, and, unable to suppress her emotions, she trembled and wept beneath her veil.

When Jesus, himself shedding tears full of loving compassion, cried out for sinners to come to him, many of his hearers were transported with emotion. There was a movement in the circle and the crowd pressed around him. Magdalene also, and following her example the other women likewise, took a step nearer. But when Jesus exclaimed: "Ah! If even one soul would come to me!" Magdalene was so moved that she wanted to fly to him at once. She stepped forward; but her companions, fearing some disturbance, held her back, whispering: "Wait! Wait!" This movement of Magdalene attracted scarcely any notice among the bystanders, since the attention of all was riveted upon Jesus's words. Jesus, aware of Magdalene's agitation, uttered words of consolation meant only for her. He said: "If even one germ of penance, of contrition, of love, of faith, of hope has, in consequence of my words, fallen upon some poor, erring heart, it will bear fruit, it will be set down in favor of that poor sinner, it will live and increase. I myself shall nourish it, shall cultivate it, shall present it to my Father." These words consoled Magdalene while they pierced her inmost soul, and she stepped back again among her companions. It was now about six o'clock, and the sun had already sunk low behind the mountain.

Meanwhile, some of the disciples accompanied Jesus to the sick, numbers of whom had been brought thither. The Pharisees, scandalized, impressed, astonished, enraged, went back to Gabara. Simon Zabulon, the chief of the synagogue, reminded Jesus of the invitation to sup in his house. Jesus replied that he would be there. The Pharisees murmured against Jesus and criticized him the whole way down the mountain, finding fault with his doctrine and his manners. Each was ashamed to allow his neighbor to remark the favorable impression that had been made upon him, and so by the time they reached the city, they had again entrenched themselves in their own self-righteousness. Magdalene and her companions followed Jesus. The former went among the people and took her place near the sick women as if to render them assistance. She was very much impressed, and the misery that she witnessed moved her still more. Jesus turned first to the men, among whom for a long time he healed diseases of all kinds. The hymns of thanksgiving from the cured and their attendants as they moved away, rang on the breeze. When he approached the sick females, the crowd that pressed around him and the need that he and his disciples had of space forced Magdalene and the holy women to fall back a little. Nevertheless, Magdalene sought by every opportunity, by every break in the crowd, to draw near to him, but Jesus constantly turned away from her. He healed some women afflicted with a flow of blood. But how express the feelings of Magdalene, so delicate, so effeminate, whose eyes were quite unused to the sight of human suffering!

It was dusk before Jesus and the disciples, preceded and followed by crowds of people, started at last down the mountain for Gabara. Magdalene, obeying only her impulse, without regard to appearances, followed close after Jesus in the crowd of disciples, and her four companions, unwilling to separate from her, did the same. She tried to keep as close to Jesus as she possibly could, though such conduct was quite unusual in females. Some of the disciples called Jesus's attention to the fact, remarking at the same time what I have just observed. But Jesus, turning around to them, replied: "Let them alone! It is not your affair!" And so he entered the city.

When he reached the hall in which Simon Zabulon had prepared the feast, he found the forecourt filled with the sick and the poor who had crowded thither on his approach, and who were loudly calling upon him for help. Jesus at once turned to them, exhorting, consoling, and healing them. Meanwhile Simon Zabulon, with some other Pharisees, made his appearance. He begged Jesus to come in to the feast, for they were awaiting him. "Thou hast," he continued, "already done enough for today. Let these people wait till another time, and let the poor go off at once." But Jesus replied: "These are my guests. I have invited them, and I must first see to their entertainment. When thou didst invite me to thy feast, thou didst invite them also. I shall not go into thy feast until they are helped, and then even I will go in only with them." Then the Pharisees had to go and prepare tables around the court for the cured and the poor. Jesus cured all, and the disciples led those that wished to remain to the tables prepared for them, and lamps were lighted in the court.

Magdalene and the women had followed Jesus hither. They stood in one of the halls of the court adjoining the entertainment hall. Jesus, followed by some of the disciples, went to the table in the latter and from its sumptuous dishes sent various meats to the tables of the poor. The disciples were the bearers of these gifts; they likewise served and ate with the poor. Jesus continued his instructions during the entertainment. The Pharisees were in animated discussion with him when Magdalene, who with her companions had approached the entrance, all of a sudden darted into the hall. Inclining humbly, her head veiled, in her hand a little white flask closed with a tiny bunch of aromatic herbs instead of a stopper, she glided quickly into the center of the apartment, went behind Jesus, and poured the contents of her little flask over his head. Then catching up the long end of her veil, she folded it, and with both hands passed it lightly once over Jesus's head, as if wishing to smooth his hair and to arrest the overflow of the ointment. The whole affair occupied but a few instants, and after it Magdalene retired some steps.

The discussion, carried on so hotly at the moment, suddenly ceased. A hush fell upon the company, and they gazed upon Jesus and the woman. The air was redolent with the fragrance of the ointment. Jesus was silent. Some of the guests put their heads together, glanced indignantly at Magdalene, and exchanged whispers. Simon Zabulon especially appeared scandalized. At last Jesus said to him: "Simon, I know well of what thou art thinking! Thou thinkest it improper that I should allow this woman to anoint my head. Thou art thinking that she is a sinner, but thou art wrong. She, out of love, has fulfilled what thou didst leave undone. Thou hast not shown me the honor due to guests."

Then he turned to Magdalene, who was still standing there, and said: "Go in peace! Much has been forgiven thee." At these words Magdalene rejoined her companions, and they left the house together. Then Jesus spoke of her to the guests. He called her a good woman full of compassion. He censured the criticizing of others, public accusations, and remarks upon the exterior fault of others while the speakers often hid in their own hearts much greater, though secret, evils. Jesus continued speaking and teaching for a considerable time and then returned with his followers to the inn.

Magdalene was deeply touched and impressed by all she had seen and heard. She was interiorly vanquished. And because she was possessed of a certain impetuous spirit of self-sacrifice, a certain greatness of soul, she longed to do something to honor Jesus and to testify to him her emotion. She had noticed with chagrin that neither before nor during the meal had he, the most wonderful, the holiest, of teachers—he, the most compassionate, the most miraculous helper of humankind—received from these Pharisees any mark of honor, any of those polite attentions usually extended to guests, and therefore she felt herself impelled to do what she had done. The words of Jesus, "If even one would be moved to come to me!" still lingered in her memory.

The little flask, which was about a hand in height, she generally carried with her as do the grand ladies of our own day. Magdalene's dress was white, embroidered with large red flowers and tiny green leaves. The sleeves were wide, gathered in and fastened by bracelets. The robe was cut wide and hung loose in the back. It was open in front to just above the knee, where it was caught by straps, or cords. The bodice, both back and front, was ornamented with cords and jewels. It passed over the shoulders like a scapular and was fastened at the sides; under it was another colored tunic. The veil that she usually wound about her neck she had, on entering the banquet hall, opened wide and thrown over her whole person.

When Magdalene returned to the inn with her companions, Martha took her to another about an hour distant and near the baths of Bethulia. There she found Mary and the holy women awaiting her coming. Mary conversed with her. Magdalene gave an account of Jesus's discourse, while the two other women related the circumstances of Magdalene's anointing and Jesus's words to her. All insisted on Magdalene's remaining and going back with them, at least for awhile, to Bethany. But she replied that she must return to Magdalum to make some arrangements in her household, a resolution very distasteful to her pious friends. She could not, however, cease talking of the impressions she had received and of the majesty, force, sweetness, and miracles of Jesus. She felt that she must follow him, that her own life was an unworthy one, and that she ought to join her sister and friends. She became very thoughtful, she wept from time to time, and her heart grew lighter. Nevertheless, she could not be induced to remain, so she returned to Magdalum with her maid. Martha accompanied her a part of the way, and then joined the holy women who were going back to Capernaum.

Magdalene was taller and more beautiful than the other women. Dinah, however, was much more active and dexterous, very cheerful, ever ready to oblige, like a lively, affectionate girl, and she was moreover very humble. But the Blessed Virgin surpassed them all in her marvelous beauty. Although in external loveliness she may have had her equal, and may have even been excelled by Magdalene in certain striking features, yet she far outshone them all in her indescribable air of simplicity, modesty, earnestness, sweetness, and gentleness. She was so very pure, so free from all earthly impressions that in her one saw only the reflex image of God in his creature.

Magdalene was soon again in her old track. She received the visits of men who spoke in the usual disparaging way of Jesus, his journeys, his doctrine, and of all who followed him. They ridiculed what they heard of Magdalene's visit to Gabara, and looked upon it as a very unlikely story. As for the rest, they declared that they found Magdalene more beautiful and charming than ever. It was by such speeches that Magdalene allowed herself to be infatuated and her good impressions dissipated. She soon sank deeper than before, and her relapse into sin gave the devil greater power over her. He attacked her more vigorously when he saw that he might possibly lose her. She became possessed, and often fell into cramps and convulsions.

On the morning of Saturday, November 11, AD 30, Jesus taught unmolested in the synagogue. Today Jesus taught in parables (Matthew 13:18–30, 34–43). After the close of the sabbath, the Pharisees began to dispute with him in the forecourt of the synagogue. They accused him of blasphemy for having forgiven Mary Magdalene her sins three days before at the meal arranged by the Pharisee Simon Zabulon. Their accusations caused a great uproar, during which Jesus left quietly. He went to his mother's house and talked with her and the other women there. The streets were again filled with the sick. Some had come before the sabbath, and some till now had not believed, but on the report of the possessed man's cure they had themselves transported thither from all quarters of the city. Many of them had been there before, but had not been cured. They were weak, tepid, slothful souls, more difficult to convert than great sinners of more ardent nature. Magdalene was converted only after many struggles and relapses, but her last efforts were generous and final. Dinah the Samaritan turned at once from her evil ways, and the Suphanite, after sighing long for grace, was suddenly converted. All the great female sinners were very quickly and powerfully converted, as was also the sturdy Paul, to whom conversion came like a flash of lightning. Judas on the contrary was always vacillating, and at last fell into the abyss.

A month later, on Saturday, December 9, AD 30, Jesus next visited his mother, with whom were then stopping Susanna Alpheus, Mary, the daughter of Cleophas of Nazareth, Susanna of Jerusalem, Dinah the Samaritan, and Martha. Jesus told them that he was going away the next morning. Martha was very sad on account of Magdalene's relapse into sin and the state of demoniacal possession in which she then was. She asked Jesus whether she should go to her, but he told her to wait awhile. Magdalene was now often like one beside herself. She yielded to fits of anger and pride, struck all that came in her way, tormented her maids, and was always arrayed in the most wanton attire. I saw her striking the man that lived as master in her house, and I beheld him returning her blows with ill-treatment. At times she fell into frightful sadness, she wept and lamented. She ran about the house seeking for Jesus and crying out: "Where is the teacher? Where is he? He has abandoned me!" and then fell into convulsions like epileptic fits. One may imagine the pain of her brother and sister at beholding one of a noble family, one so richly endowed by nature, given up to so frightful a state.

Magdalene's Second Conversion and After

JUST over two weeks later, on Monday, December 25, AD 30, at the inn in Dothaim, Jesus met Martha and Lazarus and some other women and disciples from Jerusalem. About an hour to the south of the inn at Dothaim lay the little town of Azanoth. It was built on an eminence upon which was a teacher's chair and, in earlier times, it had often been the scene of the prophets' preaching. Through the activity of the disciples, the report had been spread throughout the whole region that Jesus was about to deliver a great instruction in that place, and in consequence of this report multitudes were gathered there from all Galilee. Martha, attended by her maid, had journeyed to Magdalene in the hope of inducing her to be present at the instruction, but she was received very haughtily by her sister, with whom things had come to the worst. She was, on Martha's arrival, engaged at her toilet, and sent word that she could not speak to her then.

Martha awaited her sister's appearance with unspeakable patience, occupying herself meanwhile in prayer. At last the unhappy Magdalene presented herself, her manner haughty, excited, and defiant. She was ashamed of Martha's simple attire. She feared that some of her guests might see her, consequently she requested her to go away as soon as possible. But as Martha begged to be allowed to rest in some corner of the house, she and her maid were conducted to a room in one of the side buildings where, either through design or forgetfulness, they were allowed to remain without food or drink. It was then afternoon. Meanwhile Magdalene adorned herself for the banquet, at which she was seated on a richly decorated chair, while Martha and her maid were in prayer. After the revelry Magdalene went at last to Martha, taking with her something on a little blue-edged plate and something to drink. She addressed Martha angrily and disdainfully, her whole demeanor expressive of pride, insolence, uneasiness, and interior agitation.

Martha, full of humility and affection, invited Magdalene to go with her once more to the great instruction Jesus was going to deliver in the neighborhood. All Magdalene's female friends, Martha urged—those whom she had lately met—would be there and

55

very glad to see her. She herself (Magdalene) had already testified to the esteem in which she held Jesus, and she should now gratify Lazarus and herself (Martha) by going once more to hear him preach. She would not soon again have the opportunity of hearing the wonderful prophet and at the same time of seeing all her friends in her own neighborhood. She had shown by her anointing of Jesus at the banquet at Gabara that she knew how to honor greatness and majesty. She should now again salute him whom she had once so nobly and fearlessly honored in public, etc. It would be impossible to say how lovingly Martha spoke to her erring sister, or how patiently she endured her shamefully contemptuous manner. At last Magdalene replied: "I shall go, but not with you! You can go on ahead, for I will not be seen with one so miserably clothed. I shall dress according to my position, and I shall go with my own friends." At these words the two sisters separated, for it was very late.

Next morning Magdalene sent for Martha to come to her room while she was making her toilet. Martha went, patient as usual and secretly praying that Magdalene might go with her and be converted. Magdalene, clothed in a fine woollen garment, was sitting on a low stool, while two of her maids were busily engaged washing her feet and arms and perfuming them with fragrant water. Her hair was divided into three parts above the ears and at the back of the head, after which it was combed, brushed, oiled, and braided. Over her fine woollen undergarment was put a green robe embroidered with large yellow flowers, and over that again a mantle with folds. Her headdress was a kind of crimped cap that rose high on the forehead. Both her hair and her cap were interwoven with numberless pearls, and in her ears were long pendants. Her sleeves were wide above the elbow, but narrow below and fastened with broad, glittering bracelets. Her robe was plaited. Her under-bodice was open on the breast and laced with shining cords. During the toilet, Magdalene held in her hand a round, polished mirror. She wore an ornament on her breast. It was covered with gold, and encrusted with cut stones and pearls. Over the narrow-sleeved underdress she wore an upper one with a long flowing train and short, wide sleeves. It was made of changeable violet silk, and embroidered with large flowers, some in gold, others in different colors. The braids of her hair were ornamented with roses made of raw silk, and strings of pearls, interwoven with some kind of stiff transparent stuff that stood out in points. Very little of the hair could be seen through its load of ornamentation. It was rolled high around the face. Over this headdress Magdalene wore a rich hood of fine, transparent material. It fell on the high headdress in front, shaded the cheeks, and hung low on the shoulders behind. Martha took leave of her sister, and went to the inn near Damna in order to tell Mary and the holy women the success she had had in her efforts to persuade Magdalene to be present at the instruction about to be given in Azanoth. With the Blessed Virgin about a dozen women had come to Damna, among them Anna Cleophas, Susanna Alpheus, Susanna of Jerusalem, Veronica, Johanna Chusa, Mary Mark, Dinah, Maroni, and the Suphanite.

On Tuesday, December 26, AD 30, Jesus, accompanied by six apostles and a number of the disciples, started from the inn at Dothaim for Azanoth. On the way he met the holy women coming from Damna. Lazarus was among Jesus's companions on this occasion. After Martha's departure, Magdalene was very much tormented by the devil, who wanted to prevent her going to Jesus's instruction. She would have followed his suggestions, were it not for some of her guests, who had agreed to go with her to Azanoth to witness what they called a great show. Magdalene and her frivolous, sinful companions rode on asses to the inn of the holy women near the baths of Bethulia. Magdalene's splendid seat, along with cushions and rugs for the others, followed packed on asses.

Next morning Magdalene, again arrayed in her most wanton attire and surrounded by her companions, made her appearance at the place of instruction, which was about an hour from the inn at which she was stopping. With noise and bustle, loud talk and bold staring about, they took their places under an open tent far in front of the holy women. There were some men of their own stamp in their party. They sat upon cushions and rugs and upholstered chairs, all in full view, Magdalene in front. Their coming gave rise to general whispering and murmurs of disapprobation, for they were even more detested and despised in these quarters than in Gabara. The Pharisees especially, who knew of her first remarkable conversion at Gabara and of her subsequent relapse into her former disorders, were scandalized and expressed their indignation at her daring to appear in such an assembly.

Jesus, after healing many sick, began his long and severe discourse. The details of his sermon I cannot now recall, but I know that he cried woe upon Capernaum, Bethsaida, and Chorazin. He said also that the queen of Sheba had come from the South to hear the wisdom of Solomon, but here was one greater than Solomon. And lo, the wonder! Children that had never yet spoken, babes in their mothers' arms, cried out from time to time during the instruction: "Jesus of Nazareth! Holiest of prophets! Son of David! Son of God!" Which words caused many of the hearers, and among them Magdalene, to tremble with fear.

Making allusion to Magdalene, Jesus said that when the devil has been driven out and the house has been swept, he returns with six other demons, and rages worse than before. These words terrified Magdalene. After Jesus had in this way touched the hearts of many, he turned successively to all sides and commanded the demon to go out of all that sighed for deliverance from his thralldom, but that those who wished to remain bound to the devil should depart and take him along with them. At this command the possessed cried out from all parts of the circle: "Jesus, thou Son of God!"—and here and there people sank to the ground unconscious. Magdalene also, from her splendid seat upon which she had attracted all eyes, fell in violent convulsions. Her companions in sin applied perfumes as restoratives, and wanted to carry her away. Desiring to remain under the empire of the evil one, they were themselves glad to profit by the opportunity to retire from the scene.

But just then some persons near her cried out: "Stop, Master! Stop! This woman is dying." Jesus interrupted his discourse to reply: "Place her on her chair! The death she is now dying is a good death, and one that will vivify her!" After some time another word of Jesus pierced her to the heart and she again fell into convulsions, during which dark forms escaped from her. A crowd gathered round her in alarm, while her own immediate party tried once again to bring her to herself. She was soon able to resume her seat on her beautiful chair and then she tried to look as if she had suffered only an ordinary fainting spell. She had now become the object of general attention, especially as many other possessed back in the crowd had, like her, fallen in convulsions, and afterward rose up freed from the evil one. But when for the third time Magdalene fell down in violent convulsions, the excitement increased, and Martha hurried forward to her. When she recovered consciousness she acted like one bereft of her senses. She wept passionately and wanted to go to where the holy women were sitting. The frivolous companions with whom she had come hither held her back forcibly, declaring that she should not play the fool, and they at last succeeded in getting her down the mountain. Lazarus, Martha, and others who had followed her, now went forward and led her to the inn of the holy holy women. The crowd of worldlings who had accompanied Magdalene had already made their way off.

Before going down to his inn, Jesus healed many blind and sick. Later on, he taught again in the school, and Magdalene was present. She was not yet quite cured, but profoundly impressed, and no longer so wantonly arrayed. She had laid aside her superfluous finery, some of which was made of a delicate scalloped material like pointed lace, and so perishable that it could be worn only once. She was now veiled. Jesus in his instruction appeared again to speak for her special benefit and, when he fixed upon her his penetrating glance, she fell once more into unconsciousness, and another evil spirit went out of her. Her maids bore her from the synagogue to where she was received by Martha and Mary, who took her back to the inn. She was now like one distracted. She cried and wept. She ran through the public streets saying to all she met that she was a wicked creature, a sinner, the refuse of humanity. The holy women had the greatest trouble to quiet her. She tore her garments, disarranged her hair, and hid her face in the folds of her veil.

When Jesus returned to his inn with the disciples and some of the Pharisees, and while they were taking some refreshments standing, Magdalene escaped from the holy women, ran with streaming hair and uttering loud lamentations, made her way through the crowd, cast herself at Jesus's feet, weeping and moaning, and asked if she might still hope for salvation. The Pharisees and disciples, scandalized at the sight, said to Jesus that he should no longer suffer this reprobate woman to create disturbance everywhere, that he should send her away once for all. But Jesus replied: "Permit her to weep and lament! Ye know not what is passing in her"—and he turned to her with words of consolation. He told her to repent from her heart, to believe and to hope, for that she should soon find peace. Then he bade her depart with confidence.

Martha, who had followed with her maids, took her again to her inn. Magdalene did nothing but wring her hands and lament. She was not yet quite freed from the power of the evil one, who tortured and tormented her with the most frightful remorse and despair. There was no rest for her—she thought herself forever lost. Upon her request, Lazarus went to Magdalum in order to take charge of her property, and to dissolve the ties she had there formed. She owned, near Azanoth and in the surrounding country, fields and vineyards which Lazarus, on account of her extravagance, had previously sequestered.

The following day, Wednesday, December 27, AD 30, to escape the great crowd that had gathered here, Jesus went at night with his disciples into the neighborhood of Damna, where there was an inn, as well as a lovely eminence upon which stood a chair for teaching. Next morning, when the holy women came thither accompanied by Magdalene, they found Jesus already encompassed by people seeking his aid. When his departure became known, the crowds awaiting him at Azanoth, as well as new visitors, came streaming to Damna, and fresh bands continued to arrive during the whole instruction.

Magdalene, crushed and miserable, now sat among the holy women. Jesus inveighed severely against the sin of impurity and said that it was that vice that had called down fire upon Sodom and Gomorrah. But he spoke of the mercy of God also and of the present time of pardon, almost conjuring his hearers to accept the grace offered them. Thrice during this discourse did Jesus rest his glance upon Magdalene, and each time I saw her sinking down and dark vapors issuing from her. The third time, the holy women carried her away. She was pale, weak, annihilated as it were, and scarcely recognizable. Her tears flowed incessantly. She was completely transformed, and passionately sighed to confess her sins to Jesus and receive pardon.

The instruction over, Jesus went to a retired place, whither Mary herself and Martha led Magdalene to him. She fell on her face weeping at his feet, her hair flowing loosely around her. Jesus comforted her. When Mary and Martha had withdrawn, she cried for pardon, confessed her numerous transgressions, and asked over and over: "Lord, is there still salvation for me?" Jesus forgave her sins, and she implored him to save her from another relapse. He promised so to do, gave her his blessing, and spoke to her of the virtue of purity, also of his mother, who was pure without stain. He praised Mary highly in terms I had never before heard from his lips, and commanded Magdalene to unite herself closely to her and to seek from her advice and consolation. When Jesus and Magdalene rejoined the holy women, Jesus said to them: "She has been a great sinner, but for all future time, she will be the model of penitents."

Magdalene, through her passionate emotion, her grief and her tears, was no longer like a human being, but like a shadow tottering from weakness. She was, however, calm, though still weeping silent tears that exhausted her. The holy women comforted her with many marks of affection, while she in turn craved pardon of each. As they had to set out for Nain, and Magdalene was too weak to accompany them, Martha, Anna Cleophas, and Mara the Suphanite went with her to Damna in order to rest that night and follow the others next morning. The holy women went through Cana to Nain.

Jesus and the disciples went across through the valley of the baths of Bethulia, four or five hours farther on, to Gath-Hepher, a large city that lay on a height between Cana and Sepphoris. They passed the night outside the city at an inn that was near a cave called "John's cave."

On Sunday, January 7, AD 31, from Beth-Horon, which was six hours distant from Jerusalem, Jesus went straight on to Bethany, stopping at no place on the way excepting Anathoth. Lazarus had already returned to Bethany from Magdalum, where he had put everything in order and engaged a steward for the castle and other property. To the man who had lived with Magdalene he had assigned a dwelling situated on the heights near Ginea and sufficient means for his support. The gift was gladly accepted.

As soon as she arrived in Bethany, Magdalene went straight to the dwelling of her deceased sister, Silent Mary, by whom she had been very much beloved, and spent the whole night in tears. When Martha went to her in the morning, she found her weeping on the grave of her sister, her hair unbound and flowing around her.

The women of Jerusalem also had returned to their homes, all making the journey on foot. Magdalene, though exhausted by her malady and the shocks she had received, and wholly unaccustomed to such traveling, insisted upon walking like the others. Her feet bled more than once. The holy women who, since her conversion, showed her unspeakable affection, were often obliged to come to her assistance. She was pale and exhausted from weeping. She could not resist her desire to express her gratitude to Jesus, so she went over an hour's journey to meet him, threw herself at his feet, and bedewed them with repentant and grateful tears. Jesus extended his hand to her, raised her, and addressed to her words of kindness. He spoke of her deceased sister, Silent Mary. He said that she should tread in her footsteps and do penance as she had done, although she had never sinned. Magdalene then returned home with her maid by another way.

Well over a week later, Thursday, January 18, AD 31, Jesus was on his way from Bethzur with Lazarus and the disciples to Bethany. They stopped at several places along their route, among them at Emmaus. Jesus taught here and there on the way among the people who were busy tying up the hedges, which were already green. Martha, Magdalene, and a widow named Salome came to meet them at almost an hour's distance from Bethany. Salome had long dwelt in Bethany with Martha. Through one of Joseph's brothers and like Susanna, she was related to the holy family. She was later on present at Jesus's sepulcher. They, Martha, Magdalene, and Salome, had been at Lazarus's inn in the desert, whence they returned at dusk to Bethany. Magdalene occupied the little apartments of Silent Mary's dwelling. She often sat in a very narrow little room that appeared to be formed in a tower. It was a retired corner intended for penitential exercises. She still wept freely. True, she was no longer actually sick, but from contrition and penance she had become quite pale and reduced. She looked like one crushed by sorrow.

On the sabbath two weeks later, Saturday, March 24, AD 31, Jesus taught at Lazarus's, and then all went to walk in the gardens. Jesus talked of his passion and said in plain terms that he was the Christ. His words increased his hearers' reverence and admiration for him, while Magdalene's love and contrition reached their height. She followed Jesus everywhere, sat at his feet, stood and waited for him everywhere. She thought of him alone, saw him alone, knew only her Redeemer and her own sins. Jesus frequently addressed to her words of consolation. She was very greatly changed. Her countenance and bearing were still noble and distinguished, though her beauty was destroyed by her penance and tears. She sat almost always alone in her narrow penance chamber, and at times performed the lowest services for the poor and sick.

On Thursday, June 7, AD 31, Jesus visited Sion to comfort the poor and oppressed. In the morning, he healed the sick, while the disciples distributed what money and goods they had to the poor. In the afternoon, Jesus and the disciples went to Nain. Here, on Monday, November 13, AD 30, he had raised the youth Martialis from the dead. Martialis's mother—the rich widow Maroni—had put one of her properties at Jesus's disposal to be used by him and his disciples as an inn. Jesus and the disciples visited this house. Martha, Mary Magdalene, Veronica, Johanna Chusa, and Mara the Suphanite were waiting there. Jesus told them of his visit to Cyprus, speaking with special warmth of the Roman commandant in Salamis. Magdalene and the Suphanite were nothing like as beautiful as they used to be. They were pale and thin, and their eyes red from weeping. Martha was very energetic, and in business affairs very talkative. Johanna Chusa was a tall, pale, vigorous woman, grave in manner, but at the same time active. Veronica had in her deportment something very like St. Catherine; she was frank, resolute, and courageous.

The Death and Raising of Lazarus

THE *next period during which Mary Magdalene plays a leading role is that of the death of her brother Lazarus (July 15, AD 32) and his subsequent raising (July 26, AD 32), with all the events connected thereto. Since the lengthy account of these events in Anne Catherine's visions is told in "Lazarus and His Friends (The Secret Disciples)" in* People of the New Testament II, *it is not repeated here.*

Mary Magdalene at Events Leading to the Passion

ON the morning of Wednesday, January 21, AD 33, Jesus taught and healed in Jericho. The Virgin Mary, Peter's wife and step-daughter, and Andrew's wife set off back to Galilee, and the other holy women also returned to their homes. There was a great throng of people in Jericho, as word had already spread that Jesus was there. When the crowd became too great, Jesus went with the three apostles to Bethel, where the patriarch Jacob saw on a hill the ladder reaching from earth to heaven. It was already dark when they arrived and approached a house wherein trusty friends were awaiting them: Lazarus and his sisters, Nicodemus, and John Mark, who had come hither from Jerusalem secretly. The master of the house had a wife and four children. The house was surrounded by a courtyard in which was a fountain. Attended by two of his children, the master opened the door to the guests, whom he conducted at once to the fountain and washed their feet. As Jesus was sitting on the edge of the fountain, Magdalene came forth from the house and poured over his hair a little flat flask of perfume. She did it standing at his back, as she had often done before. I wondered at her boldness. Jesus pressed to his heart Lazarus, who was still pale and haggard.

At the Solemn Entrance into Jerusalem

WHEN toward evening on Thursday, March 19, AD 33, the Jerusalem gate was again opened, the holy women went back to Bethany, and Jesus followed later with the apostles. Magdalene, worried because Jesus and his followers had had no refreshment in Jerusalem, now prepared a meal for them herself. It was already dark when Jesus entered the courtyard of Lazarus's dwelling. Magdalene brought him a basin of water, washed his feet, and dried them with a towel that was hanging over her shoulder. The food that she had prepared did not amount to a regular meal, it was merely a luncheon. While the Lord was partaking of it, she approached and poured balm over his head. I saw Judas, who passed her at this moment, muttering his dissatisfaction, but she replied to his murmurs by saying that she could never thank the Lord sufficiently for what he had done for her and her brother.

The following day, full of trouble, Jesus went back with the apostles to Bethany for the sabbath. While he was teaching in the Temple, the Jews had been ordered to keep their houses closed, and it was forbidden to offer him or his disciples any refreshment. On reaching Bethany, they went to the public house of Simon, the healed leper, where a meal awaited them. Magdalene, filled with compassion for Jesus's fatiguing exertions, met the Lord at the door. She was clothed in a penitential robe and girdle, her flowing hair concealed by a black veil. She cast herself at his feet and with her hair wiped from them the dust, just as one would clean the shoes of another. She did it openly before all, and many were scandalized at her conduct.

After Jesus and the disciples had prepared themselves for the sabbath—that is, put on the garments prescribed and prayed under the lamp—they stretched themselves at table for the meal. Toward the end of it Magdalene, urged by love, gratitude, contrition, and anxiety, again made her appearance. She went behind the Lord's couch, broke a little flask of precious balm over his head and poured some of it upon his feet, which she again wiped with her hair. That done, she left the dining hall. Several of those present were scandalized, especially Judas, who excited Matthew, Thomas, and John Mark to displeasure. But Jesus excused her on account of the love she bore him. She often anointed him in this way. Many of the facts mentioned only once in the gospels happened frequently.

A week later, on Friday, March 27, AD 33, Jesus exhorted the apostles not to give way to their natural fears upon what he had recently said to them, namely, that they would all be dispersed; they should not forget their neighbor and should not allow one sentiment to veil, to stifle another; and here he made use of the similitude of a mantle. In general terms he reproached some of them for murmuring at Magdalene's anointing. Jesus probably said this in reference to Judas's first definitive step toward his betrayal, which had been taken just after that action of hers—also, as a gentle warning to him for the future, since it would be after Magdalene's last anointing that he would carry out his treacherous design. That some others were scandalized at Magdalene's prodigal expression of love arose from their erroneous severity and parsimony. They regarded this anointing as a luxury so often abused at worldly feasts, while overlooking the fact that such an action performed on the holy of holies was worthy of the highest praise.

Magdalene's Last Anointing of Jesus

ON the morning of Wednesday, April 1, AD 33, Jesus instructed a large number of the disciples, more than sixty, in the court before Lazarus's house. In the afternoon, about three o'clock, tables were laid for them in the court, and during their meal Jesus and the apostles served. I saw Jesus going from table to table handing something to this one, something to that, and teaching all the time. Judas was not present. He was away making purchases for the entertainment to be given at Simon's. Magdalene also had gone to Jerusalem, to buy precious ointment. The Blessed Virgin, to whom Jesus had that morning announced his approaching death, was inexpressibly sad. Her niece, Mary Cleophas, was always around her, consoling her. Full of grief, they went together to the disciples' inn.

This morning Jesus spoke of many things with his apostles. As they did not understand everything, he commanded them to write down what they could not comprehend, saying that when he would send his Spirit to them, they would recall those points and be able to seize their meaning. At last he spoke of his Holy Mother. He said that through compassion she would suffer with him all the cruel torture of his death, that with him she would die his bitter death, and still would have to survive him fifteen years. And thus Jesus went on instructing his followers with extraordinary love, counseling them on everything. I saw many of them dispersing toward evening.

It was during this instruction that Magdalene came back from Jerusalem with the ointment she had brought. She had gone to Veronica's and stayed there while Veronica saw to the purchase of the ointment, which was of three kinds, the most precious that could be procured. Magdalene had expended upon it all the money she had left. One was a flask of the oil of spikenard. She bought the flasks together with their contents. The former were of a clear, whitish, though not transparent material, almost like mother-of-pearl, though not mother-of-pearl. They were in shape like little urns, the swelling base ornamented with knobs, and they had screw-tops. Magdalene carried the vessels under her mantle in a pocket which hung on her breast suspended by a cord that passed over one shoulder and back across the back.

John Mark's mother went back with her to Bethany, and Veronica accompanied them a part of the way. As they were going through Bethany, they met Judas who, concealing his indignation, spoke to Magdalene. Magdalene had heard from Veronica that the Pharisees had resolved to arrest Jesus and put him to death, but not yet, on account of the crowds of strangers and especially the numerous pagans that followed him. This news Magdalene imparted to the other women. The women were at Simon's helping to prepare for the entertainment, for which Judas had purchased everything necessary. He had entirely emptied the purse today, secretly thinking that he would get all back again in the evening. From a man who kept a garden in Bethany he bought vegetables, two lambs, fruit, fish, honey, etc.

The dining hall used at Simon's today was different from that in which Jesus and his friends had dined once before, that is, on the day after the Triumphal Entrance into the Temple. Today they dined in an open hall at the back of the house that looked out upon the courtyard. It had been ornamented for the occasion. In the ceiling was an opening which was covered with a transparent veil and which looked like a little cupola. Under this ceiling ornamentation stood the seat for Jesus. The guests reclined during this repast on low crossbenches, which in the back had a support, and in front an arm upon which to lean. Jesus reclined at the middle of the table upon a seat to himself. On this occasion the women ate in an open hall to the left. Looking obliquely across the courtyard they could see the men at table.

When all was prepared, Simon and his servant, in festal robes, went to conduct Jesus, the apostles, and Lazarus. Simon wore a long robe, a girdle embroidered in figures, and on his arm a long fur-lined maniple. The servant wore a sleeveless jacket. Simon escorted Jesus; the servant, the apostles. Several large drinking glasses stood on the table, and beside each, two smaller ones. There were three kinds of beverages: one greenish, another red, and the third yellow. I think it was some kind of pear juice. The lamb was served first. It lay stretched out on an oval dish, the head resting on the forefeet. The dish was placed with the head toward Jesus. The holy women were seated around their own table. Magdalene, who was in tears all the time, sat opposite the Blessed Virgin. There were seven or nine present.

Jesus taught during the whole meal. It was nearing the close of his discourse; the apostles were stretched forward in breathless attention. Simon, whose services were no longer needed, sat motionless, listening to every word, when Magdalene rose quietly from her seat among the holy women. She had around her a thin, bluish-white mantle, something like the material worn by the three holy kings, and her flowing hair was covered with a veil. Laying the ointment in a fold of her mantle, she passed through the walk that was planted with shrubbery, entered the hall, went up behind Jesus, and cast herself down at his feet, weeping bitterly. She bent her face low over the foot that was resting on the couch, while Jesus himself raised to her the other that was hanging a little toward the floor. Magdalene loosened the sandals and anointed Jesus's feet on the soles and upon the upper part. Then with both hands drawing her flowing hair from beneath her veil she wiped the Master's anointed feet, and replaced the sandals.

Magdalene's action caused some interruption in Jesus's discourse. He had observed her approach, but the others were taken by surprise. Jesus said: "Be not scandalized at this woman!" and then addressed some words softly to her. She now arose, stepped behind him and poured over his head some costly water, and that so plentifully that it ran down upon his garments. Then with her hand she spread some of the ointment from the crown down the hind part of his head. The hall was filled with the delicious fragrance. The apostles whispered together and muttered their displeasure—even Peter was vexed at the interruption.

Magdalene, weeping and veiled, withdrew around behind the table. When she was about to pass before Judas, he stretched forth his hand to stay her while he indignantly addressed to her some words on her extravagance, saying that the purchase money might have been given to the poor. Magdalene made no reply. She was weeping bitterly. Then Jesus spoke, bidding them let her pass, and saying that she had anointed him for his death, for later she would not be able to do it, and that wherever this gospel would be preached, her action and their murmuring would also be recounted. Magdalene retired, her heart full of sorrow. The rest of the meal was disturbed by the displeasure of the apostles and the reproaches of Jesus. When it was over, all returned to Lazarus's.

The next day, Holy Thursday, April 2, AD 33, I saw Jesus speaking alone with his Blessed Mother, and I remember some of the words that passed between them. He had, he said, sent Peter the believing and John the loving to Jerusalem in order to prepare for Passover. Of Magdalene, who was quite out of herself from grief, he said: "She loves unspeakably, but her love is still encompassed by the body, therefore has she become like one quite out of her mind with pain." He spoke also of the treacherous scheming of Judas, and the Blessed Virgin implored mercy for him.

At the Time of Gethsemane

LATER, in the company of some of the apostles Peter, James, and John at the time of his Agony in the garden of Gethsemane, Jesus told them that on the morrow he was going to die. In another hour, his enemies would seize him, drag him before the Courts of Justice, abuse him, deride him, scourge him, and put him to death in the most horrible manner. He begged them to console his mother. He recounted to them in bitter anguish all that he would have to suffer until the evening of the next day and again begged them to comfort his mother and Magdalene. He stood thus speaking for some moments, but the apostles kept silence, not knowing what to reply. When he wanted to return to the grotto, he had not the power to do so. I saw that John and James had to lead him. When he entered it, the apostles left him and went back to their own place. It was then a quarter past eleven.

During this agony of Jesus, I saw the Blessed Virgin overwhelmed with sorrow and anguish in the house of Mary Mark. She was with Magdalene and Mary Mark in a garden adjoining the house. She had sunk on her knees on a stone slab. She was perfectly absorbed in her own interior, quite diverted in thought from everything around her, seeing only, feeling only, the sufferings of her divine Son. She had sent messengers to obtain news of him, but unable to await their coming, in her anguish of heart she went with Magdalene and Salome out into the valley of Jehosaphat. I saw her walking along veiled, her arms often outstretched toward the Mount of Olives, where she saw in spirit Jesus agonizing and sweating blood. It seemed as if she would with her outstretched hands wipe his sacred face.

In answer to these interior and vehement movements of her soul toward her Son, I saw that Jesus was stirred with thoughts of her. He turned his eyes in her direction as if seeking help from her. I saw this mutual sympathy under the appearance of rays of light passing to and fro between them. The Lord thought also of Magdalene and felt for her in her distress. He glanced toward her, and his soul was touched at sight of her. He therefore ordered the disciples to console her, for he knew that her love for him, after that of his mother, was greater than that of anyone else. He saw what she would have to suffer for him in the future, and also that she would never more offend him. Later, the Blessed Virgin, Magdalene, and Salome, accompanied by some of the disciples who had seen the approach of the soldiers, left the valley of Jehosaphat and returned to the house of Mary Mark.

At the Judgment Hall of Caiaphas

THE Blessed Virgin, united in constant, interior compassion with Jesus, knew and experienced in her soul all that happened to him.

She suffered everything with him in spiritual contemplation, and like him was absorbed in continual prayer for his executioners. But at the same time her mother-heart cried uninterruptedly to God that he might not suffer these crimes to be enacted, that he might ward off these sufferings from her most blessed Son, and she irresistibly longed to be near her poor, outraged Jesus. When then John, after the frightful cry: "He is guilty of death!" left the judgment hall of Caiaphas and went to her at Lazarus's in Jerusalem, not far from the corner gate; and when, by his account of the terrible sufferings of her Son, he confirmed what she already well knew from interior contemplation, she ardently desired to be conducted together with Magdalene (who was almost crazed from grief), and some others of the holy women, to where she might be near her suffering Jesus. John, who had left the presence of his divine Master only to console her who was next to Jesus with him, accompanied the Blessed Virgin when led by the holy women from the house. Magdalene, wringing her hands, staggered with the others along the moonlit streets, which were alive with people returning to their homes.

As Jesus is Taken to Pilate

NOT very far from the house of Caiaphas, crowded together in the corner of a building and waiting for the coming procession, were the blessed and afflicted mother of Jesus, Magdalene, and John. Mary's soul was always with Jesus, but wherever she could approach him in body also, her love gave her no rest. It drove her out upon his path and into his footsteps. After her midnight visit to Caiaphas's tribunal, she had in speechless grief tarried only a short time in the cenacle, for scarcely was Jesus led forth from prison for the morning trial when she too arose. Enveloped in mantle and veil, and taking the lead of John and Magdalene, she said: "Let us follow my son to Pilate. My eyes must again behold him." Taking a bypath, they got in advance of the procession, and here the Blessed Virgin stood and waited along with the others.

As Jesus approached her, Mary lamented as any mother might have done: "Alas! Is this my son? Ah! Is this my son! O Jesus, my Jesus!" The procession hurried by. Jesus cast upon his mother

71

a side glance full of emotion. She became unconscious of all around, and John and Magdalene bore her away. But scarcely had she somewhat recovered herself when she requested John to accompany her again to Pilate's palace.

When Jesus is Before Pilate

THE Blessed Virgin, standing with Magdalene and John in a corner of the forum hall, had with unspeakable pain beheld the whole of the dreadful scene just described, had heard the clamorous shouts and cries. And now when Jesus was taken to Herod, she begged to be conducted by John and Magdalene back over the whole way of suffering trodden by her divine Son since his arrest the preceding evening. They went over the whole route—to the judgment hall of Caiaphas, to the palace of Annas, and thence through Ophel to Gethsemane on the Mount of Olives. On many places where Jesus had suffered outrage and injury, they paused in heartfelt grief and compassion, and wherever he had fallen to the ground the Blessed Mother fell on her knees and kissed the earth. Magdalene wrung her hands, while John in tears assisted the afflicted mother to rise, and led her on further. This was the origin of that devotion of the Church, the holy way of the cross, the origin of that sympathetic meditation upon the bitter passion of our divine Redeemer even before it was fully accomplished by him.

Magdalene in her grief was like an insane person. Immeasurable as her love was her repentance. When, in her love, she longed to pour out her soul at the feet of Jesus, as once the precious balm upon his head, full of horror she descried between her and the Redeemer the abyss of her crimes; then was the pain of repentance in all its bitterness renewed in her heart. When, in her gratitude, she longed to send up like a cloud of incense her thanksgiving for forgiveness received, she saw him, full of pains and torments, led to death. With unspeakable grief she comprehended that Jesus was undergoing all this on account of her sins, which he had taken upon himself in order to atone for them with his own blood. This thought plunged her deeper and deeper into an abyss of repentant sorrow. Her soul was as it were dissolved in gratitude and love, in sorrow and bitterness, in sadness and lamentation, for she saw and felt the ingratitude, the capital crime of her nation, in delivering its Savior to the ignominious death of the cross. All this was expressed in her whole appearance, in her words and gestures. John suffered and loved not less than Magdalene, but the untroubled innocence of his pure heart lent a higher degree of peace to his soul.

As Jesus is Taken
from Herod Back to Pilate

IT was a quarter after eight in the morning of Good Friday, April 3, AD 33, when the procession with the maltreated Jesus again crossed the Forum (though from another side, probably the eastern) to Pilate's palace. The Blessed Virgin, her elder sister Mary Heli with her daughter Mary Cleophas, Magdalene, and several other holy women—in all about twenty—were, while the following events were taking place, standing in a hall from which they could hear everything, and where they could slip in and out. John was with them in the beginning. Mary, Magdalene, John, and the holy women, trembling and weeping, were presently in a corner of that hall. Although the mother of Jesus knew that there was no help for humankind excepting by his death, yet she was, as the mother of the most holy Son, full of anxiety, full of longing for the preservation of his life. Jesus had become man voluntarily to undergo crucifixion; still, when led to death, though innocent, he suffered all the pangs and torments of his frightful ill-treatment just as any human being would have suffered.

At the Place of the Scourging

THE Virgin Mary saw her lacerated Son driven past her by the executioners. With his garment he wiped the blood from his eyes in order to see his Mother. She raised her hands in agony toward him and gazed upon his blood-stained footprints. Then, as the mob moved over to another side, I saw the Blessed Virgin and Magdalene approaching the place of scourging. Surrounded and hidden by the other holy women and some well-disposed people standing by, they cast themselves on their knees and soaked up the sacred blood of Jesus with the linens until not a trace of it could be found.

Personal Appearance
of Mary and of Magdalene

I SAW the Blessed Virgin with cheeks pale and haggard, her nose pinched and long, her eyes almost bloodshot from weeping. It is astonishing, as well as indescribable, how plain, straightforward, and simple she was in appearance. Although since yesterday evening—and even during the whole night—she had in fright, in anguish, and in tears, been wandering through the valley of Jehosaphat and the crowded streets of Jerusalem, still was her dress in perfect order, her whole appearance marked by extreme propriety. There was not even a fold of her garments that did not bespeak sanctity. Everything about her was so upright and simple, so dignified, so pure, and so innocent. Her look as she gazed around was so noble, and as she turned her head a little, her veil fell in soft and graceful folds. Her movements were not eager and, though under the influence of the most grievous anguish, all her actions were performed simply and gently. Her garments were damp with the dew of the night and her own innumerable tears, but they were spotless and in perfect order. Her beauty was indescribable and altogether superhuman, for beauty in her was made up of immaculate purity, truth, simplicity, dignity, and holiness. Magdalene on the contrary was just the reverse. She was taller and, both in figure and carriage, exhibited much more style. Her beauty however was now destroyed owing to her violent repentance and intense grief. She was, if not decidedly ugly, at least painful to look upon, on account of the unrestrained fury of her passions. Her garments, wet and stained with mud, hung torn and disordered around her; her long hair floated loose and dishevelled under her wet, tossed veil. She was perfectly changed in appearance. She thought of nothing but her grief, and looked almost like one bereft of sense. There were many people here from Magdalum and the surrounding country who had known her in her early splendor, who had seen her in her wasting life of sin, and who had lost sight of her in her long retirement. Now they pointed her out with the finger and mocked at her forlorn appearance. Yes, there were some from Magdalum base enough even to throw mud at her as she passed along. But she did not notice it, so absorbed was she in her own sorrow.

On the Way to Golgotha

AFTER that most painful meeting with her divine Son carrying his cross before the dwelling of Caiaphas, the most afflicted Mother was conducted by John and the holy women, Johanna Chusa, Susanna, and Salome, to the house of Nazareth in the vicinity of the corner gate. Here the other holy women, in tears and lamentations, were gathered around Magdalene and Martha. Some children were with them. They now went all together, in number seventeen, with the Blessed Virgin—careless of the jeers of the mob, grave and resolute, and by their tears awe-inspiring—across the forum, where they kissed the spot upon which Jesus had taken up the burden of the cross. Thence they proceeded along the whole of the sorrowful way trodden by him and venerated the places marked by special sufferings.

The sufferings of the most afflicted Mother of Sorrows on this journey, at the sight of the place of execution and her ascent to it, cannot be expressed. They were twofold: the pains of Jesus suffered interiorly and the sense of being left behind. Magdalene was perfectly distracted, intoxicated and reeling, as it were, with grief, precipitated from agony to agony. From silence long maintained she fell to lamenting, from listlessness to wringing her hands, from moaning to threatening the authors of her misery. She had to be continually supported, protected, admonished to silence, and concealed by the other women.

The Blessed Virgin endured all Jesus's torture with him. She was pale as a corpse, and low moans of agony sounded from her lips. The Pharisees were mocking and jesting at the side of the low wall by which she was standing, therefore John led her to the other holy women at a still greater distance from the circle. Magdalene was like one out of her mind. She tore her face with her fingernails till her eyes and cheeks were covered with blood.

The Sun Obscured •
Second and Third Sayings from the Cross

THE mother of Jesus, Mary Cleophas, Mary Magdalene, and John were standing around Jesus's cross, between it and those of the thieves, and looking up at the Lord. The Blessed Virgin, overcome by maternal love, was in her heart fervently imploring Jesus to let her die with him. At that moment, the Lord cast an earnest and compassionate glance down upon his mother and, turning his eyes toward John, said to her: "Woman, behold, this is thy son! He will be thy son more truly than if thou hadst given him birth."

The hour of the Lord was now come. He was struggling with death, and a cold sweat burst out on every limb. John was standing by the cross and wiping Jesus's feet with his handkerchief. Magdalene, utterly crushed with grief, was leaning at the back of the cross. The Blessed Virgin, supported in the arms of Mary Cleophas and Salome, was standing between Jesus and the cross of the good thief, her gaze fixed upon her dying Son. Jesus spoke: "It is consummated!" and raising his head he cried with a loud voice: "Father, into thy hands I commend my spirit!"

The sweet, loud cry rang through heaven and earth. Then he bowed his head and gave up the spirit. I saw his soul like a luminous phantom descending through the earth near the cross down to the sphere of limbo. John and the holy women sank, face downward, prostrate on the ground. When Jesus's hands became stiff, his mother's eyes grew dim, the paleness of death overspread her countenance, her feet tottered, and she sank to the earth. Magdalene, John, and the others, yielding to their grief, fell also with veiled faces.

At the Descent from the Cross

THE Most Holy Virgin and Magdalene were seated upon the right side of the little mound between the cross of Dismas[1] and that of Jesus. The other women were busied arranging the spices and

---

[1] According to Anne Catherine, Dismas was the name of the good thief, and Gesmas that of the bad.

linens, the water, the sponges, and the vessels. Cassius also drew near when he saw Abenadar approaching, and imparted to him the miracle wrought on his eyes. All were extremely touched. Their movements were marked by an air of solemn sadness and gravity. They worked with hearts full of love, but without many words. Sometimes the silence in which the sacred duties were quickly and carefully being rendered was broken by a deep sigh or a vehement exclamation of woe. Magdalene gave way unrestrainedly to her grief. Her emotion was violent. No consideration, not even the presence of so many around her, could make her repress it.

When the blows of the hammer by which the nails were driven out [by Abenadar] resounded, Mary and Magdalene as well as all that had been present at the crucifixion were pierced with fresh grief, for the sound reminded them of that most cruel nailing of Jesus to the cross. They shuddered, as if expecting again to hear his piercing cries, and grieved anew over his death proclaimed by the silence of those blessed lips. As soon as the sacred body was taken down, the men wrapped it in linen from the knees to the waist and laid it on a sheet in his mother's arms which, in anguish of heart and ardent longing, were stretched out to receive it.

As the Body of Jesus is Prepared for Burial

THE Blessed Virgin was seated upon a large cover spread upon the ground, her right knee raised a little, and her back supported by a kind of cushion made, perhaps, of mantles rolled together. There sat the poor mother, exhausted by grief and fatigue, in the position best suited for rendering love's last, sad duties to the remains of her murdered Son. The men laid the sacred body on a sheet spread upon the mother's lap. The venerable head of Jesus rested upon her slightly raised knee, and his body lay outstretched upon the sheet. Love and grief in equal degrees struggled in the breast of the Blessed Mother. She held in her arms the body of her beloved Son, whose long martyrdom she had been able to soothe by no loving ministrations; and at the same time she beheld the frightful maltreatment exercised upon it, she gazed upon its wounds now close under her eyes. She pressed her

77

lips to his bloodstained cheeks while Magdalene knelt with her face bowed upon his feet. The other holy women helped in various ways, presenting when necessary vessels of water, sponges, towels, ointments, and spices. When not so engaged they remained at a little distance, attentively watching what was going on. Among them were Mary Cleophas, Salome, and Veronica, but Magdalene was always busied around the sacred body.

John lent constant assistance to the Blessed Virgin. He went to and fro between the women and the men, now helping the former in their task of love, and afterward assisting the latter in every way to prepare all things for the burial. Everything was thought of. The women had leathern water bottles, which they opened, and pressed the sides together to pour out their contents, also a vessel nearby on burning coals. They gave Mary and Magdalene clear water and fresh sponges as required, squeezing into leathern bottles those that had been used. I think the round lumps that I saw them squeezing out must have been sponges. Mary washed and purified all the wounds, while Magdalene, kneeling before her, frequently lent assistance, though for the most part she remained at Jesus's feet, bathing them for the last time, more with her tears than with water, and wiping them with her hair.

I saw Mary taking the hands of Jesus in her own left hand, reverently kissing them, and then filling the wide wounds made by the nails with ointment, or sweet spices. The ears, nostrils, and wound of Jesus's side, she likewise filled with the same. Magdalene was busied principally with the feet of Jesus. She repeatedly wiped and anointed them, but only to bedew them again with her tears, and she often knelt long with her face pressed upon them.

When the Blessed Virgin had anointed all the wounds, she bound up the sacred head in linen, but the covering for the face, attached to that of the head, she did not as yet draw down. With a gentle pressure she closed the half-broken eyes of Jesus and kept her hand upon them for a little while. Then she closed the mouth, embraced the sacred body of her Son, and weeping bitter tears, allowed her face to rest upon his. Magdalene's reverence for Jesus did not permit her to approach her face to his. She pressed it to his feet only.

The men raised the sacred body in the sheet upon which it was resting in the lap of his mother and carried it down to the place where the burial preparations were to be made. Mary's grief, which had been somewhat assuaged by her loving ministrations to Jesus, now burst forth anew, and, quite overcome, she rested with covered head in the arms of the women. Magdalene, as if fearing that they wanted to rob her of her Beloved, with outstretched hands ran some steps after the sacred body, but soon she turned back again to the Blessed Virgin.

John once more conducted the Blessed Virgin and the other holy women to the sacred remains of Jesus. Mary knelt down by Jesus's head, took a fine linen scarf that hung around her neck under her mantle (which she had received from Claudia Procula, Pilate's wife), and laid it under the head of her Son. Then she and the other holy women filled in the spaces between the shoulders and the head, around the whole neck and up as far as the cheeks with herbs, some of those fine threadlike plants, and a costly powder, all of which the Blessed Virgin bound up carefully in the fine linen scarf. Magdalene poured the entire contents of a little flask of precious balm into the wound of Jesus's side, while the holy women placed aromatic herbs in the hands and all around and under the feet.

The holy women sat down upon a seat opposite the entrance of the grotto. The four men carried the Lord's body down into it, set it down, strewed the stone couch with sweet spices, spread over it a linen cloth, and deposited the sacred remains upon it. The cloth hung down over the couch. Then, having with tears and embraces given expression to their love for Jesus, they left the cave. The Blessed Virgin now went in, and I saw her sitting on the head of the tomb, which was about two feet from the ground. She was bending low over the corpse of her child and weeping. When she left the cave, Magdalene hurried in with flowers and branches, which she had gathered in the garden and which she now scattered over the sacred body. She wrung her hands, and with tears and sighs embraced the feet of Jesus. When the men outside gave warning that it was time to close the doors, she went back to where the women were sitting.

On the Eve of the Resurrection

WHEN the morning sky began to clear with a streak of white light, I saw Magdalene, Mary Cleophas, Johanna Chusa, and Salome, enveloped in mantles, leaving their abode near the cenacle. They carried spices packed in linen cloths, and one of them had a lighted lantern. They kept all hidden under their mantles. The spices consisted of fresh flowers for strewing over the Sacred Body, and also of expressed sap, essences, and oils for pouring over it. The holy women walked anxiously to the little gate belonging to Nicodemus.

The holy women, when the Lord arose from the dead, were near the little gate belonging to Nicodemus. They knew nothing of the prodigies that were taking place; they did not know even of the guard at the sepulcher, for they had remained shut up in their house the whole of the preceding day, the sabbath. They anxiously inquired of one another: "Who will roll away for us the stone from the doors?" Full of longing desire to show the last honors to the sacred body in the tomb, they had entirely lost sight of the stone. They wanted to pour nard water and precious balm over the sacred body and scatter their flowers and aromatic shrubs upon it; for to the spices of yesterday's embalming, which Nicodemus alone had procured, they had contributed nothing. They wished therefore to offer now to the body of their Lord and Master the most precious that could be obtained. Salome had shared with Magdalene in defraying most of the cost. She was not the mother of John, but another Salome, a rich lady of Jerusalem, a relative of Joseph. At last the holy women concluded to set the spices on the stone before the tomb and to wait till some disciple would come who would open it for them. And so they went on toward the garden.

When, as they approached, the holy women noticed the lanterns of the guard and the soldiers lying around, they became frightened and went a short distance past the garden toward Golgotha. Magdalene, however, forgetful of danger, hurried into the garden. Salome followed her at some distance, and the other two waited outside. Magdalene, seeing the guard, stepped back at first a few steps toward Salome, then both made their way

together through the soldiers lying around and into the sepulcher. They found the stone rolled away, but the doors closed,
probably by Cassius. Magdalene anxiously opened one of them,
peered in at the tomb, and saw the linens lying empty and apart.
The whole place was resplendent with light, and an angel was sitting at the right of the tomb. Magdalene was exceedingly troubled. She hurried out of the garden of the sepulcher, off through
the gate belonging to Nicodemus, and back to the apostles.
Salome, too, who only now entered the sepulcher, ran at once
after Magdalene, rushed in fright to the women waiting outside
the garden, and told them of what had happened.

Though amazed and rejoiced at what they heard from Salome,
they could not resolve to enter the garden. It was not until Cassius
told them in a few words what he had seen, and exhorted them to
go see for themselves, that they took courage to enter. Cassius
was hurrying into the city to acquaint Pilate of all that had taken
place. He went through the gate of execution. When with beating
heart the women entered the sepulcher and drew near the holy
tomb, they beheld standing before them the two angels of the
tomb in priestly robes, white and shining. The women pressed
close to one another in terror and, covering their faces with their
hands, bowed tremblingly almost to the ground. One of the
angels addressed them. They must not fear, he said, nor must they
look for the crucified here. He was alive, he had arisen, he was no
longer among the dead.

Then the angel pointed out to them the empty tomb, and
ordered them to tell the disciples what they had seen and heard,
and that Jesus would go before them into Galilee. They should,
continued the angel, remember what the Lord had said to them in
Galilee, namely, "The Son of Man will be delivered into the hands
of sinners. He will be crucified and, on the third day, he will rise
again." The holy women, shaking and trembling with fear,
though still full of joy, tearfully gazed at the tomb and the linens,
and departed, taking the road toward the gate of execution. They
were still very much frightened. They did not hurry, but paused
from time to time and looked around from the distance, to see
whether they might not possibly behold the Lord, or whether
Magdalene was returning.

Meanwhile Magdalene reached the cenacle like one beside herself and knocked violently at the door. Some of the disciples were still asleep on their couches around the walls, while several others had risen and were talking together. Peter and John opened the door. Magdalene, without entering, merely uttered the words: "They have taken the Lord from the tomb! We know not where" —and ran back in great haste to the garden of the sepulcher. Peter and John followed her, but John outstripped Peter.

Magdalene was quite wet with dew when she again reached the garden and ran to the tomb. Her mantle had slipped from her head down on her shoulders, and her long hair had fallen around loose. As she was alone, she was afraid to enter the sepulcher at once, so she waited out on the step at the entrance. She stooped down, trying to see through the low doors into the cave and even as far as the stone couch. Her long hair fell forward as she stooped, and she was trying to keep it back with her hands, when she saw the two angels in white priestly garments sitting at the head and the foot of the tomb, and heard the words: "Woman, why weepest thou?" She cried out in her grief: "They have taken my Lord away! I know not where they have laid him!"

Saying this and seeing nothing but the linens, she turned weeping, like one seeking something, and as if she must find him. She had a dim presentiment that Jesus was near, and even the apparition of the angels could not turn her from her one idea. She did not appear conscious of the fact that it was an angel that spoke to her. She thought only of Jesus; her only thought was: "Jesus is not here! Where is Jesus?" I saw her running a few steps from the sepulcher and then returning like one half-distracted and in quest of something. Her long hair fell on her shoulders. Once she drew the whole mass on the right shoulder through both hands, then flung it back and gazed around.

About ten steps from the sepulcher and toward the east, where the garden rose in the direction of the city, she spied in the gray light of dawn, standing among the bushes behind a palm tree, a figure clothed in a long, white garment. Rushing toward it, she heard once more the words: "Woman, why weepest thou? Whom seekest thou?" She thought it was the gardener. I saw that he had a spade in his hand and on his head a flat hat, which had a piece of

82

something like bark standing out in front as a protection from the sun. It was just like that I had seen on the gardener in the parable which Jesus, shortly before his passion, had related to the women in Bethany.

The apparition was not resplendent. It looked like a person clad in long, white garments and seen at twilight. At the words: "Whom seekest thou?" Magdalene at once answered: "Sir, if thou hast taken him hence, show me where thou hast laid him! I will take him away!" And she again glanced around, as if to see whether he had not laid him someplace near. Then Jesus, in his well-known voice, said: "Mary!" Recognizing the voice, and forgetting the crucifixion, death, and burial now that he was alive, she turned quickly and, as once before, exclaimed: "Rabboni!" (Master!). She fell on her knees before him and stretched out her arms toward his feet. But Jesus raised his hand to keep her off, saying: "Do not touch me, for I am not yet ascended to my Father. But go to my brethren and say to them: I ascend to my Father and to your Father, to my God and to your God." At these words the Lord vanished.

It was explained to me why Jesus said: "Do not touch me," but I have only an indistinct remembrance of it. I think he said it because Magdalene was so impetuous. She seemed possessed of the idea that Jesus was alive just as he was before, and that everything was as it used to be. Upon Jesus's words that he had not yet ascended to his Father, I was told that he had not yet, since his resurrection, presented himself to his heavenly Father, had not yet thanked him for his victory over death and for redemption. I understood by those words that the first fruits of joy belong to God. It was as if Jesus had said that Magdalene should recollect herself and thank God for the mystery of redemption just accomplished and his conquest over death. After the disappearance of the Lord, Magdalene rose up quickly and again, as if in a dream, ran to the tomb. She saw the two angels, she saw the empty linens, and hurried, now certain of the miracle, back to her companions.

It may have been about half-past three o'clock when Jesus appeared to Magdalene. Scarcely had she left the garden when John approached, followed by Peter. John stood outside the entrance of the cave and stooped down to look, through the outer doors of the sepulcher, at the half-opened doors of the tomb, where he saw the linens lying. Then came Peter. He stepped down into the sepulcher and went to the tomb, in the center of which he saw the winding sheet lying. John now followed Peter to the tomb, saw the same things, and believed in the resurrection. All that the Lord had said, all that was written in the scriptures, was now clear to them.

As long as the sacred body lay in the tomb, the two angels sat one at the head, the other at the foot, and when Magdalene and the two apostles came they were still there. Now for the first time I saw the guards arise from where they were lying on the ground. They took their lances, also the lanterns that were hanging on poles at the door of the entrance and shedding their light into the cave, and hurried in evident fear and trepidation to the gate of execution and into the city.

Meanwhile Magdalene had reached the holy women and told them of the Lord's apparition. Then she too hurried on to the city through the neighboring gate of the execution, but the others went again to the garden, outside of which Jesus appeared to them in a white flowing garment that concealed even his hands. He said: "All hail!" They trembled and fell at his feet. Jesus waved his hand in a certain direction while addressing to them some words, and vanished. The holy women then hastened through the Bethlehem gate on Zion to tell the disciples in the cenacle that they had seen the Lord and what he had said to them. But the disciples would not at first credit Magdalene's report, and until the return of Peter and John they looked upon the whole affair as the effect of women's imagination.

On the evening of the same day, many of the disciples and all the apostles excepting Thomas assembled with Nicodemus and Joseph of Arimathea in the hall of the Last Supper, the doors being closed. They seemed to be engaged in some after-celebration of mourning or thanksgiving, for the Passover solemnities ended today in Jerusalem. The Blessed Virgin was, during the whole celebration, with Mary Cleophas and Magdalene in the hall outside, which opened into the Supper Room. Peter preached at intervals during the prayers.

Later I saw the Mother of God in Bethany. She was quiet and grave, more deeply absorbed in feelings of holy awe than in natural sorrow. Mary Cleophas was remarkably amiable and, of all the women, most like Mary. Magdalene, in her sorrow and love, was above all fear. She was perfectly heroic and without a thought of danger. She took no rest, but often left the house, hurried through the streets with streaming hair, and wherever she found listeners, whether in their homes or in public places, she accused them as the murderers of the Lord, vehemently recounting all they had done to the Savior and announcing to them his resurrection. If she found no one to listen to her, she wandered through the gardens and told it to the flowers, the trees, and the fountains. Oftentimes a crowd gathered around her, some offering her compassion, others insulting her on account of her past life. She was little esteemed by the crowd, for she had once given great scandal. I saw that her present violent conduct scandalized some of the Jews, and about five of them wanted to seize her, but she passed straight through them and went on as before. She had lost sight of the whole world, she sighed only after Jesus.

At the Second Love Feast (*Agape*)

AFTER the close of the sabbath, the apostles having laid aside their robes of ceremony, I saw a great meal spread in the outer hall. It was a love feast, such as had taken place on the preceding Sunday. And now I saw the Blessed Virgin, Magdalene, and another woman come into the house. The Blessed Virgin and Magdalene entered the hall, Peter and John going to meet them. The third woman remained in the antechamber. The entrance hall was opened into the Supper Room, also some of the side halls. The exterior doors leading into the courtyard, as well as those of the court itself, were shut. A great many disciples were gathered in the side halls. As soon as Mary and Magdalene entered, the doors were closed and all ranged for prayer. The holy women remained reverently standing on either side of the door, their arms crossed upon their breast.

Later, when the Risen Christ grasped Thomas's hand, I saw that his wounds were not like bloody marks, but like little radiant suns. The other disciples were greatly touched by this scene. They leaned forward, but without crowding, to see what the Lord was allowing Thomas to feel. I saw the Blessed Virgin during the whole time of Jesus's stay perfectly motionless, as if absorbed in calm, deep interior recollection. Magdalene appeared more agitated, yet manifesting far less emotion than did the disciples.

At the Love Feast (*Agape*) in Bethany and in the House of the Last Supper

ON Thursday, April 16, AD 33, I saw the apostles in Bethany, whither they were followed by about three hundred of the faithful, among them fifty women. They had given over their goods to the community. The Blessed Virgin also had come from Jerusalem to Bethany and was stopping in Martha and Magdalene's house. There was a great love feast of bread-breaking and passing round of the cup held in the open hall of Lazarus's court.

During the period from April 19–May 11, AD 33, Peter's wife and daughter, Mark's wife, and other women came from Bethsaida to Bethany, where they dwelt under tents. They had no communication whatever with the men. They came into the presence of the apostles only for instruction, and employed themselves in weaving and twisting long strips of stuff and coarse covers for tents, many of them working at the same time upon one piece. The Blessed Virgin also, along with Martha and Magdalene, worked at embroidery, sometimes reclining, sometimes walking about, work in hand.

Magdalene and Martha gave up their houses at Bethany to the new converts, and Lazarus delivered over all that he owned to the community.

On Wednesday, May 13, AD 33, the love feast over, all assembled outside the hall under the trees. Jesus addressed to them a long instruction, and ended by giving them his blessing. To his Blessed Mother, who was standing in front of the holy women, he extended his hand. All were very much affected, and I felt that Magdalene ardently longed to embrace Jesus's feet. But she restrained her desire, for his demeanor was so grave that he inspired holy fear. When he left them, they wept very much. It was not however an exterior weeping; it was like the weeping of the soul. The assembly broke up before midnight.

At Jesus's Ascension into Heaven

ON the night before his wonderful ascension, Thursday, May 14, AD 33, I saw Jesus in the inner hall of the house of the Last Supper with the Blessed Virgin and the eleven. The disciples and the holy women were praying in the side halls. In the Supper Room the communion table was standing under the lighted lamp, and on it the Passover bread and chalice. The apostles were in their robes of ceremony. The Blessed Virgin was opposite Jesus who, as on Maundy Thursday, was consecrating bread and wine. I saw the blessed sacrament entering the mouths of the apostles in the form of a luminous body, and Jesus's words at the consecration of the wine flowing into the chalice like a stream of red light. During the last days, Magdalene, Martha, and Mary Cleophas received the blessed sacrament.

On the eighth day after Pentecost, May 31, AD 33, I saw the apostles busily engaged the whole night in the house of the Last Supper, praying, etc. At daybreak they went with many of the disciples into the Temple, to which the Blessed Virgin and the holy women had preceded them. The Blessed Virgin and the other women had left the Temple some time previously in order to kneel alone before the blessed sacrament and pray. Magdalene prayed in the entrance hall sometimes standing, sometimes kneeling, or again prostrate on the ground, her arms outstretched. The other women had retired into their cells adjoining the church of Bethsaida.

Before his ascension, Christ Jesus had made known to his most holy Mother what she should say at the end of her earthly career to the apostles and some of the disciples who should be with her. He told her also that she should bless them, and that it would conduce very much to their welfare and eternal salvation. He entrusted to her also certain spiritual labors for the general good, which being accomplished, her longing after heaven was to be realized. Jesus had at the same time made known to Magdalene that she was to live concealed in the wilderness and that Martha was to establish a community of women. He added that he himself would always be with them.

After the Ascension

SHORTLY after the ascension, Mary Magdalene went into the wilderness, to the region where John the Baptist had lived, but somewhat more to the south. At first she frequented huts roundabout in which she sometimes found food. She veiled herself, so as not to be recognized. Later she ventured further, into a wild and rocky region where she lived entirely apart in a cave. There I saw satan in the form of a dragon seek to terrify her by belching fire upon her—but the dragon had each time to swallow again its own fire and give ground.

The Journey to Gaul

ABOUT three years after Pentecost, persecution of Christians by the Jews intensified, and while Mary Magdalene was visiting her brother and sister in Bethany, the three were arrested. On this occasion Lazarus, Martha, and Mary Magdalene were taken into custody, as well as the sisters' maidservants Marcella and Sarah and two other people who were visiting Lazarus at the time: one of the seventy-two disciples, named Maximin, and the man born blind who was healed by Jesus, Celidonius, sometimes known as Sidonius. These seven were arrested and taken to the Mediterranean coast (somewhere close to present-day Tel-Aviv), where they were put into a little boat, towed far out to the sea, and cut loose. The intention was that they should perish, but this did not happen. Through divine providence the little boat made it across the Mediterranean, the family, servants, and companions coming ashore at a place in the south of France now called St. Maries-de-la-Mer. (This story is partially recounted also in "Martha.")

Having been raised from the dead, Lazarus possessed an extraordinary power, as did Mary Magdalene, and Martha too, after having spent so much time in the presence of Jesus. When Lazarus spoke, it was a powerful experience for all who heard. While Sarah stayed behind in St. Maries-de-la-Mer, the rest of the group went to the town of Massilia (present-day Marseilles), further eastward along the coast. There they lived, and because of Lazarus's presence and the power of his speech a whole community was soon converted to the new religion of Jesus Christ, the messiah, who had died and risen from the dead. Lazarus baptized them and became the bishop of this first community of Christians in Europe. Lazarus remained as bishop of Marseilles, Magdalene retired to lead the life of a hermit in a cave at Saint-Baume, east of Marseilles, and Martha traveled with her maidservant Marcella north of Marseilles and founded a community there.

Further Regarding Gaul

AFTER the ascension Lazarus was always to be found among the disciples. Three years after the death of Christ Jesus, he and Martha were captured by the Jews, and on the evening of that same day Magdalene also was caught as she was on her way to visit her siblings.

Together with Lazarus, who was already a priest, the disciple Maximin and another man whose name I have forgotten[1] were taken into custody also, along with Marcella, the former maidservant of Magdalene, and the maidservant of Martha (Sarah).[2] They were seven in all: three men and four women.

I saw how, mistreated by the Jews all the while, they were taken to the seashore and made to board a small, leaky vessel lacking both rudder and sail. This unseaworthy vessel was tied to a larger ship, which towed them far out in the sea before cutting them loose. The small company prayed and sang together, and in due course I saw them make land far away on the coast of France, near a place where the water lapped gently upon the shore. After disembarking, they pushed the little vessel back out to sea.

At a distance of well over an hour stood a great city, toward which they now turned their steps. Those who came upon them

---

[1] Celidonius, the "man born blind" (see below).

[2] Here Anne Catherine adds: "Marcella had been with Magdalene in her earlier, secular life. The women who had come into community with Martha were also driven away from somewhere." For details, see "Martha."

as they made their way looked on, but did not approach them. They had completed their sea journey with supernatural swiftness, during which they had carried with them only some few small jugs. When they drank from these they were quickened, similarly to what had transpired on the way to the promised land.[1]

When they arrived, a pagan festival was underway. The seven visitors proceeded to seat themselves among colonnades in an open space before the temple. For some time they remained there; and then, after all had refreshed themselves from the small jugs just mentioned, Martha took the initiative to admit into their circle and address the people who had meanwhile gathered around them, describing how they came to be there, adding words also regarding Jesus. Martha was animated and lively. At another time I saw people hurling stones at the seven to drive them away—but they remained unharmed, sitting peacefully in their place till the dawning of a new day. Eventually others of the company undertook to communicate with those native to the place, gradually winning more and more of them over as friends.

The following day an official arrived from a great structure I took to be a civic building, and commenced to interrogate them. The whole day they remained there beneath the arches, speaking with the many passers-by who continued to congregate around them.

On the third day the whole company was led by the official to the civic building, after which they were divided into two groups and stationed at two locations: the men remained with the official in the civic building; the women were taken to a house in the city, where they were well met and provided with refreshment. All the while I saw them teaching wherever they went; the head official had let it be known throughout the city that none should do these visitors harm.

Soon many of the local people sought baptism, to which end Lazarus employed a great basin that stood in the open space before the temple; indeed, the temple itself soon seemed quite

---

[1] Presumably a reference to the heavenly manna that sustained the children of Israel during the Exodus.

abandoned. It seems to me that the head official of the city was baptized also. I also saw that they did not stay together there. Lazarus and his male companions remained in this place where, as bishop, Lazarus taught the doctrine of Christ Jesus.

Magdalene separated herself from the others and withdrew in the wilderness at some great distance from the city, where she lived in a cave. For her part, Martha made her way with Marcella and the other woman (Sarah) more toward the east, to a wild, stony region where many women were living in a row of small huts built among the cliffs. The three were well received by these women, and in due course a convent was established there.

The two companions of Lazarus eventually came to live elsewhere, but I cannot recall where. Sometimes I saw Magdalene come together with one of them—Maximin, as it seems to me—at a place midway between their respective places of residence, where she received the blessed sacrament.

The name of the third man who had come ashore with Magdalene and the others was Celidonius. He was the man born blind whom Jesus healed and who thereafter remained with the disciples. I looked into the image of his healing in order to better determine who he was, and it was then I was told his name.

Magdalene's Cave and Burial

IN vision I beheld in the wild mountains around Marseilles the great cave of Magdalene.[1] It was supported by pillars that seemed to have grown there. Its walls were perforated with natural openings in which one could sit. There was an altar of grass or turf, from which grew a green cross with living branches; no body was thereon, but from its midpoint hung a crown.

Magdalene's sleeping place was not within this cave, but next

[1] At this point Anne Catherine described in considerable detail the geological features and lay of the land around the place where Magdalene's cave was located. The mountains in the distance gave the appearance of two curved towers. The cave itself was not to be seen from the elevated mountain valley, for it was set high up on the back side of a peak. It is not possible to bring to clarity here all Anne Catherine had to say on this subject. CB

to it, in a portion of the mountainside that Magdalene had apparently herself hewn out. It was like a storage cache carved into the mountain, before which a wattle door could be drawn closed, rendering it quite difficult to detect.

I saw Magdalene in death lying upon something like a trestle of lattice-work woven of a kind of wood that seemed to be what I know as Kreuzbeere.[1] She was clothed in a gown of green leaves, with a cap of the same upon her head, around which wound her hair, excepting a lock that fell down behind. She was lying on her back, and in her crossed arms held a wooden crucifix. This crucifix which she held in death was forked in shape,[2] and green; upon it was woven a body. She was not gaunt, but strong and well-developed, tanned and tough from long exposure to the elements. Beside her upon the ground lay a pair of clean earthenware dishes; the doors to her bivouac were drawn open.

Two hermits entered bearing poles across which cords had been fastened, the whole covered with a large blanket. In this latter they neatly wrapped the corpse, which they then bore some good distance to Martha and her cloister. Magdalene had still a large brown blanket.[3]

[1] Kreuzbeere, or crossberry (or gooseberry), so-called on account of its triple spines, which often have a cruciform arrangement.

[2] In the notes, in place of the word "forked" stands this drawing: Υ

[3] Anne Catherine reported further that over her cave Maximin later had a church built in which some remains of Magdalene were preserved: the head (one cheek was missing but on the other some flesh remained), an arm, hair, and also a container with soil (she could not tell just what kind of soil). She saw other places also where remains of Magdalene were kept, but could not recall where.

Maroni

MARONI was a wealthy widow from the town of Nain. She was the sister of the wife of the apostle James the Greater and the mother of the youth of Nain,[1] who at the age of twelve Jesus raised from the dead at the entrance to the city of Nain around 9 AM on Monday, November 13, AD 30 (as described in Luke 7:11–17), and who, after this miracle had taken place, not only lodged Jesus and the disciples both at her summer estate and her great house in Nain, but also generously placed a portion of her wealth at the disposal of the community—in which she then became one of the most active women. At her request and with the help of his own mother, Jesus then healed from a distance Maroni's friend the widow Mary of Nain from possession, after which she also entered the circle of the holy women. Maroni was the daughter of an uncle, on the father's side, of Peter, and so she was a cousin of Peter's wife. Her first husband was the son of a sister of Elizabeth, who herself was the daughter of a sister of the mother of Anne. Maroni's first husband having died without children, she had married Eliud,[2] a relation of Anne, and left Chisloth, near Tabor, to take up her abode at Nain, which was not far off, where she soon lost her second husband.

✛ ✛ ✛ ✛ ✛

IN the company of three disciples, Jesus traveled on Wednesday, August 2, AD 30, to the town of Nain. Maroni had been informed

[1] According to Anne Catherine, the youth's name was Martialis. He later became a disciple and was one of the group of disciples who accompanied the apostle Peter to Rome.

[2] Regarding this family connection, Anne Catherine provides the following background: "To the north of Mount Tabor was situated the city of Tabor, whence the mountain derived its name, and about an hour westward in the direction of Sepphoris was another fortified place, Casaloth, which was in the valley on the south side of the mountain, northward from Nain and in the direction of Apheke. I have heard a more modern name given to this place, and

93

by Andrew and Nathaniel of Jesus's near approach, and she was awaiting his arrival. With another widow, she now went out to the inn to welcome him. They cast themselves veiled at his feet. Maroni begged Jesus to accept the offer of the other good widow, who wished to put all she possessed into the treasury of the holy women for the maintenance of the disciples and for the poor, whom she herself also wanted to serve. Jesus graciously accepted her offer, while he instructed and consoled her and her friend. They had brought some provisions for a repast, which along with a sum of money they handed over to the disciples. The latter was sent to the women at Capernaum for the common treasury. Jesus took some rest here with the disciples, for he had on the preceding day taught in Engannim with indescribable effort and had cured the sick, after which he had journeyed thence to Nain, a distance of about seven hours. A widow lately introduced to Jesus told him of another widow named Mary who likewise desired to give what she possessed for the support of the disciples. But Jesus replied that she should keep it till later when it would be more needed.[1]

Upon leaving a leper's hut[2] in Capernaum on the morning of Friday, November 10, AD 30, Jesus went to an inn in the valley of the doves, south of Capernaum, where he met Maroni, the widow of Nain, who begged him to come and heal her twelve-year-old son. In the afternoon he returned to Capernaum and

---

I saw that relatives of Jesus once dwelt there, namely, a sister of Elizabeth, who, like the maidservant of Mary Mark, bore the name of Rhoda. She had three daughters, one named Mara or Maraham and two sons. Maraha was one of the three widows, friends of Mary, and her two sons—Arastaria and Cocharia—were later among the disciples. One of Rhoda's sons married Maroni, and died without issue. His widow, in obedience to the law, entered into a second marriage with one of her first husband's family named Eliud, a young nephew of Anne. Thereafter she lived at Nain and by her second husband had one son, who was called Martialis. She was now a widow for the second time, the so-called widow of Nain whose son Martialis was raised from the dead by Jesus."

[1] See "Mary of Nain" for more details on this widow.

[2] Earlier this same morning, Jesus had approached by the Roman centurion Cornelius, whose servant was desperately ill. Jesus praised Cornelius for his faith and healed the servant from afar (Matthew 8:5–13, Luke 7:1–10). Jesus then went to a leper's hut and healed the leper, as described in Mark 1:40–45.

taught in the synagogue as the sabbath began. Suddenly a man who was possessed ran in and caused a great commotion, and Jesus healed him (Mark 1:21–28). Seeing this, the Pharisees—utterly astounded—gave up a plan they had to lay hands on Jesus, who then turned off into the street that led to the heart of the city, and for about an hour cured numbers of sick that had been brought together, also some possessed. After that Jesus, with several of the disciples, left the city and went to a little valley beyond Magdala not far from Damna. There they found a public inn, at which were Maroni and the pagan Lais of Nain[1] and her two daughters, Sabia and Athalia, both of whom Jesus, when at Meroz, had from a distance delivered from the devil. Maroni now came beseeching Jesus to go to her son Martialis, a boy of twelve years, who was so ill that she feared to find him dead on her return. Jesus told her to go home in peace, that he would follow her—but when, he did not say. Maroni had brought with her presents for the inn. She immediately hurried back home with her servant. She had about nine hours to travel. She was a wealthy woman and very good, a mother to all the poor children in Nain.

After some disputations next day with Sadducees and Pharisees in the Temple, where he also taught regarding his reasons for teaching in parables, Jesus and the disciples continued along the road to Nain. This road crossed the valley of Magdalum above Peter's fishery to the east of the mountain that looked down upon Gabara, and then ran into the valley eastward of Bethulia and Gischala. Jesus may have journeyed with the disciples nine to ten hours when that evening (Sunday, November 12, AD 30) they put up at a shepherd inn about three or four hours from Nain. They had crossed the brook Kishon once. Jesus taught the whole way, explaining to his disciples in particular how they would be able to detect false teachers (Matthew 7:15–20).

Nain was a beautiful little place with well-built houses, and was sometimes known also as Engannim. It lay upon a charming hill on the brook Kishon to the south, about an hour from Mount Tabor and facing Endor on the southwest. Jezreel was more to

---

[1] See "Lais" for further details.

the south, but was hidden by intervening heights. The beautiful plain of Esdrelon stretched out before Nain, which was almost three or four hours distant from Nazareth. The country here was uncommonly rich in grain, fruit, and wine, and Maroni owned a whole mountain covered with the most beautiful vineyards. At the time, Jesus had with him about thirty companions, and since the path over the hill was rather narrow some went on before and others behind him.

Just before nine in the morning of the following day (Monday, November 13, AD 30), Jesus and his companions drew near to Nain and encountered the funeral procession at the gate. A crowd of Jews enveloped in mourning mantles passed out of the city gate with the corpse. Four men were carrying the coffin, in which reposed the remains upon a kind of frame made of crossed poles curved in the middle. The coffin was in shape something like the human form, light like a woven basket, with a cover fastened to the top. Jesus passed through the disciples who, formed into two rows on either side of the road, advanced to meet the coming procession, and said: "Stand still!" Then as he laid his hand upon the coffin, he said: "Set the coffin down." The bearers obeyed, the crowd fell back, and the disciples ranged on either side. Maroni, the mother of the dead youth, with several of her female friends, was following the corpse. They too paused just as they were passing out of the gate a few feet from where Jesus was standing. They were veiled and showed every sign of grief. Maroni stood in front shedding silent tears. She may indeed have been thinking: "Ah, he has come too late!" Jesus said to her most kindly and earnestly: "Woman, weep not!" The grief of all present touched him, for the widow was much loved in the city on account of her great charity to orphans and the poor. Still there were many wicked and malignant people around, and numbers of others came flocking from the city. Jesus called for water and a little branch. Someone brought to a disciple, who handed them to Jesus, a little vessel of water and a twig of hyssop. Jesus took the water and said to the bearers: "Open the coffin and loosen the bands!" While this command was being executed, Jesus raised his eyes to heaven and spoke the words recorded in Matthew 11:25–30. Jesus said to the youth, "Arise!" There then occurred the miraculous raising from the dead of the youth of Nain—the twelve-year-old Martialis,[1] son of the widow Maroni—described in Luke 7:11–17.

Jesus took Martialis by the hand and led him to the arms of his mother Maroni, who was hastening toward him. As he restored him to her, he said: "Here, you have your thy son back, but I shall demand him of you when he shall have been regenerated in baptism." Maroni was so transported with joy, amazement, and awe, that she uttered no thanks at the moment. Her feelings found vent only in tears and embraces. The procession accompanied her to her home, the people chanting a hymn of praise. Jesus followed with the disciples. He entered the widow's house, which was very large and surrounded by gardens and courts. Friends came crowding from all quarters, all pressing eagerly to see the youth. Now began at once a joyous and most abundant distribution of gifts to the poor, who had gathered around the house to offer congratulations. Clothing, linen, corn, bread, lambs, birds, and money were given out plentifully. Meanwhile Jesus instructed the crowds assembled in the courtyards of the widow. Tables were spread both in the house and courts, and at them all were feasted. Peter, as the widow's relative—for she was the daughter of his father-in-law's brother—was especially happy and at home in the house. He discharged in a certain degree the office of father of the family. Jesus frequently addressed questions and words of instruction to the resuscitated boy.

The meal over, Jesus went with the disciples to the beautiful garden of the widow Maroni at the southern end of the city. The maimed and sick lined his whole route, and he cured them all. The streets were alive with excitement. It was already growing dark when Jesus entered the garden where Maroni with her relatives and domestics,[2] several doctors of the law, Martialis, and some other boys were gathered. There were several summer houses in the garden. Before one more beautiful than the others, whose roof was supported on pillars, and which might be shut in

---

[1] A more complete account of the raising of Martialis, and what Anne Catherine subsequently saw of his later life, will be found in the entry devoted to him in *People of the New Testament III*.

[2] Elsewhere Anne Catherine mentions that "the three widows" were present.

by movable screens, was a torch placed high under the palm trees. Its flames lighted up the whole hall, and glistened beautifully on the long, green leaves. Near the trees, on which fruit was still hanging, one could see as distinctly and clearly by the light of the torch as by day. At first Jesus taught and explained walking around; afterward, he entered the summer house. He often spoke to Martialis in the hearing of others. It was a wonderfully beautiful evening in that garden. The night was advanced when Jesus and his followers returned to Maroni's house, in whose side buildings all found lodgings.

Next morning, Tuesday, November 14, AD 30, news of Jesus's presence in Nain and the resurrection of the boy spread, and crowds of people, among them many sick, gathered into the city from the whole country around. They completely filled the street in front of Maroni's residence, where they stood in long rows. Jesus cured part of them the next morning. He also spoke of the sanctity of marriage and helped to reconcile several couples whose wives were seeking divorce from their husbands. Around midday, when Jesus left Nain accompanied by his disciples, Maroni, her boy and her domestics, all the cured, and many good people of the city accompanied him, singing psalms and bearing green branches before him.

Some weeks later, on Wednesday, November 29, AD 30, the day after the sermon on the mount, Jesus continued his preaching of the day before on the mountain, especially regarding the second beatitude (Matthew 5:4). Mary, Mary Cleophas, Maroni of Nain, and two other women, as well as all the twelve disciples who later became apostles were there. Indeed, hereafter Maroni was often in the community of the holy women, particularly Susanna Alpheus, Susanna of Jerusalem, Veronica, Johanna Chusa, Mary Mark, Dinah the Samaritan, and the Mara the Suphanite— especially the latter two. She was also to be seen in the company of Martha and Lazarus in Bethany.

On a subsequent visit to Nain (Friday, June 8, AD 31), Jesus first visited several people and then went to Maroni's garden. Here he gave the holy women advice about their inner life and their work serving the community of Christians. The next day, Jesus and the disciples took a sabbath walk together through the fields around

Nain. The season about this time in Nain was indescribably delightful. After giving some moving teachings to the disciples, they all went again to Maroni's garden, where too came the holy women. Jesus told them about the reconciliation that had taken place among the married couples in Mallep, and related matters.

Much later, late in the evening on Good Friday (April 3, AD 33), I saw the Blessed Virgin and her companions knocking at the cenacle and being admitted, then Abenadar; and by degrees most of the apostles and several of the disciples entered. The holy women retired to the apartments occupied by the Blessed Virgin. They took some refreshment and spent some moments in tears and mourning, relating to one another all that had happened. The men changed their garments, and I saw them standing under the lamp celebrating the sabbath. Then they ate lambs at the different tables around the cenacle, but without any ceremony. It was not the paschal lamb. They had already eaten that yesterday. All were in great trouble and sadness. The holy women also prayed with Mary under a lamp. Later, when it had grown quite dark, Lazarus, Martha, the widow Maroni of Nain, Dinah the Samaritan, and Mara the Suphanite were admitted. They were come from Bethany to keep the sabbath. Once more was sorrow renewed by the narrations of each.

Veronica • Seraphia

VERONICA, earlier called Seraphia,[1] was from Jerusalem, the daughter of a brother of Zechariah of Hebron (the father of John the Baptist), into whose ancestral house near the Jerusalem fish-market Joachim and Anna had moved when they brought their little daughter to the Temple. Thus, Veronica was cousin to John the Baptist. She was related also to the old priest Simeon, and a friend of his sons, who had acquired from their father an inclination, or secret love, for the messiah. Veronica was a tall, beautiful, and courageous woman, with a great love for Jesus. She was already an adult, though not yet married, when the twelve-year-old Jesus was teaching in the Temple. At that time Jesus's parents had searched for him everywhere among his relatives, but he had remained behind with four older boys. During those days, when not at the Temple, Jesus had stayed in the same house by the Jerusalem gate where Mary had stayed the day before her purification, and again for two nights with some elderly people when Jesus was a small child. While the twelve-year-old Jesus was staying there, it was Veronica who sent him meals. This small house or inn of elderly people was a kind of establishment. It was situated east of the Mount of Olives, and often used later as a refuge by Jesus and the disciples. Later, in fact the very last time Jesus was to teach in the Temple, Veronica secretly brought him food there.[2]

---

[1] Seraphia received the Latin name Veronica—that is, *vera icon*, meaning "true icon"—because of her veil, which on Good Friday received an imprint of the face of Jesus.

[2] A second account provides some additional details: "Veronica, earlier called Seraphia, was a cousin of John the Baptist, her father being the son of Zechariah's brother. She was from Jerusalem. When Mary, a little girl of four years, was placed among the young girls at the Temple, I saw Joachim, Anne, and some that had accompanied them going into Zechariah's paternal house not far from the fish market. A very old relative of the family now occupied it, Zechariah's uncle, perhaps, and Seraphia's grandfather. At the time of Mary's

Later, Veronica married Sirach, a member of the Sanhedrin, who was descended from the chaste Susanna (whose story is told in Chapter 13 of the book of Daniel). To begin with, Sirach was hostile toward Jesus and his followers, and would keep Veronica locked up at home whenever he noticed she was helping Jesus and the disciples. But then he received instruction from Joseph of Arimathea and Nicodemus—members of the Sanhedrin also—and on this account his attitude toward Jesus changed. He then allowed Veronica to follow Jesus and serve the community of the disciples.[1] They had three children, two of whom later became

espousals with Joseph, I saw that Seraphia was older than the Blessed Virgin. She was related also to the aged Simeon who had prophesied at Jesus's Presentation in the Temple, and from early youth she was brought up with his sons. Simeon had inspired these young people with a longing after the messiah. This waiting for salvation was, for a long time, like a secret affection among many good people; others at that time had no idea of such things. When Jesus at the age of twelve remained behind in Jerusalem to teach in the Temple, I saw Seraphia older than the mother of Jesus and still unmarried. She sent Jesus food to a little inn outside of Jerusalem, where he put up when he was not in the Temple. It was at this same inn, a quarter of an hour from Jerusalem and on the road to Bethlehem, that Mary and Joseph, when going to present Jesus in the Temple after his birth, spent one day and two nights with the two old people. They were Essenes, and the wife was related to Johanna Chusa. They were acquainted with the holy family and Jesus. Their inn was an establishment for the poor. Jesus and the disciples often took shelter there; and in his last days, when he was preaching in the Temple, I often saw food sent thither by Seraphia. But at that time there were other occupants in it."

[1] We have also this second account with additional details: "Seraphia married late in life. Her husband Sirach, a descendant of the chaste Susanna, was a member of the council belonging to the Temple. He was at first very much opposed to Jesus, and Seraphia, on account of her intimate connection with Jesus and the holy women, had much to suffer from him. He had even on several different occasions confined her for a long time in a prison cell. Converted at last by Joseph of Arimathea and Nicodemus, he became more lenient, and allowed his wife to follow Jesus. At Jesus's trial before Caiaphas, both last night and this morning, he had, in company with Nicodemus, Joseph of Arimathea, and all well-disposed people, declared himself for our Lord, and with them left the Sanhedrin. Seraphia was still a beautiful, majestic woman, although she must have been over fifty years old. At the triumphant entrance of Jesus into Jerusalem, which we celebrate on Palm Sunday, I saw her among the other women with a child on her arm. She took her veil from her head and spread it joyfully and reverently in the Lord's path."

disciples, while the third fell away. Her son Amandor was one of the first disciples of Jesus.[1]

It was Veronica who purchased the holy vessel from the Temple and gave it to be used at the Last Supper. Thus did this vessel (later called the Grail cup), which had been given originally by Melchizedek to Abraham and was then handed down through the ages as a most holy and sacred artifact, eventually come into the hands of Jesus for the institution of the eucharist at the Last Supper.

The cloth of Veronica that received the image of Christ was not so much a veil as a linen neck scarf,[2] which she had worn around her shoulders on Good Friday as Jesus was carrying the cross through the streets of Jerusalem. Beholding Jesus's battered and bloody face, Veronica had offered this scarf, reaching out with it toward his face as a sign of her empathy for his suffering. He pressed it to his face and thus it was that the cloth miraculously received an imprint thereof.

Veronica's scarf remained at first with the holy women, but when Magdalene, Martha, Lazarus, and some others were exiled (arriving ultimately at Marseilles), it was passed on to Mary, and later brought to Rome by some apostles. There is another account that the scarf remained with the holy women, that the apostle Thaddeus took it with him to King Abgar,[3] and that it came later to Constantinople and is now in Turin, where the burial sheet of Christ is. Anne Catherine beheld yet another episode, given below, in which Veronica took the scarf to Rome, along with Nicodemus and Epaphras.[4]

---

[1] Amandor was received as a disciple by Jesus in Bethsaida on Thursday, August 4, AD 29, along with the Essene youth Eustachius, and the son of the widow Lea, Kolaya. Amandor, Eustachius, and Kolaya were his first three disciples.

[2] Such scarfs were customarily worn as a sign of sympathy with another's sorrow.

[3] See "Judas Thaddeus" in *People of the New Testament II*.

[4] "Epaphras was a simple servant of the disciples, having formerly been engaged in the Temple as a servant and messenger of the priests. He was with the apostles in the cenacle during the first days after Jesus's resurrection, when he saw the Risen One, as he frequently did afterward."

The Scarf Goes to Rome

IN the third year after Christ's ascension, the Roman emperor sent officials to Jerusalem to collect proofs of the rumors abroad regarding Jesus's death and resurrection. One of these officials took back with him to Rome Nicodemus, Veronica, and a relative of Johanna Chusa, the disciple Epaphras.

I saw Veronica in the emperor's presence. He was sick, and he lay on a raised couch before which hung a curtain. It was a small square room with no window in it, the light being admitted through the roof, from which hung cords attached to shutters that could be opened or closed at pleasure. Veronica was alone with the emperor, his attendants having withdrawn into the antechamber.

I saw that Veronica had brought with her, besides the veil, one of the linens from Jesus's tomb. She unfolded the former before

the emperor. It was a long, narrow strip of stuff, which she had once worn as a scarf around her head and neck. The impression of Jesus's face was on one end of it, and when she held it up before the emperor, she grasped its whole length in one hand. The countenance of Jesus was visible on one side, and was arranged as I have drawn in the picture here. The face of Jesus thereon was not a clean, distinct portrait, for it was impressed on the cloth in blood; it was also broader than a painted likeness would have been, for Jesus had pressed the veil or scarf all around his face.

On the other cloth that Veronica had with her I saw the impression of Jesus's scourged body. I think this was one of the cloths upon which Jesus had been washed for burial.

I did not see the emperor touch these linens, or that they were applied to him in any way. He was cured by the mere sight of them. In gratitude for this favor he wanted to keep Veronica in Rome, make her rich presents, give her a house, faithful servants, etc. But all the reward she asked was permission to return to Jerusalem and to die where Jesus had died. I saw that she did return, with the companions of her journey.

During the persecution of the Christians in Jerusalem, toward the end of the third year after their return—when Lazarus and his sisters were driven into exile—I saw Veronica flee with some other women. But she was overtaken and cast into prison, where she was tortured as a martyr for the truth, for Jesus. Veronica, who had so often fed Jesus (in both the early and the final years of his earthly life) with earthly bread—even as with his own flesh and blood he had nourished her to eternal life—perished of starvation.

ON Sunday, July 24, and Monday, July 25, AD 29, Jesus traveled eastward toward Mount Tabor, after visiting Mount Carmel. At the foot of the west side of Mount Tabor was the little town Chisloth-Tabor. Here Jesus taught in the synagogue concerning the baptism of John. Five people accompanied Jesus here, among them some future disciples. The Mother of God, Mary Cleophas, the mother of Parmenas, and two other women, I saw going to Nazareth at this time, while Johanna Chusa and Veronica, together with her son Amandor—who later on joined the disciples—were on their way to the same place from Jerusalem. They were going to visit Mary, with whom they had become acquainted on their yearly journeys to the holy city. They expected Jesus to arrive there when he returned from his journey to Lebanon.

Nearly two months later, on Wednesday, September 21, AD 29, Jesus left Bethel early and arrived that evening at a little village called Giah on Mount Amma, facing the Gibeon desert. There he ate a meal and talked with several people, who asked him about the prophet from Nazareth. Then he continued on his way, arriving that night at Lazarus's castle in Bethany. He was greeted there not only by Lazarus but also by Nicodemus, John Mark, and the aged Obed (a relative of the prophetess Anna), who were guests of Lazarus at the time. Among the women gathered there also, as guests of Martha, were Veronica, Mary Mark, and Susanna of Jerusalem. Jesus greeted them all, and they took a meal together before retiring for the night.

One month later, on Thursday, October 20, AD 29, after spending some time in Phasael with Jairus,[1] Jesus, making his way to Bethany, stopped at an inn in the vicinity and there gave his disciples a long instruction in which he alluded to the trials in store for him and all his followers. He told them that they should now leave him and weigh well whether they would be able to stand by him in his future sufferings. Lazarus came out to meet him. The disciples departed for their homes, Aram and Themeni[2] alone accompanying him further to Bethany, where many friends from Jerusalem were awaiting him, among them the holy women and Veronica.

Nine weeks later, on Tuesday, December 27, AD 29, about a hundred guests had gathered in Cana to attend the wedding. That evening, Jesus taught in the synagogue concerning the significance of marriage, husbands and wives, continence, chastity, and spiritual union. Later, Jesus addressed the bridal pair. All the relatives of Anne and Joachim had come from around Galilee to Cana. Mary Mark, John Mark, Obed, and Veronica had come from Jerusalem. Jesus himself brought about twenty-five of his disciples with him. Besides the wine, Jesus had engaged to supply the second course of the banquet as well, and for all this his mother and Martha provided. This second course consisted of birds, fish, honey, and fruits. Veronica had brought with her from Jerusalem a basket of the choicest flowers and the most skillfully-made confections.

Two months later, on Thursday, February 9, AD 30, Jesus taught in Jezreel and performed many miracles before a great concourse of people. All the disciples from Galilee were here assembled to meet him. Nathaniel Chased, Nathaniel the bridegroom, Peter, James, John, the sons of Mary Cleophas—all were there. Lazarus, Martha, Veronica, and Johanna Chusa, who had arrived earlier from Jerusalem, had in the meanwhile visited Magdalene at her castle of Magdalum to persuade her to go with them to Jezreel in order to see, if not to hear, the wise, the admirable, the most eloquent, Jesus. Magdalene had yielded to the persuasions of

---

[1] See "Jairus the Essene, of Phasael" in *People of the New Testament III*.

[2] "Aram and Themeni were the nephews of Joseph of Arimathea on his mother's side. They had been John's disciples but had followed Jesus when, on his way to Gilgal, he had passed John's place of baptism."

the women and, surrounded by much vain display, accompanied them thither.

About five weeks after this, on the morning of Sunday, March 19, AD 30, Jesus and Lazarus went to Jerusalem. On this same morning Martha went to Jerusalem to notify Mary Mark and the other women that Jesus was coming with Lazarus to the house of the former. Jesus and Lazarus arrived toward midday. There were present at the dinner besides Veronica, Johanna Chusa, and Susanna, the disciples of Jesus and of John belonging to Jerusalem, John Mark, Simeon's sons, Veronica's son Amandor, and Joseph of Arimathea's nephews Aram and Themeni, about nine men in all. Jesus spoke of the nearness of the kingdom of heaven, of his disciples' call, of their following him, and even hinted at his own passion.

Nearly six months later, before daybreak on Friday, July 21, AD 30, Jesus and Lazarus were directing their steps between Hay and Gilgal through the desert of Jericho, while the disciples went ahead by another route. When within a few hours of Bethany Lazarus went on ahead and Jesus continued his journey alone. At this time there were assembled at Bethany with Lazarus and the five disciples from Jerusalem, about fifteen disciples and followers of Jesus and seven women. The men consisted of Saturnin, Nicodemus, Joseph of Arimathea, his nephews, Simeon's sons, and those of Johanna Chusa, Veronica, and Obed respectively. Among the women were Veronica, Johanna Chusa, Susanna, Mary Mark the widow of Obed, Martha, and the discreet old servant of the last named, who afterward joined the holy women who cared for the wants of the Master and his disciples. All were gathered in a large, subterranean vault of Lazarus's castle, quietly and, it seemed, secretly awaiting the coming of Jesus. Toward evening Jesus arrived and entered the garden by a back gate. Jesus accompanied Lazarus through a long, shady walk up to the house and down into the vaulted chamber. The women drew their veils and bowed low on their knees before him, while the men inclined profoundly. Jesus greeted all and blessed them, after which they took their place at table. The women sat on cushions at one side of the table, their feet crossed under them.

The following Monday, July 24, AD 30, Veronica, Johanna

Chusa, and Obed's widow arrived at an inn and prepared a luncheon. Jesus and the disciples partook of it standing, after which they girded themselves and recommenced their journey.

The following week, on Wednesday, August 2, AD 30, accompanied by three disciples, Jesus went to the town of Nain. There he met the widow of Nain—Maroni—whose sister was married to James the Greater. Maroni introduced Jesus to another widow who, like herself, wished to serve his work and help the community of his followers. This latter widow told Jesus of another woman named Mary who likewise desired to give what she possessed for the support of the disciples. But Jesus replied that she should keep it till later when it would be more needed. This woman was an adulteress, and had been, on account of her infidelity, repudiated by her husband, a rich Jew of Damascus. She had heard of Jesus's mercy to sinners, was very much touched, and had no other desire than to do penance and be restored to grace. She had visited Martha, with whose family she was distantly related, had confessed to her her transgression, and begged her to intercede for her with the mother of Jesus. She gave over to her also a part of her wealth. Martha, Johanna Chusa, and Veronica, full of compassion for the sinner, interested themselves in her case, and took her at once to Mary's dwelling at Capernaum. Mary sent in behalf of the unhappy creature a messenger to Jesus, who replied that he would come in good time and heal her.

Two months later, on Tuesday, October 3, AD 30, Jesus was preparing to leave the town of Ainon after having spent some time there. But before he left with his disciples Jesus had an interview with Mara the Suphanite in her own house. He gave her salutary advice. Mara was entirely changed. She was full of love, zeal, humility, and gratitude; she busied herself with the poor and the sick. When journeying after her cure through Ramoth and Basan, Jesus had sent a disciple to Bethany to inform the holy women of it and of her reconciliation, in consequence of which announcement Veronica, Johanna Chusa, and Martha had been to visit her.

Three weeks later, on Wednesday, October 25, AD 30, Jesus was teaching from a mountain near Meroz. Disputing with the Pharisees, he referred to the two commandments: love of God and love of neighbor (Matthew 22:36–40). During the healing of the sick, Manahem, the blind disciple of Coreae—who had been restored to sight and whom Jesus had sent with a message to Lazarus—returned from Bethany with the two nephews of Joseph of Arimathea. Jesus gave them an interview. The holy women had sent by them money and gifts of various kinds to Jesus. Dinah the Samaritan had visited the holy women at Capernaum, bringing with her a rich contribution. Veronica and Johanna Chusa had also visited Mary. On their return journey they called to see Magdalene, whom they found very much changed. She was depressed in spirits, her folly apparently undergoing a struggle with her good inclinations.

After the passage of two weeks, on Tuesday, November 7, AD 30, Jesus was preparing for the sermon on the mount, which he would deliver the following day on the mountain beyond Gabara. Some sixty disciples, friends, and relatives of Jesus came to Gabara in expectation of this occasion. Among them was Mary Magdalene, who had been persuaded to come by her sister Martha, using such inducements as: You will behold a very wonderful spectacle: the crowds of people, the marvelous eloquence of the prophet, the sick, the cures that he effects, the hardihood with which he addresses the Pharisees! Veronica, Mary Chusa, and Jesus's mother, who wishes you so well—we all are convinced that you will thank us for the invitation. I think it will cheer you up a little. Oh, if you would only pass some time with us in Bethany! You must at least come to Damna with me tomorrow morning. There you will find all the women of our party at the inn.

Toward the end of the following month, on Tuesday, December 26, AD 30, Jesus made his way to the hill near Azanoth, where he had announced that he would teach. On the way he met his mother and some of the holy women—among them were Anna Cleophas, Susanna Alpheus, Susanna of Jerusalem, Veronica, Joanna Chusa, Mary Mark, Maroni, Mara the Suphanite, and Dinah the Samaritan. Martha had succeeded in persuading Mary Magdalene to come—it had taken great patience—and she arrived with great pomp and ceremony at the hill.

Susanna Cleophas (Susanna of Jerusalem)

SUSANNA of Jerusalem was a daughter of Cleophas, born to him
out of wedlock. Cleophas was an older brother of Joseph. As did
the Virgin Mary, so also Susanna lived as a temple virgin.[1] Later
she became wealthy, married to Matthias, a relative of the later
apostle Matthias, who took the place of Judas Iscariot in the circle
of twelve at Pentecost. Right at the outset of Christ's ministry,
Susanna of Jerusalem belonged to the circle of friends around
Lazarus and Martha in Bethany, often accompanying Martha on
her travels to help the disciples. Susanna also supported the community with generous donations. When Dinah the Samaritan
woman first converted, she repaired to an inn lying between
Jerusalem and Jericho where many other holy women resided at
that time, among them Susanna. Dinah sought Susanna out to
help her remain upright in her faith and teach her, for she was

---

[1] Elsewhere Brentano reports these words of Anne Catherine, regarding
first Mary, then Susanna: "Beth-Horon is a large town, inhabited by Levites.
Very fine, big grapes grow here, and many other fruits as well. The holy family stayed with friends in a well-kept house. The man was a schoolteacher; it
was a Levite school, and there were a number of children in the house. These
women and children were from Nazareth, Sepphoris, Zebulon, and thereabouts; some of them had already been in Anne's house during the examina-
tion (of Mary); for instance, Mary's elder sister (Mary Heli) and her little
daughter Mary Cleophas, and Anne's sister from Sepphoris with her daughters. The stay here was made the occasion of great rejoicing over the child
Mary. She was led into a big room accompanied by the other children and
placed on a raised seat with a canopy, arranged for her like a little throne. The
schoolteacher and others again asked her all manner of questions, putting
wreaths on her head. All were astonished by the wisdom of her answers. I also
heard about the cleverness of another girl who had passed through here a
short time ago on her way home from the Temple School. Her name was Susanna, and later she followed Jesus with the holy women. It was her place that
Mary was to take in the Temple, for there was a limited number of such
places. Susanna was fifteen years old when she left the Temple, and thus about
eleven years older than Mary."

still struggling mightily against fleshly desires. She remained with Susanna for a considerable time, and in the end achieved a full conversion.

On Monday, December 25, AD 30, at the time of the second conversion of Magdalene, after he had assisted and prepared her, Martha took leave of her sister and went to the inn near Damna, in order to tell Mary and the holy women the success she had had in her efforts to persuade Magdalene to be present at the instruction about to be given in Azanoth. With the Blessed Virgin about a dozen women had come to Damna, among them Anna Cleophas, Susanna Alpheus, Susanna of Jerusalem, Veronica, Johanna Chusa, Mary Mark, Dinah, Maroni, and the Suphanite.

Mary and Other Holy Women Receive Christ's Body

Salome of Jerusalem

SALOME of Jerusalem was a widow at the time of the crucifixion on Golgotha. Like Susanna of Jerusalem, Salome was related to the holy family through a brother of Joseph. Salome of Jerusalem lived for a long time at the home of Martha in Bethany. In the company of Mary Magdalene, Mary Cleophas, and Johanna Chusa, Salome was in the garden of the holy sepulcher on Easter Sunday morning and experienced the Risen Christ there.

Mary Mark

MARY MARK was a relative of the old priest Simeon, who blessed the baby Jesus in the Temple (Luke 2:22–35). She lived with her son John Mark northeast of Jerusalem. Their house lay beyond the city, about a quarter of an hour from the Temple, on the eastern side and opposite the Mount of Olives. It was not far from the home of Joseph of Arimathea, and near a stone-cutter's yard, in a retired quarter of the city little frequented by Pharisees. Jesus was often a guest at Mary Mark's home, often with several disciples. It was not necessary to enter the city in order to reach it, and was the site of many gatherings of the holy women during the years of the ministry. The Virgin Mary stayed there frequently, and also directly prior to the passion. More relating to this house and its significance will be found in the section on Mary Mark's son John Mark.[1] Mary Mark was very active among the holy women, seeing after the needs of Jesus and the disciples through the ministry, and was present at Golgotha, helped with the preparation of Jesus's body for burial, and at the internment stood facing the Virgin. She had a maidservant who bore the name of Rhoda.

---

[1] References to Mary Mark are numerous, scattered, and usually brief throughout Anne Catherine's visions, so rather than list them all, a brief summary is provided. See also "John Mark" in *People of the New Testament II*.

As can be read in the article on John Mark, Luke had also a friendly relationship with Mary Mark, and it was from her house that Luke and Cleophas set out on the morning of April 6, AD 33, the day after the resurrection, soon to encounter the Risen One as they made their way along the road to Emmaus.[1]

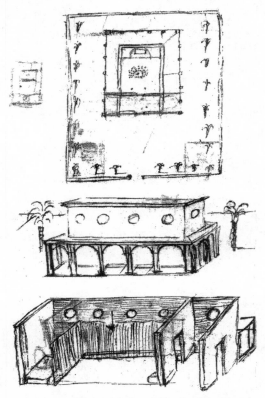

The House of Mary Mark and Her Son John Mark

[1] "Luke was present on the day of the resurrection at the *agape*, or love feast, and the instruction upon the blessed sacrament delivered by Matthew in the evening at Lazarus's, in Bethany. After the instruction he went, troubled and doubting, to Jerusalem where he spent the night in John Mark's house. There he met several other disciples, among them Cleophas. The disciples were talking about Jesus's resurrection and expressing their doubts. Luke and Cleophas, especially, were wavering in their faith. Moreover, as the command of the high priests was again made known that no one should harbor the disciples of Jesus or provide them with food, it was then that both resolved to go together to Emmaus."

Johanna Chusa

JOHANNA CHUSA, a tall, pale woman, very serious in her manner—but at the same time strong and energetic—was a niece of the prophetess Anna, who was in the Temple when Simeon blessed the child Jesus (Luke 2:36–38). She was the wife of Chusa, the steward who ran the household of Herod Antipas. Johanna's son had already made the acquaintance of the twelve-year-old Jesus when he (Jesus) remained behind in the Temple, and later was one of Jesus's secret disciples in Jerusalem.

Johanna was frequently at the home of Lazarus and Martha in Bethany and was one of Martha's most industrious helpers. Jesus often dined at the home of Johanna Chusa with his disciples. It was Johanna who, together with Veronica and Mary of Hebron (a niece of Elizabeth), went to Herod's castle at Machaerus to retrieve the head of Elizabeth's son, John the Baptist. She was also one of the four holy women to bear witness to the Risen Christ in the garden of the holy sepulcher on Easter Sunday morning, which Anne Catherine describes thus:

When the morning sky began to clear with a streak of white light, I saw Magdalene, Mary Cleophas, Johanna Chusa, and Salome, enveloped in mantles, leaving their abode near the cenacle. They carried spices packed in linen cloths, and one of them had a lighted lantern... The holy women walked anxiously to the little gate belonging to Nicodemus... During the dispersion of the disciples and the passion of the Lord, Martha had a heavy duty to fulfill and she still discharged it. Though torn with grief, she had to see to everything, to lend a helping hand everywhere. She had to feed the dispersed and wandering, attend to their wants, provide nourishment for all. Her assistant in all this, as well as in the cooking, was Johanna Chusa.

Regarding relatives of Joanna Chusa, Anne Catherine says that much earlier, when Mary was but a child, toward evening as the holy family was about a quarter of an hour's distance from Jerusalem, making its way there for Mary's purification, they turned and entered a small house that lay next to a large inn. The owners were a married couple without children, and by them the holy travelers were welcomed with extraordinary joy. The house lay between the brook Kidron and the city. The husband was a gardener; he clipped the hedges and kept the road in order. The wife was a relative of Johanna Chusa. They appeared to be Essenes. Much later, in the third year after Christ's ascension, when the Roman emperor sent officials to Jerusalem to collect proofs of the rumors afloat in connection with Jesus's death and resurrection, one of these officials took back with him to Rome Nicodemus, Veronica, and the disciple Epaphras—another relative of Johanna Chusa.[1]

Johanna did not live long after the passion, for some Jews out of malice began immediately to pursue and secretly put away the early Christians. Johanna was imprisoned on one occasion, but then released. She was killed sometime later as the result of such persecution.

The following vignettes from Anne Catherine's visions provide a sampling of Joanna Chusa's activities during the years of Jesus's ministry:

ON Sunday–Monday, July 24–25, AD 29, Veronica, Johanna Chusa, and the son of Veronica (Amandor)—who later joined the disciples—were on their way to Jerusalem, where they were going to visit Mary, with whom they had become acquainted on their yearly journeys to the holy city.

Six weeks later, on the morning of Tuesday, September 6, AD 29, the five disciples then traveling with Jesus went into Nazareth to visit their relatives and acquaintances. Jesus, however, stayed with Eliud the Essene,[2] with whom he prayed and very confidentially conversed, for to that simple-hearted, pious man many mysteries had been revealed. At that time there were four women in Mary's house besides herself: her niece, Mary Cleophas; Johanna Chusa, a cousin of Anna the prophetess; the relative of Simeon,

---

[1] See "Veronica" for a full account of this story.
[2] See "Eliud the Essene" in *People of the New Testament III*.

Mary, mother of John Mark; and the widow Lea. Veronica was no longer there, nor was Peter's wife, whom I had lately seen at the place where the publicans lived.

Two weeks later, on Tuesday, September 20, AD 29, Jesus went to Bethany, a distance of perhaps six miles, and entered a mountainous region along the way. It was the winter season, foggy and cloudy by day, and sometimes white frost by night. Jesus enveloped his head in a scarf, and journeyed straight on toward the east. I saw Mary and four holy women—Mary Cleophas, Johanna Chusa, Mary Mark, and Lea—leaving the house and wending their way through a field near Tiberias. They had with them two servants from the fishery. One went on ahead, the other followed, both laden with baggage which they carried on a pole across the shoulder, a pack in front and another behind. They, too, were going to Bethany by the usual route, which ran by Shechem to the right.

The holy women walked generally in single file, a couple of steps apart. They went in this way probably because most of the roads, excepting the broad highways, were narrow, intended for foot passengers, and led through the mountains. They walked quickly with a firm step, not swaying from side to side, as the country people do here. Very probably this is because from early youth the inhabitants of that country are accustomed to making long journeys on foot. They had their gowns tucked up to about the middle of the calf, their lower limbs bandaged tightly down to the ankle, and bound to the soles of their feet were thick, padded sandals. Over the head was a veil, the ends of which were fastened into the scarf wound round the neck. This scarf was crossed on the breast, thence carried behind and caught in the girdle; sometimes the wearers ran their hands into its folds and there let them rest. The man, going on before the travelers, prepared the way for them. He opened the hedges, removed stones from the path, laid bridges, gave orders at the inns and, in fine, saw to everything. The one who followed put everything again into its first order.

Jesus left Bethel for Bethany early the next day, Wednesday, September 21, AD 29, arriving that evening at a little village called Giah on Mount Amma, facing the Gibeon desert. There, he ate a meal and talked with several people who asked him about the prophet from Nazareth. Then he continued on his way, arriving after nightfall at Lazarus's castle in Bethany. That same night I saw the Blessed Virgin, Johanna Chusa, Mary Cleophas, the widow Lea, and Mary Salome passing the night at an inn between the desert Gibea and the desert Ephron, about five hours from Bethany. They slept under a shed enclosed on all sides by light walls. It contained two apartments. The front one was divided off into two rows of alcoves, of which the holy women took possession; the back served as a kitchen. Before the inn was an open hut in which a fire was burning.

On the following day, Thursday, September 22, AD 29, Jesus taught walking about the courtyards and gardens of Lazarus's castle. He spoke earnestly, feelingly, and lovingly, though his manner was full of dignity and he uttered no unnecessary word. All loved him and followed him, though not without a sentiment of awe. At about half-past one the Blessed Virgin arrived with Johanna Chusa, Lea, Mary Salome, and Mary Cleophas. The servant had in advance announced their approach.

Nearly three months later, on Friday, December 16, AD 29, Jesus, with some disciples of John then in his company, directed his steps to Kibzaim, where he arrived before the sabbath. Kibzaim lay in a valley between two branches of a mountain range that extended through the middle of the country, and assumed in this place almost the exact shape of a wolf's claw. The people were good, hospitable souls, and well-inclined to Jesus, whose coming they were expecting. Jesus put up near the school with one of the head men. There arrived also to salute Jesus, Lazarus, Martha, Joanna Chusa, the son of Simeon (who was employed at the Temple), and the old servant of the first named. They were on their way to the wedding at Cana and had been informed by messengers that they would here meet Jesus.

Just over seven weeks later, on Thursday, February 9, AD 30, Jesus taught in Jezreel (where one month before he had publicly healed the sick) and performed many miracles before a great concourse of people. All the disciples from Galilee were here assembled to meet him. Nathaniel Chased, Nathaniel the bridegroom, Peter, James, John, the sons of Mary Cleophas, all were there. Lazarus, Martha, Veronica, and Johanna Chusa, who had come before from Jerusalem, had visited Magdalene at her castle of Magdalum to persuade her to go with them to Jezreel in order to see, if not to hear, the wise, the admirable, the most eloquent, and most beautiful Jesus, of whom the whole country was full. Magdalene had yielded to the persuasions of the women and, surrounded by much vain display, accompanied them thither.

The morning after Jesus's arrival at the castle of Lazarus, Sunday, March 19, AD 30, Martha went to Jerusalem to notify Mary Mark and the other women that Jesus was coming with her brother to the house of the former. Jesus and Lazarus arrived toward midday. There were present at the dinner besides Veronica, Johanna Chusa, and Susanna, the disciples of Jesus and of John belonging to Jerusalem, John Mark, Simeon's sons, Veronica's son, and Joseph of Arimathea's nephews, about nine men in all. Jesus spoke of the nearness of the kingdom of God, of his disciples' call, of their following him, and even hinted at his own passion.

Some four months later, before daybreak on Sunday, July 16, AD 30, Jesus and his disciples left Adama and went to a nearby mountain, where it had been made known beforehand that he would teach on the day after the sabbath. A multitude had already gathered there and, as Jesus arrived, he was greeted with cries such as: "Thou art the true prophet, the helper!" Shortly after nine, Jesus began to teach. He spoke of, among other things, the parable of the sowing of the seed (Matthew 13:24–30). He taught until evening. The sons of Johanna Chusa and Veronica came here to Jesus. They had been sent by Lazarus, to warn him against the two spies whom the Pharisees had dispatched from Jerusalem to Adama. The disciples brought them to Jesus during a pause in the instruction. He told them not to be at all disquieted on his account, that he would fulfill his mission, and he thanked them for their devotedness.

Five days later, again before daybreak, on Friday, July 21, AD 30, Jesus and Lazarus directed their steps between Hay and Gilgal through the desert of Jericho, on their way to Bethany. The other disciples had gone ahead by another route. When within a few hours of Bethany, Lazarus went on ahead and Jesus continued his journey alone. When he arrived, there were assembled at Bethany with Lazarus and the five disciples from Jerusalem, about fifteen disciples and followers of Jesus and seven women: Saturnin, Nicodemus, Joseph of Arimathea, his nephews, Simeon's sons, and those of Johanna Chusa, Veronica, and Obed respectively. Among the women were Veronica, Johanna Chusa, Susanna, Mary Mark the widow of Obed, Martha, and the discreet old servant of the last named, who afterward joined the holy women who cared for the wants of the Master and his disciples. That night, when all was still in the castle, Jesus went to the Mount of Olives, to the cave in the garden of Gethsemane, where he was to pray on the night before the passion began.

Six months later, on Tuesday, January 9, AD 31, Jesus went with his companions to Jutta, the Baptist's birthplace. It was five hours' distance from the inn outside Jerusalem and one hour from Hebron. Mary, Veronica, Susanna, Johanna Chusa, John Mark, Lazarus, Joseph of Arimathea, Nicodemus, and several of the disciples from Jerusalem were there awaiting Jesus. And now Jesus disclosed to them the fact that John had been put to death by Herod. Deep grief seized upon them all.

The following Monday, January 15, AD 31, Saturnin, Joseph Barsabbas, and two other disciples—who had gone from Galilee to Machaerus, then to Jutta, and lastly had come hither in quest of Jesus—arrived. With many expressions of grief they related the murder of the Baptist. Soon after, accompanied by the sons of Mary Heli, Joseph of Arimathea's nephews, those of Zechariah, and the sons of Joanna Chusa and Veronica, they set out for Machaerus, taking Jutta on their route. They took with them an ass laden with all that was necessary for carrying out their design. Machaerus now, with the exception of a few soldiers, was quite deserted. Next day, Tuesday, January 16, AD 31, as it became known at Machaerus, through the domestics of Herodias, where John's head had been thrown, Johanna Chusa, Veronica, and one of the Baptist's relatives journeyed thither in order to make search for it. But until the vaulted sewer could be opened and drained, the head, which was resting on a stone projecting from the wall, could not be reached.

Three days later, on the morning of Friday, January 19, AD 31, Jesus and a group of disciples went to Jerusalem, first visiting the house of Johanna Chusa. Around ten in the morning, he went to the Temple and taught there without arousing any opposition. After sharing a light meal with his disciples in the early afternoon at the house of Johanna Chusa, Jesus and the disciples went to the pool of Bethesda, where Jesus imparted instructions to the sick, healing a number of them. On the way out, he healed the paralyzed man who had been ill for thirty-eight years (John 5:1–15). By then, the sabbath had already begun. So Jesus went to the Temple and taught there again. In the evening, around sunset, John the Baptist's body was buried at Jutta, in the vault of Zechariah, the disciples having returned from Machaerus with it the day before.

Three months later, on Thursday, April 19, AD 31, as Jesus was continuing his sermon on the mount, the Pharisees began to proclaim Jesus as a "disturber of the peace," saying that they had the sabbath, the festival days, and their own teaching, and that they did not need the innovations of this upstart. They threatened to complain to Herod, who would certainly put a stop to Jesus's activities. Jesus answered that he would continue to teach and heal, in spite of Herod, until his mission was complete. That evening, as Jesus and the disciples ate together, Lazarus told of the journey the women had made to Machaerus from Hebron and Jerusalem. Indeed, one of them, Johanna Chusa, had just succeeded in recovering the head of John the Baptist from Herod's castle.

Almost two years later, while at the disciples' inn outside Bethany on Sunday, February 8, AD 33—as the passion approached—three men came to Jesus from Jerusalem: Obed, the son of the old man Simeon, a temple servant and a disciple in secret; the second, a relative of Veronica; and the third, a relative of Joanna Chusa. This last-mentioned became, later on, bishop of Kedar. For a time also he lived as a hermit near the date trees that, on her flight into Egypt, had bent down their fruit to Mary that she might partake of it.

When late in the night of Thursday, April 2, AD 33—the day before Good Friday—a shouting band hurried from Ophel by torchlight to meet the approaching procession sent out to arrest the Master, the disciples lurking around dispersed in all directions. I saw that the Blessed Virgin, in her trouble and anguish, with

Martha, Magdalene, Mary Cleophas, Mary Salome, Mary Mark, Susanna, Johanna Chusa, Veronica, and Salome, again directed her steps to the valley of Jehosaphat. They were to the south of Gethsemane, opposite that part of the Mount of Olives where was another grotto in which Jesus had formerly been accustomed to pray.

The following day, Good Friday (April 3, AD 33), after that most painful meeting with her divine Son carrying his cross before the dwelling of Caiaphas, the most afflicted mother was conducted by John and the holy women, Johanna Chusa, Susanna, and Salome, to the house of Nazareth in the vicinity of the corner gate. Here the other holy women, in tears and lamentations, were gathered around Magdalene and Martha. Some children were with them. They now went all together, in number seventeen, with the Blessed Virgin, careless of the jeers of the mob, grave and resolute, and by their tears awe-inspiring, across the forum, where they kissed the spot upon which Jesus had taken up the burden of the cross. Later, they went up the hill of Golgotha by the gently sloping western side and stood in three groups, one behind the other, outside the wall enclosing the circle. The mother of Jesus, her niece Mary Cleophas, Salome, and John stood close to the circle around the crosses. Martha, Mary Heli, Veronica, Johanna Chusa, Susanna, and Mary Mark stood a little distance back around Magdalene.

It may have been almost nine o'clock on the eve of the resurrection, Saturday, April 4, AD 33, in a solitary place near the gate, that I saw the Blessed Virgin suddenly halt in her hurried walk. She gazed as if ravished with joyous longing up at the top of the wall. Floating down toward her in the midst of a great multitude of the souls of the ancient patriarchs, I saw the most holy soul of Jesus, resplendent with light and without trace of wound. Turning to the patriarchs and pointing to the Blessed Virgin, he uttered the words: "Mary, my mother!" and appeared to embrace her. Inexpressibly consoled, she hurried back to the women, whom she found busied preparing ointment and spices on a table. I saw lying on a table bunches of all kinds of herbs mixed and put in order, little flasks of ointment and nard water, and several flowers growing in pots, among which I remember one, a striped iris, or lily. The women packed them all in linen cloths. During Mary's absence, Magdalene, Mary Cleophas, Johanna Chusa, and Mary Salome had gone to the city to buy all these things. They wanted to go early next morning to scatter them over the body of Jesus in its winding sheet and pour upon it the perfumed water.

Early on the morning of the resurrection, Sunday, April 5, AD 33, when the morning sky began to clear with a streak of white light, I saw Magdalene, Mary Cleophas, Johanna Chusa, and Salome, enveloped in mantles, leaving their abode near the cenacle. They carried the spices packed in linen cloths, and one of them had a lighted lantern. They kept all hidden under their mantles. The holy women walked anxiously to the little gate belonging to Nicodemus.

On the occasion of his apparition through the closed doors in the evening of Saturday, April 11, AD 33, Jesus taught the apostles that addition to the service of the sabbath which relates to the blessed sacrament. The Blessed Virgin was taken to Jerusalem by Mary Mark; and Veronica, who now went round with her openly, accompanied them, along with Johanna Chusa from Bethany.

Dinah the Samaritan Woman

THE first to have been converted by Jesus was Dinah the Samaritan woman, who is known to us through her lengthy conversation with Jesus and subsequent conversion at Jacob's well in Sichar[1] on Wednesday, July 26, AD 30.[2] Dinah was an intelligent woman of some standing in the world, the offspring of a mixed marriage—a Jewish mother and a pagan father—born at a country seat near Damascus. She lost her parents at an early age and was cared for by a dissolute nurse by whom her evil passions had been fostered. Later Dinah had five husbands, one after the other. Some died of grief, others were put out of the way by her new lovers. The last of these, a rich merchant who was a relative of one of her former husbands, lived in Shechem, whither she followed him and superintended his household, for purposes of convenience calling herself Salome. They were not espoused, but this fact was not known to the people of Shechem, who on account of her intelligence, beauty, and good nature held Dinah in high esteem. The husband was a vigorous man of about thirty-six years with ruddy face and reddish beard. Dinah was living with this man at the time of her conversion at Jacob's well.[3]

From her marriages Dinah had three daughters and two half-

---

[1] There remains some certainly regarding the name of the town nearest to Jacob's well. Most commentators have supposed that Shechem, now called Nablous, was the town here called Sichar. But Shechem lies a mile and a half west of Jacob's well, whereas Sichar, now called Askar, lies scarcely half a mile north of the well. It was a small town, loosely called a city, and adjoined the land that Jacob gave to Joseph—Joseph's tomb being about one hundred yards east of it. It may be presumed for the purpose of nomenclature in these visions that Sichar was nearest the actual well, whereas the larger town of Shechem was the scene of most of the other events Anne Catherine relates regarding Dinah and other Samaritans.

[2] John 4:4–42.

[3] "Many things in Dinah's life were similar to those in Magdalene's, but she had fallen more deeply than the latter. Still, I once saw that in the beginning of

grown sons, all of whom had remained with the relatives of their respective fathers when their mother was obliged to leave Damascus. Dinah's sons at a later period joined the seventy-two disciples. Following her conversion, Jesus introduced Dinah to his mother and she joined the circle of holy women, becoming one of the most industrious helpers in the community. Along with Magdalene, Mary Cleophas, Seraphia (Veronica), and Mara the Suphanite, she was among the most beautiful women of the community, although the Virgin outshone them all.

Anne Catherine had much to say about Dinah at the time of her conversion, and in her later role as one of the holy women. She also expanded at some length on how the life of Dinah was prophetic—that Jesus had spoken to the entire sect of Samaritans in her person, that they were attached to their errors by as many ties as she had committed adulteries (see below). Anne Catherine had also a special love for Dinah, who it seems must have reciprocated, for on three occasions—even while busied with visions of the daily life of Jesus—Anne Catherine reports that Dinah visited her. She appeared as a bride dressed in white, with a crown upon her head, bowing in deep humility before Jesus. On one occasion Anne Catherine suddenly perceived Dinah in this form as though looking in at her through the window as she lay upon her sickbed. And on another occasion, while distracted by some domestic disturbance, Anne Catherine looked up suddenly through her tears and said: "See! There stands the Samaritan woman. And Jesus also! She bows ever before him on his way, and with such humility. She is so different now, white as snow and nobly dressed. This is not yet, however, but still to come."

Magdalene's evil career at Magdala, one of her lovers lost his life at the hand of a rival. Dinah was an uncommonly gifted, open-hearted, easily influenced, pleasing woman of great vivacity and impetuosity, but she was always disturbed in conscience. She was living now more respectably, that is with this her reputed husband, in a house that stood alone and surrounded by a moat near the gate leading from Shechem to the spring house. Though not held in contempt by the inhabitants, still they did not have much communication with her. Her manners were different from theirs, her costume elaborate and studied, all of which, however, they pardoned in her, as she was a stranger."

Dinah's Conversion
at the Well and Related Events

ON Wednesday, July 26, AD 30, Jesus crossed the little river that forms the boundary of Samaria and, leaving Mount Garizim to the right, approached Shechem. Andrew, James the Greater, and Saturnin accompanied him, the others having scattered in different directions. Jesus went to nearby Sichar, close by Jacob's well, which was situated on a little hill in the inheritance of Joseph to the north of Mount Garizim and south of Mount Ebal. Sichar lay about a quarter of an hour to the west in a valley that ran along the west side of the city for about an hour. About two good hours northward from Sichar stood the city of Samaria upon a mountain. Another Samaritan city, Shechem, lay about an hour closer by.

Several deeply-rutted roads ran from different points around the little hill and up to the octangular buildings that enclosed Jacob's well, which was surrounded by trees and grassy seats. The spring house was encircled by an open, arched gallery under which about twenty people could find standing room. Directly opposite the road leading from Sichar, and under the arched roof, was the door—usually kept shut—that opened into the spring house proper. There was an aperture in the cover of the latter, which could be closed at pleasure. The interior of the little spring house was quite roomy. The well was deep and surrounded by a stone rim high enough to afford a seat. Between it and the walls, one could walk about freely. The well had a wooden cover, which when opened disclosed a large cylinder just opposite the entrance and lying across the well. From it hung the bucket, which was unwound by means of a winch. Opposite the door was a pump for raising the water to the top of the wall of the spring house, whence it flowed out to the east, south, and west under the surrounding arches into three little basins dug in the earth. They were intended for travelers to perform their ablutions and wash their feet; also for watering beasts of burden.

It was toward midday when Jesus and the three disciples reached this hill. Jesus sent them on to the larger town of Shechem to procure food, for he was hungry, while he himself ascended the hill alone to await them. The day was hot, and Jesus was very tired and thirsty. He sat down a short distance from the well on the side of the path that led up from Sichar. Resting his head upon his hand, he seemed to be patiently waiting for someone to open the well and give him to drink.

And now I saw a Samaritan woman of about thirty years, a leathern bottle hanging on her arm, coming up the hill from Sichar to draw water. She was beautiful,[1] and I remarked how briskly and vigorously, and with what long strides, she mounted the hill. Her costume appeared somewhat studied, and there was an air of distinction about it. Her dress was striped blue and red and embroidered with large yellow flowers; the sleeves above and below the elbow were fastened by yellow bracelets, and were ruffled at the wrist. She wore a white stomacher ornamented with yellow cords. Her neck was entirely concealed by a yellow woolen collar thickly covered with strings of pearl and coral. Her veil, very fine and long, was woven of some rich, woolen material. It hung down her back, but by means of a string could be drawn together and fastened around her waist. When thus worn, it formed a point behind, and on either side folds in which the elbows could comfortably rest. When both sides of the veil were fastened on the breast, the whole of the upper part of her person was enveloped as if in a mantle. Her head was bound with fillets that entirely concealed the hair. From her headdress there arose above the forehead something like a little tower or crown. Tucked up behind it lay the forepart of the veil which, when let down over her face, reached to the breast. She had her large, brownish goat- or camel-hair apron, with its open pockets, thrown up over her right arm, so that the leather bottle hanging on that arm was partly concealed. This apron was similar to those usually worn at such work as drawing water. It protected the dress from the bucket and water bottle. The bottle was of leather, and like a

---

[1] Elsewhere Anne Catherine said of Magdalene: "She was taller and more beautiful than the other women, but Dinah was much more active and dexterous, very cheerful, ever ready to oblige, like a lively, affectionate girl, and moreover very humble. But the Blessed Virgin surpassed them all in her marvelous beauty."

seamless sack. It was convex on two sides, as if lined with a firm, arched, wooden surface; but the two others, when the bottle was empty, lay together in folds like those of a pocketbook. On the two firm sides were leather-covered handles through which ran a leather strap used for carrying it on the arm. The mouth of the bottle was narrow. It could be opened like a funnel for receiving the contents, and closed again like a work pouch. When empty, the bottle hung flat on the side, but when filled it bulged out, holding as much as an ordinary water bucket.[1]

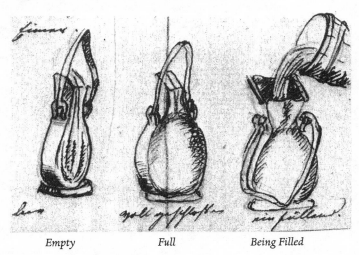

| Empty | Full | Being Filled |

It was under this guise that I saw the woman briskly ascending the hill to get water from Jacob's well for herself and others. I took a fancy to her right away. She was so kind, so frank, so open-hearted. She was called Dinah, was the child of a mixed marriage, and belonged to the sect of Samaritans.[2] She lived in Shechem,

---

[1] In Brentano's notes we find the above illustration of the water vessels Dinah carried to Jacob's well.

[2] The Samaritans were a people that lived in what had been the Northern Kingdom of Israel. Hundreds of years previously, after the death of King Solomon in 975 BC, the nation of Israel split into north and south. The northern ten tribes of Israel were collectively called Israel, and their capital city was Samaria. The southern tribes of Judah and Benjamin were collectively called Judah, and their capital city was Jerusalem. A distance of thirty miles separated

but it was not her birthplace. Her peculiar circumstances were unknown to the inhabitants, among whom she went by the name of Salome. Both she and her husband were very much liked on account of their open, friendly, and obliging manners.

The windings of the path by which she mounted the hill prevented Dinah's seeing Jesus until she actually stood before him. There was something unsettling in the sight as he sat there exhausted and alone on the path leading to Jacob's well. He wore a long, white robe of fine wool like an alb, bound with a broad girdle. It was a garment such as the prophets wore, and which the disciples usually carried for him. He made use of it only on solemn occasions when he preached, or fulfilled some prophecy.

Dinah coming thus suddenly upon Jesus was startled. She lowered her veil and hesitated to advance, for Jesus was sitting full in her path. I saw passing through her mind the characteristic thoughts: "A man! What is he doing here? Is it a temptation?" She saw that Jesus was a Jew as, beaming with benevolence, he graciously drew his feet back, for the path was narrow, with the words: "Pass on, and give me to drink!"

These words touched the woman, since the Jews and the Samaritans were accustomed to exchange only glances of mutual

---

the two cities. Ancestrally, Samaritans claim descent from the Israelite tribes of Ephraim and Manasseh (the two sons of Joseph, son of Jacob) as well as from the priestly tribe of Levi. But the Samaritans were a racially mixed society, with pagan ancestry also. Although they worshipped Jahweh as did the Jews, their religion was not mainstream Judaism. They accepted only the first five books of the bible (the Pentateuch) as canonical, and their temple was on Mount Gerazim instead of on Mount Zion in Jerusalem. The Samaritans of Jesus's day were strict monotheists, but nevertheless, because of their imperfect adherence to Judaism and their partly pagan ancestry, were despised by ordinary Jews. Rather than contaminate themselves by passing through Samaritan territory, Jews traveling between Galilee and Judea would take the longer, six-day journey along the Jordan river valley rather than a shorter, more direct route through Samaria. By speaking—contrary to Jewish custom—with a Samaritan (Dinah), Jesus indicated that a new attitude must be taken toward the Samaritans, as also by passing through their towns instead of crossing the Jordan to avoid them. When asked whom to regard as our neighbor, Jesus told the story of the good Samaritan precisely because Samaritans were despised.

aversion, and so she still lingered, saying: "Why are you here all alone at this hour? If anyone should happen to see me here with you, he would be scandalized." To which Jesus answered that his companions had gone on to the city to purchase food. Dinah said: "Indeed! The three men whom I met? But they will find little at this hour. What the Shechemites have prepared for today, they need for themselves." She spoke as if it were either a feast or a fast that day in Shechem and named another place to which they should have gone for food. But Jesus again said: "Pass on, and give me to drink!" Then Dinah passed by him. Jesus arose and followed her to the well, which she unlocked. While going thither, she said: "How can you, being a Jew, ask a drink from a Samaritan?" And Jesus answered her: "If you knew the gift of God and who he is that says to you: 'Give me to drink,' you would perhaps have asked of him, and he would have given you living water."

Then Dinah loosened the cover and the bucket, meanwhile saying to Jesus, who had seated himself on the rim of the well: "Sir, you have nothing wherein to draw, and the well is deep. Whence then have you living water? Are you greater than our father Jacob who gave us this well, and drank thereof himself, and his children and his cattle?" As she uttered these words, I had a vision of Jacob digging the well and the water springing up.

The woman understood Jesus's words to refer to the water of this well and so, as she was speaking, she put the bucket on the cylinder, which turned heavily, lowered it, and drew it up again. She pushed up her sleeves with the bracelets until they puffed out high above the elbow, and in this way with bare arms she filled her leather bottle out of the bucket. Then, taking a little vessel made of bark and shaped like a horn, she filled it with water and handed it to Jesus, who, sitting on the rim of the well, drank it and said to her: "Whosoever drinks of this water, shall thirst again, but those that drink of the water I shall give them, shall not thirst forever. Yes, the water that I will give them shall become in them a fountain of water springing into life everlasting."

Dinah replied eagerly: "Sir, give me that living water, that I may no more thirst nor have to come with so much fatigue to draw." She was struck by his words "living water" and had a presentiment, though without being fully conscious of it, that Jesus meant

128

by the "living water" the fulfillment of the Promise. And so it was under prophetic inspiration that she uttered her heartfelt prayer for that living water.

I have always felt and understood that those persons with whom the Redeemer treated are not to be considered as mere individuals. They perfectly represented a whole race of people, and they did so, because they belonged to the plenitude of time. And so in Dinah the Samaritan there stood before the Redeemer the whole Samaritan sect, so long separated from the true faith of Israel—from the fountain of living water.[1]

When Dinah had thus spoken, Jesus said to her: "Go home, call thy husband, and come back hither!" and I heard him give the command twice, because it was not to instruct her alone that he had come. In this command the Redeemer addressed the whole sect: "Samaria, call hither him to whom you belong, him who by a holy contract is lawfully bound to you."

Dinah replied to the Lord: "I have no husband!" By this, Samaria confessed to the bridegroom of souls that she had no contract, that she belonged to no one.

Jesus replied: "You have said well, for you have had five husbands, and he with whom you now live is not your husband. You have spoken truly." In these words the messiah said to the sect: "Samaria, you speak the truth. You have been espoused to the idols of five different nations, and your present alliance with God is no marriage contract."

Here Dinah, lowering her eyes and hanging her head, said: "Sir, I see that you are a prophet," and she drew down her veil. Thereby the Samaritan sect recognized the divine mission of the Lord, and confessed its own guilt.

---

[1] Anne Catherine added: "Jesus at the well of Jacob thirsted after the chosen souls of Samaria, in order to refresh them with the living waters from which they had cut themselves off. It was that portion of the rebellious sect still open to salvation that here thirsted after this living water, and, in a certain way, reached out an open hand to receive it. Samaria spoke through Dinah: 'Give me, O Lord, the Blessing of the Promise! Help me to obtain the living water from which I may receive more consolation than from this temporal well of Jacob, through which alone we still have communication with the Jews.'"

As if Dinah understood the prophetic meaning of Jesus's words "and he with whom you live is not your husband"—that is, your actual connection with the true God is imperfect and illegal, the religion of the Samaritans has by sin and self-will been separated from God's Covenant with Jacob—she pointed toward the south, to the temple not far off on Mount Garizim, and said questioningly: "Our Fathers adored on that mountain, and you say that Jerusalem is the place where we must adore?"

Jesus replied with the words: "Woman! Believe me, the hour comes when neither in Garizim nor in Jerusalem will you adore the Father." In this reply he meant to say: "Samaria, the hour comes when neither here nor in the sanctuary of the Temple will God be adored, because He walks in the midst of you," and he continued: "You adore that which you know not, but we adore that which we know, for salvation is of the Jews."

Here he related to her a similitude of the wild, unfruitful suckers of trees, which shoot forth into wood and foliage, but produce no fruit. It was as if he had said to the sect: "Samaria, you have not security in your worship. You have no union, no sacrament, no pledge of alliance, no Ark of the Covenant, no fruit. The Jews— from whom the messiah will be born—have all these things, the Promise, and its fulfillment."

And again Jesus said: "But the hour comes and now is when the true adorers will adore the Father in spirit and in truth, for the Father wills such to adore him. God is a spirit, and they that adore him must adore him in spirit, and in truth." By these words Jesus meant: "Samaria, the hour come, yea, it now is, when the Father by true adorers will be honored in the Holy Spirit and in the Son, who is the way and the truth."

Dinah replied: "I know that the messiah comes. When he is come, he will tell us all things." In these words here at the well of Jacob, spoke that portion of the Samaritan sect that might lay some legitimate claim to the Promise: "I hope for, I believe in, the coming of the messiah. He will help us."

Jesus responded: "I am he, I who now speak to you!" By this he said to all Samaria that would be converted: "Samaria! I came to Jacob's well athirst for you, you water of this well. And when you gave me to drink, I promised you living water that would never let you thirst again. And you did, hoping and believing, make known to me your longing for this water. Behold, I reward you, for you have allayed my thirst after you by your desire after me! Samaria, I am the fountain of living water. I who now speak to you, am the messiah."

As Jesus pronounced the words: "I am the messiah," Dinah, trembling with holy joy, gazed at him in amazement. But suddenly recovering herself, she turned and, leaving her water bottle standing and the well open, fled down the path to Shechem, to tell her husband and all whom she met what had happened to her. It was strictly forbidden to leave the well of Jacob open, but what cared Dinah now for the well of Jacob! What cared she for her bucket of earthly water! She had received the living water, and her loving, joyous heart was longing to pour its refreshing streams over all her neighbors.

But as she was hurrying out of the spring house, she ran past the three disciples who had come with the food and had already been standing for some time at a little distance from the door, wondering what their Master could have to say for so long with a Samaritan woman. But through reverence for him, they forebore to question. Dinah ran down to Shechem and with great eagerness said to her husband and others whom she met on the street: "Come up to Jacob's well! There you will see a man that has told me all the secret actions of my life. Come, he is certainly the Christ!"

Meanwhile the three disciples approached Jesus, who was still by the well, and offered him some rolls and honey out of their basket, saying: "Master, eat!" Jesus arose and left the well with the words: "I have meat to eat which you know not."

The disciples said to one another: "Has any man brought him to eat?" and they thought to themselves: "Did that Samaritan woman give him to eat?"

Jesus would not stop to eat, but began descending the path to Shechem. The disciples followed, eating. Jesus said to them as he went on before: "My meat is to do the will of him that sent me, that I may perfect his work." By that he meant, to convert the people of Shechem, after whose salvation his soul hungered. He spoke much more to the same purport.

When near the city, Dinah the Samaritan again appeared hurrying back to meet Jesus. She joined him respectfully, but full of joy and frankness, and Jesus addressed many words to her, sometimes standing still and sometimes moving slowly forward. He unfolded to her all her past life with all the dispositions of her soul. She was deeply moved and promised that both she and her husband would abandon all and follow him. He pointed out to her many ways by which she could do penance for her sins and repair her scandals.

While Jesus was speaking with Dinah, the disciples followed at some distance, wondering what he could have to say to the woman. "We have brought him food, and that with a good deal of difficulty. Why, now, does he not eat?"

When near Shechem, Dinah left the Master and hurried forward to meet her husband and many of the citizens, who came pouring out of their houses, all curiosity to see Jesus. Full of joy, they exulted and shouted salutations of welcome to him. Jesus, standing still, motioned with his hand for silence, and addressed them kindly for some moments, telling them among other things to believe all that the woman had told them. Jesus was so remarkably gracious in his words, his glance so bright and penetrating, that all hearts beat more quickly, all were borne toward him, and they were pressing in their solicitations for him to enter and teach in their city. He promised that he would do so, but for the present passed on. This scene took place somewhere between three and four o'clock in the afternoon.

Leaving Shechem to the right, Jesus now journeyed about an hour southward to a field around which were scattered twenty shepherd huts and tents. In one of the larger huts, the Blessed Virgin, Mary Cleophas, the wife of James the Greater, and two of the widows were awaiting him. A meal was served and a young boy was brought to Jesus, and raised by him.

There then approached—and that rather timidly—several persons from Shechem, among them Dinah. They did not venture to draw near because they were not accustomed to have dealings with the Jewish shepherds. Dinah however made bold to advance first, and I saw her talking with the women and the Blessed Virgin. After the repast, Jesus and the disciples took leave of the holy

132

women, who immediately set about preparing for their return journey to Galilee, whither Jesus himself was to go the next day but one.

Jesus now returned with Dinah and the other Samaritans to Shechem, a city not very large, but with broad streets and open squares. The Samaritan house of prayer was a fine-looking building, rather more ornamented than the synagogues of small Jewish places. The women of Shechem were not so reserved as the Jewish women; they communicated more freely with the men.

As soon as Jesus entered Shechem he was surrounded by a crowd. He did not go into their synagogue but taught walking around here and there on the streets, and in one of the squares where there was an orator's chair. Everywhere was the concourse of people very great, and they were full of joy at the messiah's having come to them. Dinah, though very much moved and very recollected, was of all the women the one that approached nearest to Jesus. Her neighbors now looked upon her with special regard, as she had been the first to find Jesus. She sent to Jesus the man with whom she was living, who spoke to him a few words of exhortation. He stood before Jesus quite embarrassed and ashamed of his sins.

Jesus did not tarry long in Shechem, but went out by the opposite gate and taught here and there among the houses and gardens that extended for some distance along the valley. He put up at an inn distant from Shechem a good half-hour, promising, however, to return to the city on the following day and give them an instruction.

When Jesus went again to Shechem the following morning, Thursday, July 27, AD 30, he taught the whole day, dividing the time between the orator's chair in the city and the hills outside, and in the evening he taught again in the inn. From the whole country around came crowds to hear him, and they followed him from place to place. The cry was: "Now he is teaching here! Now he is teaching there!"

Dinah was everywhere foremost, everywhere made her way through the crowd to Jesus. She was very attentive, very earnest, and deeply impressed. She had had another interview with Jesus and was now about to separate from her reputed husband. They had resolved for Jesus's sake to consecrate all their riches to the poor and the good of the future Church. Jesus told them how to proceed in the affair. Many of the Samaritans were profoundly touched by what they had seen and heard, and they said to Dinah: "You have spoken truly. We have now heard him ourselves. He is the messiah!" The good woman was quite out of herself, and so in earnest, so joyous! I have always loved her dearly.

Several more references to Dinah will be found in the entry for Mara the Suphanite during the period from November, AD 30, to January, AD 31, during which time the two women were frequently together.

After the Crucifixion

AFTER the crucifixion, when the body of Jesus was taken down from the cross and prepared for burial, and then carried by litter to the sepulcher, with many of the other holy women in train behind, Dinah the Samaritan, Maroni of Nain, and Mara the Suphanite were with Martha and Lazarus in Bethany. Later I saw the Blessed Virgin and her companions knocking at the cenacle and being admitted, then Abenadar, and by degrees most of the apostles and several of the disciples entered.

The holy women retired to the apartments occupied by the Blessed Virgin. They took some refreshment and spent some moments in tears and mourning, relating to one another all that had happened. All were in great trouble and sadness. The holy women also prayed with Mary under a lamp. Later, when it had grown quite dark, Lazarus, Martha, the widow Maroni of Nain, Dinah the Samaritan, and Mara the Suphanite were admitted. They had come from Bethany to keep the sabbath.

In the house occupied by the Blessed Virgin there was a large hall with several little recesses cut off by hangings and movable partitions. These were private sleeping places. When the holy women returned from the sepulcher, they put everything they brought back again into its place and lighted the lamp that was hanging from the center of the ceiling. Then they gathered under it around the Blessed Virgin and took turns in praying most devoutly. They were all in deep sorrow.

After that they partook of some refreshment, and were soon joined by Martha, Maroni, Dinah, and Mary who, after celebrating the sabbath in Bethany, had come hither with Lazarus. The last-named went to the men in the cenacle.

When, with tears on both sides, the death and burial of Jesus had been recounted to the newly-arrived, and the hour was far advanced, some of the men, among them Joseph of Arimathea, left the Supper Room, called for the women that wanted to return to their homes in the city, and took their leave. The women who had remained with the Blessed Virgin now retired, each to her own screened sleeping place. They veiled their heads in long linen scarves, and sat for a little while in silent grief on the ground, leaning on the sleeping covers that were rolled up against the wall. After some moments, they arose, spread out the covers, laid aside their sandals, girdles, and some articles of dress, enveloped themselves from head to foot, as they were accustomed to do on retiring to rest, and lay down on their couches for a short sleep. At midnight they rose again, dressed, folded the couch together, assembled once more under the lamp around the Blessed Virgin, and prayed in turn.

Mara the Suphanite

ABOUT a month after Dinah's conversion there came to the city of Ainon a woman named Mara. She was a Jewess and rich, but an adulteress, and came from the region of Supha in the land of the Moabites (who were descendents of Lot). It was because she was from the region of Supha that she was called the Suphanite. She was a descendant of Orpah, the widow of Chilion (the son of Naomi and Elimelech of Bethlehem, so that Orpah was the daughter-in-law of Naomi). Upon Naomi's advice, Orpah did not accompany her to Bethlehem. Instead, Ruth—the widow of Orpah's other son Mahlon—accompanied Naomi thither. Orpah married again in Moab, and from that union sprang the family of Mara the Suphanite. Through her descent from Orpah (Ruth's sister-in-law), Mara was connected with the house of David, the ancestral line of Jesus.[1] It was shown me how this stream, deviat-

---

[1] The following summary from the book of Ruth will help clarify this lineage, and how Mara was descended—as was Jesus—from David. During a famine, a man named Elimelech took his wife Naomi and their two sons, Mahlon and Chilion, east from their home in Bethlehem in Judea to the country of Moab. After their father Elimelech's death, the sons married Moabite women named Orpah and Ruth. They lived together for about ten years, until both Mahlon and Chilion died, leaving their mother Naomi to live with her daughters-in-law. Hearing that the famine was over in Judah, Naomi decided to return to her home, and she urged her daughters-in-law to return to their own mothers in Moab, for in this way the childless widows might improve their chances to remarry and bear children. After much dispute, Orpah acceded to her mother-in-law's wishes and left her, weeping. But Ruth clung to Naomi, saying "Where you go I will go; where you lodge, I will lodge; your people shall be my people, and your God my God."

Once they reached Bethlehem, Naomi and Ruth sought food by gleaning grain from the field of a kinsman of Naomi's named Boaz. Boaz saw Ruth gleaning, and so introduced himself, telling her that his workers would protect her and share their provisions with her. Ruth thanked Boaz, but then questioned why she, a foreigner, should receive such kindness. Boaz replied that he

136

ing in her from its course and troubled by her abominable sins, was purified anew in her by the grace of Jesus and flowed once more in its direct course toward the Church.[1]

Mara's Jewish husband, who lived in Damascus, had rejected her because she had had four lovers, one after the other. Through these liaisons she had given birth to three illegitimate children—a son and two daughters—whom she had with her in Ainon at the time of her conversion. Her legitimate children had been retained by their father when he repudiated his unfaithful wife, their mother.

Mara was living at this time in a house of her own at Ainon. For a long time she had conceived sentiments of sorrow for her disorders and had done penance—her conduct being so reserved and proper that she had won the esteem of even the most respectable women of Ainon.

Hearing the preaching of John the Baptist against adultery had intensified her sense of wanting to do penance. She was often possessed by five devils. They had again seized upon her when, as a last resource, she had gone to the court where Jesus was curing the sick. The Pharisees rebuffed her and their words—which in her deep dejection she had taken as true—had driven her to the brink of despair.

She was converted in Ainon on Monday, September 4, AD 30, through her encounter with Jesus. On that day Jesus delivered Mara from the demonic influence and granted her forgiveness,

---

had learned of Ruth's faithfulness to her mother-in-law, and then prayed the God of Israel to bless Ruth for her loyalty.

Hearing of Boaz's interest in Ruth, Naomi then contrived to get Ruth married to Boaz by invoking her kinship with him. She sent Ruth to Boaz at night to offer herself to him, but Boaz, an upright man, refused to take advantage of her. Instead he helped Naomi and Ruth negotiate some rituals of inheritance, after which Boaz married Ruth. Soon they had a son, Obed, who later fathered Jesse, who fathered David, who became king of a unified Israel.

[1] "I saw," said Anne Catherine elsewhere, "how a stray branch of the stock of David was purified within Mara by the grace of Jesus, and admitted into the bosom of the Church. I cannot express how many of these roots and offshoots I see become intertwined with each other, lost to view, and then once more brought to light."

blessing also her three illegitimate children, whose hands he placed in those of their healed and fully-converted mother. Mara then bestowed upon Jesus many gifts at a banquet held in his honor in her festive house.

Upon his later return to Ainon, Jesus helped Mara reconcile with her husband. Following her conversion, Dinah and Veronica welcomed Mara warmly into the circle of holy women. A fuller account of these and other events follows below.

Her Conversion and
Later Episodes in Her Life

ON Monday, September 4, AD 30, while Jesus was busy curing the sick, a beautiful woman of middle age and in the garb of a stranger entered the large portico by the gate leading from the city. Her head and hair were wound in a thin veil woven with pearls. She wore a bodice, in shape somewhat like a heart and open at the sides, rather like a scapular thrown over the head and fastened together around the body by straps reaching from the back. Around the neck and breast it was ornamented with cords and pearls. From it fell, in folds to the ankle, two deep skirts, one shorter than the other. Both were of fine white wool embroidered with large, colored flowers. The sleeves were wide and fastened with armlets. To the shoulder straps connecting the front and back of the bodice was attached the upper part of a short mantle that fell over the arms. Over this flowed a long veil, of the whiteness of wool.

The woman, ashamed and anxious, entered slowly and timidly, her pale countenance bespeaking confusion and her eyes red from weeping. She wanted to approach Jesus, but the crowd was so great that she could not get near him. The Pharisees keeping order went to her, and she at once addressed them: "Lead me to the prophet, that he may forgive my sins and cure me!"

The Pharisees stopped her with the words: "Woman, go home! What do you want here? The prophet will not speak to you. How can he forgive you your sins? He will not busy himself with you, for you are an adulteress."

When the woman heard these words, she grew pale, her countenance assumed a frightful expression, she threw herself on the ground, rent her mantle from top to bottom, snatched her veil from her head, and cried: "Ah, then I am lost! Now they lay hold of me! They are tearing me to pieces! See, there they are!" and she named five devils who were raging against her, one of her husband, the other four of her paramours. It was a fearful spectacle. Some of the women standing around raised her from the ground, and bore her wailing to her home.

Jesus knew well what was going on but he would not put the Pharisees of this place to shame. He did not interfere but quietly continued his work of healing, for her hour had not yet come.

Soon after, accompanied by the disciples and Pharisees, and followed by the people, Jesus went through the city to the hill upon which John the Baptist had formerly taught. It was in the center of moss-covered ramparts and there were some buildings around. On the side by which they approached was a half-ruined castle, in one of whose towers Herod took up his abode during John's teaching. The whole hill was already covered with the expectant crowd.

Jesus mounted to the place where John had taught. It was covered with a large awning open on all sides. Here he delivered a long discourse in which he spoke of the mercy of God to men, particularly to his own people. Jesus did not however say so openly at Ainon as he had done at Bezek three days earlier, on Friday, September 1, AD 30, that he was himself the messiah. He spoke also of John, his imprisonment and his mission. One crowd of listeners was at intervals supplanted by another, that all might hear his words. Jesus questioned some of them as to why they wanted to receive baptism, why they had put it off till the present, and what they thought the ceremony to be. The discourse ended at about three o'clock in the afternoon.

Then Jesus and the disciples went with the Pharisees down the hill and into the city, where a great entertainment had been prepared for him in one of the public halls. But when he drew near the hall, he stopped short, saying: "I have another kind of hunger," and he asked (though he already knew) where that woman lived whom they had sent away from him in the morning. They pointed out the house, which was near the hall of entertainment.

Jesus left his companions standing where they were, while he went forward and entered the house through the courtyard. As Jesus approached, I saw the fearful torture and affliction of the woman inside. The devil, who had possession of her, drove her from one corner to another. She was like a timorous animal that would hide itself. As Jesus was traversing the court and drawing near to where she was, she fled through a corridor and into a cellar in the side of the hill upon which her house was built. In it was a vessel like a great cask, narrow above and wide below. She wanted to hide herself in it, but when she tried to do so, it burst with a loud crash. It was an immense earthen vessel.

Jesus meantime halted and cried: "Mara of Suphan, wife of... (here he pronounced her husband's name, which I have forgotten), I command you in the Name of God to come to me!"

Then the woman, enveloped from head to foot—as if the demon forced her still to hide in her mantle—came creeping to Jesus's feet on all fours, like a dog awaiting the whip. But Jesus said to her: "Stand up!" She obeyed, but drew her veil tightly over her face and around her neck as if she wanted to strangle herself.

Then Jesus said to her: "Uncover your face!" and she unwound her veil, but lowering her eyes and averting them from Jesus as if forced to do so by an interior power. Jesus, approaching his head to hers, said: "Look at me!" and she obeyed. He breathed upon her, a black vapor went out of her on all sides, and she fell unconscious before him.

Her maidservants, alarmed by the loud bursting of the cask, had hurried thither and were standing nearby. Jesus directed them to take their mistress upstairs and lay her on a bed. He soon followed with two of the disciples that had accompanied him and found her weeping bitter tears. He went to her, laid his hand on her head, and said: "Your sins are forgiven you!"

She wept vehemently and sat up. And now her three children entered the room, a boy about twelve years old, and two little girls of about nine and seven. The girls wore little short-sleeved tunics embroidered in yellow. Jesus stepped forward to meet the children, spoke to them kindly, asked them some questions, and gave them some instruction. Their mother said: "Thank the prophet! He has cured me!" whereupon the little ones fell on the ground at Jesus's feet. He blessed them, led them one by one to their mother, in order of age, and put their little hands into hers.

It seemed to me that by this action Jesus removed from the children the disgrace and thus legitimized them, for they were the fruits of adulterous unions. Jesus still consoled the woman, telling her that she would be reconciled with her husband, and counseling her thenceforth to live righteously in contrition and penance. After that he went with the disciples to the entertainment of the Pharisees.

Jesus now went into the entertainment hall in which were the Pharisees and the rest of the disciples and took his place with them at table. The Pharisees were somewhat displeased that Jesus had left them and gone to seek the woman whom they had so harshly repulsed that morning before so many people. But they said nothing, fearing to receive a reproof themselves. Jesus treated them with much consideration during the meal and taught in numerous similitudes and parables.

Toward the middle of the entertainment the three children of the Suphanite entered in their holiday dresses. One of the little girls bore an urn full of fragrant water, the other had a similar one of nard, and the boy carried a vessel. They entered the hall by the door opposite the unoccupied side of the table, cast themselves down before Jesus, and set their presents on the table in front of him. Mara herself followed with her maids but she dared not approach. She was veiled and carried a shining crystal vase with colored veins like marble in which, surrounded by upright sprays of delicate green foliage, were various kinds of costly aromatics. Her children had offered similar vases, but smaller.

The Pharisees cast forbidding glances upon the mother and children. But Jesus said: "Draw near, Mara!" and she stepped humbly behind him, while her children, to whom she had handed it, deposited her offering beside the others on the table.

Jesus thanked her. The Pharisees murmured, as later on they did at Magdalene's present to Jesus. They thought it a great waste, quite opposed to economy and compassion for the needy; however, they only wanted something to bring against the poor woman.

Jesus spoke to her very kindly, as also to the children, to whom he presented some fruit, which they took away with them. The Suphanite remained veiled and standing humbly behind Jesus. He said to the Pharisees: "All gifts come from God. For precious gifts, gratitude gives in return what it has the most precious, and that is no waste. The people that gather and prepare these spices must live." Then he directed one of the disciples to give the value of them to the poor, spoke some words upon the woman's conversion and repentance, restored her to the good opinion of all, and called upon the inhabitants of the city to treat her affectionately.

Mara spoke not a word, but wept quietly under her veil the whole time. At last she cast herself in silence at Jesus's feet, rose, and left the dining hall. Jesus took this occasion to give some instruction against adultery. Which among them, he asked, felt himself free from spiritual adultery? He remarked that John had not been able to convert Herod, but that this poor woman had of her own accord turned away from her evil life, and then he related the parable of the sheep lost and found. He had already consoled the woman in her own house, assuring her that her children would turn out well, and holding out to her the hope that she should one day join the women under Martha's supervision and work for the benefit of the inns.

Several weeks later, on September 29, AD 30, Jesus was teaching at intervals as he traveled from Succoth to Ainon. Just outside Ainon a beautiful tent had been erected and a solemn reception prepared for Jesus by Mara the Suphanite. The most distinguished personages of the city were present, also the priests, and Mara with her children. The men washed the feet of Jesus and his disciples, and costly refreshments were offered them, according to custom. Mara's children and others of their age presented the dishes of food. The women, closely veiled, prostrated before Jesus, their faces on the ground. He saluted and blessed them graciously. Mara, with tears of joy and gratitude, invited Jesus to repair to her house. When he entered the city, Mara's children, two girls and a boy, as has been said, and others of their age with long garlands of flowers and scarfs of woolen stuff, walked before him and at his side.

As Jesus, accompanied by his disciples, entered the courtyard of Mara's house—passing under a flowery arch erected for the occasion—Mara again cast herself at his feet, weeping and thanking him, her children following her example. Jesus caressed the little ones. Mara told him that Dinah the Samaritan had been there, and that the man with whom she had been living up to that time had received baptism. Mara knew Dinah, since her own husband and three legitimate children lived in Damascus, where Dinah was from. She and the Samaritan had together sounded Jesus's praises. She was radiant with joy and showed Jesus many costly robes for the use of the priests, and a high miter she herself had made for the Temple—for she was incredibly skillful at such work, and rich in money and property.

Jesus was very gracious toward her. He spoke to her of her husband, advising her to go back to him, to be reconciled with him, for her presence near him would prove of use, and her illegitimate children could be provided for elsewhere. He directed her also to send a messenger to her husband to request him to come to her. On leaving her house, Jesus went to the place of baptism, where he mounted the pulpit and taught the people.

After the sabbath there was an entertainment given to Jesus at the public banqueting hall. It had been prepared by Mara. The tables, as well as the hall, were beautifully decorated with foliage and flowers and lamps. The guests were numerous, and among them were many whom Jesus had cured. The women sat on one side behind a screen. During the meal Mara went forward with her children and placed costly perfumes on the table. She then poured a flask of fragrant balm over Jesus's head and cast herself down before him. Jesus received these attentions graciously, and related parables. No one found fault with Mara, for all loved her on account of her generosity.

Four days later, on Tuesday, October 3, AD 30, before Jesus again left Ainon with his disciples, he had an interview with Mara in her own house. He gave her salutary advice. Mara was entirely changed. She was full of love, zeal, humility, and gratitude; she busied herself with the poor and the sick. When journeying, after her cure, through Ramoth and Basan, Jesus had sent a disciple to Bethany to inform the holy women of it and of her reconciliation, in consequence of which announcement Veronica, Johanna Chusa, and Martha had been to visit her.

On his departure from Ainon, Jesus received rich presents from Mara and many other people, all of which were at once distributed to the poor. The gateway by which he left the city was decorated with an arch of flowers and garlands. The assembled crowd saluted him with songs of praise, and he was met outside the city by women and children who presented him with wreaths.

Three days later, on Tuesday, November 7, AD 30, the day before the sermon on the mount, Martha was much engaged in encouraging Magdalene to go with her there the following day. Magdalene was somewhat broken in spirits, lacking the courage to disengage herself from her surroundings. She looked pale and languid. The man with whom she lived, on account of his low and vulgar sentiments, was utterly distasteful to her. Martha treated her very prudently and affectionately. She said to her: "Dinah and Mara the Suphanite, whom you know, two amiable and clever women, invite you to be present with them at the instruction that Jesus is going to give on the mountain."

That evening, Magdalene, with Martha and Anna Cleophas, started from Magdalum to join the holy women at Damna. Magdalene rode on an ass, for she was not accustomed to walking. She was dressed elegantly, though not to such excess nor so extravagantly as at a later period when she was converted for the second time. She took a private apartment in the inn and spoke only with Dinah and Mara, who visited her by turns. I saw them together, an affable and well-bred confidence marking their conversation. There was however on the part of the converted sinners a shade of embarrassment similar to what might be experienced on a military officer's meeting a former comrade who had become a priest. This feeling soon gave way to tears and womanly expressions of mutual sympathy and they went together to the inn at the foot of the mountain.

Several days after the sermon on the mount, on the morning of Saturday, November 11, AD 30, Jesus was teaching in the synagogue. The streets were again filled with the sick. Some had come before the sabbath, and some till now had not believed—but on the report of the possessed man's cure they had themselves transported thither from all quarters of the city. Many of them had been there before but had not been cured. They were weak, tepid, slothful souls, more difficult to convert than great sinners of more ardent nature. Magdalene was converted only after many struggles and relapses, but her last efforts were generous and final. Dinah turned at once from her evil ways, and Mara, after sighing long for grace, was suddenly converted. All the great female sinners were very quickly and powerfully converted, as was also the sturdy Paul, to whom conversion came like a flash of lightning.

By now the holy women had established inns for the use of Jesus and the disciples as they journeyed. Martha and Susanna were just now visiting their inns on the way through Galilee to Samaria, for here they exercised a kind of general superintendence—the other women seeing to those established in their own respective districts. They went together to the several inns, taking with them asses laden with all kinds of household necessaries. Once when Mara accompanied them (Saturday, December 9, AD 30), the report spread among the people that Mary Magdalene now went around with the women who provided for the needs of the prophet of Nazareth and his party. Indeed, Mara was in figure very like Magdalene, and neither of them was very well-known on this side of the Jordan. Besides being called Mara, and the ill repute her past life had gained for her, the Suphanite also had anointed Jesus at a feast given by one of the Pharisees. She was consequently, even at this early date, confounded with Magdalene—a mistake that only increased with time among those not well acquainted with the community.

About a month later, on Saturday, January 5, AD 31, Jesus was sharing a meal with some Pharisees, many of whom had heard of the conversion of Magdalene, of Mara the Suphanite, and of Dinah the Samaritan. When they brought this to the attention of Jesus, he replied: "If you knew me, you would speak differently. I am come to have pity on sinners." He then contrasted external ulcers, which carry off poisonous humors and are easily healed, with internal ones, which though full of loathsome matter do not affect the appearance of the individual so afflicted.

Five months later, on Thursday, June 7, AD 31, shortly after returning from his journey to Cyprus, Jesus and the disciples journeyed to Nain. Several disciples and the youth of Nain whom Jesus had raised from the dead came to meet him near the well outside the city. Jesus had with him now about twelve disciples, though no apostles. The disciples belonging to Jerusalem had come hither from the holy city with some of the holy women, while others, having celebrated the feast of Pentecost with Mary at Nazareth, awaited at Nain on their return journey the coming of Jesus, who when he arrived put up at an inn prepared for him there in one of the houses belonging to the widow of Nain— whom he went to see shortly after his arrival. The female portion of the family came out veiled to meet him in the portico of the inner court and cast themselves at his feet. Jesus saluted them graciously and accompanied them into the reception hall. There were five women present besides the widow herself; namely, Martha, Magdalene, Veronica, Johanna Chusa, and Mara the Suphanite. They, the holy women, sat apart at the end of the hall on a kind of raised trestle like a long, low sofa. They sat cross-legged on cushions and rugs. The seat they occupied was raised high enough to show the feet upon which it rested. The women were silent until Jesus addressed them, and then each spoke in her turn. They related what was going on at Jerusalem and told Jesus of the snares Herod had laid for him. They became so animated in their recital that Jesus raised his finger and reproached them with their worldly solicitude and their judgments of others. Then he told them all about Cyprus, of those whom he had won to the truth, and spoke in words of love of the Roman commandant in Salamis. By this time Magdalene and Mara were nothing like as beautiful as they used to be. They were pale and thin, and their eyes red from weeping.

As was described at the close of the article on Dinah the Samaritan, at the time when the body of Jesus was taken down from the cross, washed and prepared, and carried on a litter to the sepulcher, Mara—along with Dinah and Maroni of Nain—were with Martha and Lazarus in Bethany. Similarly, when it had grown quite dark, she and these same others, having traveled from Bethany together, were admitted into the cenacle that same night.

The Holy Women at
Christ's Death and Resurrection

Dr. Robert Powell

THE reason for focusing here upon the holy women present at the Mystery of Golgotha is that these women—along with the only male apostle present, John of Zebedee—bore witness to the great sacrifice of the Son of God, Christ.

According to Anne Catherine, during the night Thursday/Friday of Christ's passion, the Blessed Virgin Mary, who was the center of the circle of holy women, was accompanied by the following nine women: Martha, Mary Magdalene, Mary Cleophas, Mary Salome, Mary Mark, Susanna (of Jerusalem), Johanna Chusa, Veronica (Seraphia), and Salome (of Jerusalem).

All of these holy women—and several more—were present at the crucifixion. Altogether, according to Anne Catherine, there were seventeen women present at the scene of the crucifixion—arranged in three groups: *four* who were directly beneath the cross; *six* who were a relatively short distance from the cross; and *seven* somewhat further away.

That there were *four* directly beneath the cross is confirmed by comparing the accounts of the four gospels:

Emmerich: Virgin Mary, Mary Magdalene, Mary Cleophas, and Salome (Mary Salome)

Matthew: Mary Magdalene, Mary the mother of James and Joses (Mary Cleophas),[1] the mother of the sons of Zebedee (Mary Salome)

Mark: Mary Magdalene, Mary the mother of James the Less and Joses (Mary Cleophas), Salome (Mary Salome)

Luke: His mother the Virgin Mary, Mary Magdalene, Mary the wife of Cleophas [Mary Cleophas]

John: No information given

[1] See note p. 150.

147

The *six* holy women who according to Anne Catherine were a relatively short distance from the cross were:

Martha, Mary Heli, Veronica (Seraphia), Johanna Chusa, Susanna (of Jerusalem), and Mary Mark.

Finally, Anne Catherine says that there were *seven* holy women present at the crucifixion who were somewhat further from the cross. Although she does not name these holy women, from her subsequent descriptions it can be deduced that five of this group were:

Salome (of Jerusalem), Anna Cleophas (daughter of a brother of Joseph), Maroni (the mother of the youth of Nain [Luke 7:11–17]), Dinah (the Samaritan woman with whom Jesus conversed at Jacob's well [John 4:4–42]), and Mara (the Suphanite, who had been possessed and been healed by Jesus, who then spoke of the parable of the lost sheep in reference to herself. [Matt. 18:10–14])

Taking these three groups together, it can be said that there were *fifteen* holy women present at the crucifixion (seemingly there were two more, still to be identified).

Christ's body was taken down from the cross by Joseph of Arimathea, Nicodemus, and Abenadar, the Roman centurion of Arab descent who dipped a sponge in vinegar and raised it on the end of his lance to the mouth of Jesus on the cross (John 19:28–30).

After the body was taken down, it was prepared for burial. Anne Catherine describes how the Virgin Mary attended especially to the head and chest region, and Mary Magdalene to the feet of Jesus. All the remaining holy women still present helped or watched the preparation of the body for burial. Especially helpful were Mary Cleophas, Salome (probably Mary Salome, rather than Salome of Jerusalem), and Veronica (Seraphia).

Anne Catherine explicitly says that Mary Heli, who was already old, watched this activity on the part of the holy women in preparing the body for burial. She also mentions that a small group of holy women had left the hill of Golgotha after the crucifixion and gone to the home of Lazarus in Bethany to relate to him all that had happened. These holy women were Martha (Lazarus's sister), Maroni, Dinah, and Mara.

After the body had been prepared it was carried to the tomb, about a seven-minute walk east of Golgotha. The body of Jesus was borne on a makeshift stretcher by four men: Nicodemus and Joseph of Arimathea at the front, and John and Abenadar at the rear. The holy sepulcher was situated in a cave in the rocks of a beautiful garden, and the garden and tomb both belonged to Joseph of Arimathea. The garden with the holy sepulcher was located outside the city wall, close to the Bethlehem gate in that wall, and also close to the little gate of Nicodemus. According to Anne Catherine, when on Easter Sunday morning Mary Magdalene discovered that the holy sepulcher was empty: "She hurriedly rushed through the little gate of Nicodemus into the city" to find the disciples and to tell them that 'They have taken the Lord from the tomb.'"

There was a procession of eleven or twelve holy women following the four men bearing the body. Anne Catherine names twelve women. However, two of the names appear to refer to the same woman, namely Mary Salome, who was married to Zebedee. When the "wife of Zebedee" and "Mary Salome" are both named (and they are named consecutively in the list), it would appear that Anne Catherine referred to this woman in two different ways, in which case there would have been eleven holy women in the procession.

Anne Catherine quite exactly describes the procession of the holy women following the four men. Although she does not say so explicitly, the impression she gives is that the women were arranged in pairs, headed by the Virgin Mary and Mary Heli, followed by Mary Magdalene and Mary Cleophas, and so on. Since Mary Salome is the same as Salome (the wife of Zebedee)—as the name is here given by Anne Catherine—the order of the procession was:

> Virgin Mary, Mary Heli, Mary Magdalene, Mary Cleophas, Veronica (Seraphia), Johanna Chusa, Mary Mark, Mary Salome, Salome of Jerusalem, Susanna (of Jerusalem), and Anna—a niece of Joseph (the husband of Mary).

Anne Catherine describes that a group of five women went into the city on Holy Saturday to purchase a variety of herbs, little flasks of ointment, and nard water. They wanted to go early next morning to the holy sepulcher to scatter the herbs over the body of Jesus in its winding sheet and pour upon it the perfumed water. These five women were Mary Magdalene, Mary Cleophas, Salome (of Jerusalem), Johanna Chusa, and Mary Salome. This is the order in which they are mentioned in the original German text of the visions of Anne Catherine written down by Clemens Brentano. In the English translation, the name Salome (of Jerusalem) is erroneously omitted from this list, indicating only Mary Magdalene, Mary Cleophas, Johanna Chusa, and Mary Salome.

Anne Catherine's description of Easter Sunday morning initially describes only four of this group of five holy women going to the garden of the holy sepulcher. As can be seen from the accounts in the four gospels (see summary below), four women are also named as having gone on Easter Sunday morning to the garden of the holy sepulcher. These four women named in the gospels are Mary Magdalene, Salome, Johanna (Chusa), and Mary the mother of James. Anne Catherine's account helps to clarify that the Salome named here is indeed Salome of Jerusalem (rather than Mary Salome). However, there is some ambiguity in the gospel designation "Mary the mother of James," since on the one hand Mary Cleophas was the mother of the disciples James the Less, Judas Thaddeus, and Simon, while on the other Mary Salome was the mother of the disciples James the Greater and John. As we shall see in the following, the most probable solution to this ambiguity is that with "Mary the mother of James"—the designation occurring in both Mark and Luke—is meant Mary Cleophas, noting also that in the section above summarizing the gospel accounts of the women under the cross, Mary Cleophas is referred to as "Mary the mother of James and Joses."[1] On account of this ambiguity, however, there remains the slight possibility that the fifth woman mentioned in Anne Catherine's account, Mary Salome, is the "Mary the mother of James" mentioned in one of the gospel accounts—either in Mark or Luke—in which case the other gospel reference using this designation would be

---

[1] Mary Cleophas had a son, Joseph (or Joses) Barsabbas by her second husband, Sabbas.

referring to Mary Cleophas who, according to Anne Catherine, was definitely one of the four women. However, it seems most unlikely that "Mary the mother of James" in one gospel would refer to Mary Salome, but in another gospel to Mary Cleophas.

For our considerations it is important that Mary Salome *is* mentioned later in Anne Catherine's account in the original German version. Given that Mary Salome was part of this group that went to buy the herbs, ointment, and perfumed water on Holy Saturday, and that the five women did this with the intention of going together to the holy sepulcher early the next morning, it seems a reasonable supposition that Mary Salome was indeed there, but that perhaps she followed the other four later and so was not initially mentioned in the description by Anne Catherine (although, as stated already, she *is* mentioned *later* in the original German edition).

Whereas Mary Salome's name is clearly stated later on in the description in the original German edition, only the simpler name "Salome" is indicated in the English edition. Anne Catherine described that this Salome was *not* the mother of John and his brother James. In other words, this Salome was *not* Mary Salome. This Salome (Salome of Jerusalem) is thus clearly distinguished from Mary Salome, who *was* the mother of James and John. "She was not the mother of John, but another Salome, a rich lady of Jerusalem, a relative of Joseph," who was wealthy enough to cover the major part of the cost of purchasing the herbs, ointments, and perfumed water. Anne Catherine added that it was Mary Magdalene and Salome who had shared in defraying most of the cost of the purchase.

Now let us consider more closely something also confusing in the original German text. First we read:

> Magdalene forgot all danger and hurried into the garden, and Salome followed her at some distance. It was primarily these two who had purchased the ointments. The other two women were more afraid and hung back at the entrance to the garden.

Here the first two women are clearly identified as Magdalene and Salome (of Jerusalem), who went on ahead of the other two women (Mary Cleophas and Johanna Chusa in Anne Catherine's

151

account). After describing that Magdalene and Salome went together to the holy sepulcher, and that Magdalene then—after seeing that the body of Jesus was not there—ran back to the cenacle to tell the disciples, Anne Catherine says:

> Concerning Mary Salome, who did not go further than the entrance to the sepulcher, I do not know whether she heard anything spoken by the angel [in the sepulcher]. I saw her, right after Magdalene, flee in fright from the sepulcher and garden and seek out the other women who had remained behind outside the garden, in order to let them know what had taken place.

The translator of this text into English clearly thought that Anne Catherine had made a mistake in saying "Mary Salome" instead of "Salome," and therefore concluded that "Mary Salome" should be corrected to "Salome." Moreover, later in the German text it is stated:

> The other women, when told by Mary Salome, were shocked and joyful at the same time, and hesitated a while before going into the garden.

Thus, in the original German text of Anne Catherine's description, there are *two* references to Mary Salome in the garden of the holy sepulcher that morning. The following is a comparison with the gospel accounts of the holy women present in the garden of the holy sepulcher on Easter Sunday morning:

Emmerich: Magdalene, Mary Cleophas, Johanna Chusa, Salome (of Jerusalem), Mary Salome (whom she later refers to)

Matthew: Magdalene, the other Mary*

Mark: Magdalene, Salome (of Jerusalem) Mary the mother of James*

Luke: Magdalene, Johanna (Chusa), Mary the mother of James*

John: Magdalene   (*most likely* Mary Cleophas)

The naming of Mary Salome (twice) in the original German text of Anne Catherine's description of the holy women in the garden of the holy sepulcher on Easter Sunday morning appears, then, to be a mistake—a mistake that was corrected in the English translation, where in the two places in the German text that the name Mary Salome appears, the name is given instead simply as Salome. Thus, from the English translation it appears that there were four (not five) holy women who bore witness to the resurrection early that Sunday morning, whereas from Anne Catherine's description it is evident that originally five holy women had planned to go to the garden of the holy sepulcher on Easter Sunday morning, but that only four of this group of holy women set off together (Mary Magdalene, Mary Cleophas, Johanna Chusa, and Salome of Jerusalem).

Of course, there is the possibility, already referred to, that the fifth woman belonging to the original group, Mary Salome, followed later and joined the other four in the garden of the holy sepulcher—by which time Mary Magdalene had already left and run back to the cenacle to find the disciples in order to tell them about the empty tomb. However, since (as indicated in the following) the holy women had been afraid to go out while it was still dark—fearing that the enemies of Jesus might waylay them—it seems unlikely that Mary Salome would have dared proceed alone to the garden. In this case, the corrective given in the English translation (twice changing the name "Mary Salome" to "Salome") would seem to be appropriate.

Given the significance of the holy women bearing witness to the resurrection, the most significant event of the life of the earth, it is worthwhile to consider this quite closely. The details presented in the following are based on the original German edition.

Anne Catherine describes that in the night preceding the resurrection:

> My gaze turned again to the holy women [who] wanted to go to Jesus's tomb before daybreak. Several times they had given voice to their concern about this undertaking, for they were very afraid that the enemies of Jesus might waylay them when they went out. However the Blessed Virgin . . . consoled them, that after some rest they should take courage and go to the tomb, and no harm would befall them.

Here the Virgin Mary, at the center of the entire group of holy women, counseled the five to proceed with their plan to go to the holy sepulcher before daybreak. The Virgin Mary surely knew of the significance of bearing witness to this great event that was about to take place—the event that would signify the crowning of creation through the birth of the "first born of the dead" as the archetype for all humanity.

> As the morning sky brightened with a white streak of light, I saw Magdalene, Mary Cleophas, Johanna Chusa, and Salome . . . leave their dwelling place near the cenacle.

Now, although not described in the four gospels, the Virgin Mary herself—according to Anne Catherine—had been the first to bear witness to the Risen Lord:

> It was about eleven o'clock at night when the Blessed Virgin, moved by love and ardent desire, could no longer remain in the house. . . . She traversed alone the whole way passed over by Jesus bearing the cross. . . . She went through the deserted streets and paused at every spot upon which some special suffering or outrage had befallen the Lord. . . . She was in an elevated state of love . . . entirely immersed in love and contemplation. . . . She completed her way to the top of Mount Golgotha. . . . I saw in vision the soul of Jesus in dazzling splendor between two warrior angels. . . . Now I saw the Lord arise in glory through the rock. There was an earthquake, and a warrior angel descended like lightning from heaven down to the tomb, rolled the stone to the right side and sat upon it. . . . In the very moment when the angel descended to the tomb and there was an earthquake I saw the Risen Lord appear to his mother on Golgotha. He was extraordinarily beautiful and glorious, his manner serious. . . . His wounds were large and radiant. . . . He showed her his wounds, and as she sank to the ground to kiss his feet he took her by the hand, raised her up, and disappeared. . . . Looking east I saw on the horizon above Jerusalem a white streak of light. . . .
>
> The holy women were near to the little gate of Nicodemus when the Lord rose from the dead. . . . Magdalene forgot all danger and hurried into the garden, and Salome followed her at some distance. . . . The other two women were more anxious and remained behind at the entrance to

the garden. As she approached the guards, I saw Magdalene in a state of shock hurry back some distance toward Salome. Then, however, both went together . . . into the sepulcher . . . . The whole place was resplendent with light, and an angel sat to the right of the tomb. Magdalene was deeply troubled, and I do not know if she heard any of the angel's words. I saw her immediately rush out hurriedly from the garden through the little gate of Nicodemus into the city. . . . Concerning Mary Salome, who did not go further than the entrance to the sepulcher, I do not know whether she heard anything spoken by the angel [either]. I saw her, right after Magdalene, flee in fright from the sepulcher and the garden and seek out the other women who had remained behind outside the garden, in order to let them know what had taken place. . . . The other women, when told by Mary Salome, were shocked and joyful at the same time, and hesitated a while before going into the garden.

Careful consideration of these words seems to indicate that Anne Catherine did indeed twice refer to Salome of Jerusalem as "Mary Salome," so that it would appear, here again, that the corrective made in the English translation is appropriate. Since in the subsequent description by Anne Catherine there is no further mention of the names of the holy women present in the garden of the holy sepulcher, nor of their number, it is not possible to draw a definite conclusion regarding this. However, without further evidence to the contrary, it would seem that there were actually four holy women (Mary Magdalene, Mary Cleophas, Johanna Chusa, and Salome of Jerusalem) in the garden of the holy sepulcher on Easter Sunday morning. Continuing with Anne Catherine's description:

I saw Magdalene arrive at the cenacle. . . . Peter and John opened the door. Magdalene merely uttered the words "They have taken the Lord from the tomb! We do not know where"—and ran back with great haste to the garden of the holy sepulcher. . . . Magdalene hurried . . . to the tomb. . . . She saw two angels in white priestly robes sitting at the head and the foot of the tomb. . . . She looked around and saw in the east, about ten steps from the sepulcher, . . . a long, white-clad figure in the dawn twilight. . . . Jesus said to her "Mary!" Recognizing the voice and forgetting the crucifixion, death, and burial, as if he were still living, she turned quickly . . . and exclaimed "Rabuni! (Master!)" She fell upon her knees in front of him and stretched out her arms toward his feet. Jesus, however, raised his hand in a defensive gesture toward her and said "Do not touch me! For I have not yet ascended to my Father. Go to my brothers and say to them: "I shall ascend to my Father and your Father, to my God and your God." Thereupon the Lord disappeared. . . .

Magdalene found the holy women and related to them that she had spoken with Peter and had seen the angels and now the Lord in the garden, and the women replied that they also had seen the angels. Magdalene now hurried off to the city . . . and the women went again toward the garden. . . . Close by the garden of the holy sepulcher Jesus appeared to the holy women in a flowing white robe . . . and said, "Hail to you!" Trembling they fell at his feet. . . . The Lord, addressing some words to them, gestured in a certain direction and then vanished, whereupon the holy women hurried through the Bethlehem gate to Mt. Zion, to tell the disciples in the cenacle that they had seen the Lord. . . .

Summarizing: in addition to Mary Magdalene, then, the holy women Mary Cleophas, Johanna Chusa, and Salome of Jerusalem also bore witness to the miracle of the resurrection on Easter Sunday morning (and perhaps also Mary Salome).[1]

---

[1] Also, in vision on Easter night, Saturday/Sunday, March 29/30, 1823, Anne Catherine referred to *five* holy women present at the resurrection (including Mary Salome), rather than the *four* usually mentioned as having been there.

The Angel Seated on the Stone of the Tomb

157

Noli Me Tangere: *Touch Me Not*

Magdalene Tells the Apostles the Body of Jesus is Not in the Tomb

Jesus Appears to Some of the Holy Women

The Holy Women
Establish Inns For Jesus and
the Disciples

ON Sunday, July 23, AD 30, as Jesus explained his intention to teach throughout the land, Lazarus and the women made plans how best to help Jesus in his mission. They thought of setting up inns for Jesus and the disciples at certain places and of supplying provisions and clothes. The holy women had heard with sorrow what hardships Jesus and his followers had had to endure upon their journeys, and that Jesus especially, on his last hurried journey to Tyre, had suffered such want; they had heard of his having to soften the hard crusts, which Saturnin had begged on the way, in order to be able to eat them. They had therefore offered to establish inns and furnish them with all that was necessary. Jesus accepted their offer, and came hither to make with them the necessary arrangements. As he now declared that he would henceforth publicly teach everywhere, Lazarus and the women again offered to establish inns, especially since the Jews in the cities around Jerusalem, instigated by the Pharisees, would furnish nothing to him and his disciples. They also begged the Lord to signify to them the principal stopping places on his journeys and the number of his disciples, that they might know how many inns would be needed and what quantity of provisions to supply. Jesus replied by giving them the route of his future journeys, also the stopping places and the probable number of disciples. It was decided that about fifteen inns should be made ready and entrusted to the care of confidential persons, some of them relatives either of Lazarus or of the holy family. They were scattered throughout the whole country, with the exception of the district of Cabul toward Tyre and Sidon.

The holy women then consulted together as to what district each should see to and what share each should take in the new

161

establishments, to supply furniture, covers, clothes, sandals, etc., to provide for washing and repairing, and to attend to the furnishing of bread and other necessaries. All this took place before and during the meal. Martha was in her element.

After the meal Jesus, Lazarus, the other friends, and the holy women assembled secretly in another of the subterranean halls. Jesus sat on a raised seat at one side of the hall, the men standing and sitting around him; the women were on the opposite side on steps covered with carpets and cushions. Jesus spoke of the mercy of God to His people. He had sent them prophets one after another whom they had disowned and ill-treated; now they would reject the supreme grace, and he predicted what would betide them. Some of the men withdrew at the close of this instruction and Jesus went with others into the hall and walked up and down. Martha, who was passing to and fro, approached him and had a long talk about her sister Magdalene. She related what she had heard of her from Veronica, and her own consequent anxiety.

While Jesus was walking up and down the hall with the men, the women sat playing a kind of lottery for the benefit of their new undertaking. On the elevated platform was a table on rollers around which they sat. The plane of the table, which projected into five angles like the rays of a star, covered a box about two inches in depth. From the five points to the center of this partitioned box, ran deep furrows on the surface, and between them were slits connecting the interior. Each of the women had some long strings of pearls and many other little precious stones. Each in turn placed some of them in one of the furrows on the table. Then, resting a delicate little bow on the outer end of the furrow, she shot a tiny arrow at the nearest pearl or stone. The shock received by this one communicated itself to the rest, which rolled into the other furrows or dropped through the holes into the compartments in the interior of the box. When all the pearls and stones had been shot from the surface, the table, which was upon rollers, was agitated to and fro, by which movement the contents fell into other little compartments that could be drawn out at the edge. Each of these little drawers had previously been assigned to one of the players, so that when the holy women drew them out, they saw at once what they had won for their new undertaking or which jewel they had lost.

During the game the holy women lost a very precious pearl that had fallen down among them. All moved back and looked for it most carefully. When at last they found it and were expressing their joy, Jesus came over to them and related the parable of the lost drachma and the joy of the owner upon finding it again. From their pearl, lost, carefully sought, and joyfully found, he drew a new similitude to Magdalene. He called her a pearl more precious than many others that, from the lottery table of holy love, had fallen and were going to destruction. "With what joy," he exclaimed, "will ye find again the precious pearl!" Then the women, deeply moved, asked: "Ah, Lord! Will that pearl be found again?" and Jesus answered: "Seek ye more earnestly than the woman in the parable sought the lost drachma, or the shepherd his stray sheep." Profoundly touched at this answer, all promised to seek after Magdalene more diligently than after their lost pearl, and assured him that their joy upon finding her would far exceed what they now felt.

Soon the holy women had established inns for the use of Jesus and the disciples as they journeyed. Martha and Susanna were just now visiting their inns on the way through Galilee to Samaria, for here they exercised a kind of general superintendence—the other women seeing to those established in their own respective districts. They went together to the several inns, taking with them asses laden with all kinds of household necessaries. Once when Mara accompanied them (Saturday, December 9, AD 30), the report spread among the people that Mary Magdalene now went around with the women who provided for the needs of the prophet of Nazareth and his party. Mara was in figure very like Magdalene, and neither of them was very well-known on this side of the Jordan. By this time, Magdalene and Mara were nothing like as beautiful as they used to be. They were pale and thin, and their eyes red from weeping. Martha was very energetic, and in business affairs very talkative. Johanna Chusa was a tall, pale, vigorous woman, grave in manner, but at the same time active. Veronica had in her deportment something very like St. Catherine; she was frank, resolute, and courageous. When the holy women were thus gathered together, they used to work industriously, sewing and preparing for the community all sorts of things, which were distributed among their private inns, or laid away in the storerooms. From these latter the apostles and disciples supplied their own needs, as well as those of the poor. When there was no special work of this kind to be done, the holy women spent their time in sewing for poor synagogues. They generally had with them their maidservants, who preceded or followed them on their journeys, and carried the various materials, sometimes in leathern pouches, sometimes attached to their girdle under their mantle. These maids wore tightly fitting bodices and short tunics. When the holy women were to remain some time at any place, their maids returned and awaited their coming at some of the inns along the route.

Major Women
Disciples and Relations of Jesus

Enue

LATE in the day on Friday, December 1, AD 30,[1] when it was already dark and the crowd around Jesus very great, a woman afflicted with a flow of blood, taking advantage of the darkness, made her way through the crowd, leaning on the arms of her nurses. She dwelt not far from the synagogue. The women afflicted with the same malady—though not so grievously as herself—had told her of their own cure some hours earlier. They had that day at noon, when Jesus was passing in the midst of the crowd, ventured to touch his garments, and were thereby instantly cured. Their words roused her faith. She hoped in the dusk of evening, and in the throng that would gather round Jesus on leaving the synagogue, to be able to touch him unnoticed. Jesus knew her thoughts and consequently slackened his pace. The nurses led her as close to him as possible. Standing near her were her daughter, her husband's uncle, and her sister-in-law Lea. The sufferer knelt down, leaned forward supporting herself on one hand, and, with the other reaching through the crowd,

---

[1] On this day several other significant events occurred. First, Jesus preached concerning the third beatitude, but because the sabbath was approaching he broke off early and sailed back toward Capernaum. There he taught near the south gate in a house that Peter had rented. It was here that the healing of the paralytic described in Mark 2:1–2, Luke 5:17–26 and Matthew 9:1–9 occurred. After this Jesus went to the synagogue, where he taught—this time without disruption. Jairus, whose daughter (Salome) Jesus had raised from the dead on Saturday, November 18, AD 30, was there. As Jesus left, Jairus approached him to ask help for Salome, who was again close to death. It was as he made his way to the home of Jairus to raise Salome from the dead for a second time that the widow reached out to touch his garment.

touched the hem of Jesus's robe. Instantly she felt that she was healed.[1]

Jesus at the same moment halted, glanced around at the disciples, and inquired: "Who has touched me?" To which Peter answered: "You ask, 'Who touched me?' The people throng and press upon you, as you see!" But Jesus responded: "Someone has touched me, for I know that virtue is gone out from me." Then he looked around and, as the crowd had fallen back a step, the woman could not longer remain hidden. Quite abashed, she approached him timidly, fell on her knees before him, and acknowledged in hearing of the whole crowd what she had done. Then she related how long she had suffered from a flow of blood, and that she believed herself healed by the touch of his garment. Turning to Jesus, she begged him to forgive her.

Then Jesus addressed to her these words: "Be comforted, my daughter, your faith has made you whole! Go in peace, and remain free from your infirmity!" and she departed with her friends. She was thirty years old, very thin and pale, and was named Enue. Her deceased husband was a Jew. She had only one daughter, who had been taken charge of by her uncle. He had now come to the baptism, accompanied by his niece and sister-in-law Lea. The husband of the latter was a Pharisee and an enemy of Jesus. Enue had, in her widowhood, wished to enter into a connection which to her rich relatives appeared far below her position; therefore they had opposed her.

Some months later, on the morning of Tuesday, March 6, AD 31, Jesus was teaching and healing outside Caesarea-Philippi. Meanwhile, more disciples arrived, bringing the total number with him to about sixty. Around midday Jesus and these disciples went to the house of Enue's uncle, where he was received most solemnly according to pagan customs, carpets being spread for him to walk upon, and green branches and wreaths being carried. The uncle, led by Enue and her daughter, came to meet Jesus, and the women cast themselves down before him. It was partly in answer to the prayer of this old man that Jesus had come

---

[1] Matt. 9:20–22.

to Caesarea. He and several other pagans wanted to be baptized, but they had scruples on the subject of circumcision.[1]

Over the beautifully paved inner court of the old man's house an awning of white fabric was stretched, and through an opening in the center hung a wreath. Besides the trees, the whole court was adorned with garlands of flowers. Baptism was administered under the awning. Before the ceremony, Jesus gave an instruction and spoke in private with the neophytes, who opened their hearts to him. They exposed to him their whole life and made their profession of faith in him. Jesus then absolved them from their sins, and they were baptized by Saturnin in a basin of water which Jesus had previously blessed. The ceremony was followed by a grand entertainment in which all the disciples and the friends of the family took part. The meal was conducted according to pagan customs. The table was higher than those in use among the Jews, and the guests reclined upon long, raised divans, the feet turned out, and one arm resting on a cushion. The edge of the table was indented, and before each of the guests were some small dishes, though the principal servings were on large ones in the center of the table.

Enue, since her cure, was scarcely recognizable, so well and hearty had she become. She and her daughter, who was about twenty-one years old, sat at table beside their uncle. During the entertainment, they arose and withdrew for awhile. When they returned, the mother stood somewhat back while the daughter,

---

[1] "Jesus never touched upon this point in his public discourse, but he had a private interview with the uncle. In such cases he never commanded circumcision, though at the same time he did not advocate its discontinuance. When pious old pagans, upon receiving baptism, told him in confidence of their trouble on this subject, Jesus used to console them by telling them that if they did not wish to become Jews they should remain as they were, but believe and practice what they heard from him. Such people then lived apart from both Judaism and paganism. They prayed, they gave alms, and became Christians without passing through Judaism. Even to the apostles Jesus refrained from expressing himself on this point in order not to scandalize them, so that I never remember having heard the Pharisees, who listened so closely to catch him in his words, ever accuse him on that head, no, not even at the time of his passion."

wearing a beautiful veil and carrying a little white vase of perfume, went behind Jesus, broke it, and poured the contents over
his head. Then with both hands she smoothed it right and left over
his hair and drew the part behind the ears through her hands.
After that she gathered up the end of her veil, passed it over his
head in order to dry it, and retired.

A quantity of food was then distributed to the poor outside the
house. This house was not the uncle's former residence. It was
one to which he had removed with Enue in order to avoid contact with the pagans and the frequenting of their temples; still, it
was not in the Jewish quarter. Enue had had communications
with the Jews, one of whom she had married, but he was now
deceased. It was, however, from her pagan parents that she inherited all her wealth. On leaving their old home Enue and her uncle
had left behind quantities of corn, clothes, and covers for the
poor.

The following day, Wednesday, March 7, AD 31, after the conclusion of a pagan feast that had been underway in Caesarea at the
time,[1] Jesus went thither and prepared several of the Jews, who
afterward received baptism from the disciples. The ceremony
concluded, Jesus with several of his disciples returned to the home
of Enue and her uncle and took leave of them. Humbly, reverently,
and with many tears, these worthy people bade goodbye to Jesus.
They had previously sent presents to the place outside the city
gate where Jesus continued a while longer his instructions to the
poor travelers belonging to the caravan and to others from the
city. The presents consisted of bread, corn, garments, and covers,
all of which, with whatever else they had received, Jesus caused to

---

[1] "During Jesus's stay in Caesarea, the pagans were celebrating a feast near
the fountain in the city. It had reference to the benefit they derived from the
water. During this feast incense was burned on tripods before an idol around
which was gathered a crowd of maidens wearing crowns. The idol was made
up of three or four figures sitting back to back, each having its own head,
hands, and feet. The arms down to the elbows were fastened to the body, but
the hands were outstretched. The fountain on all sides poured out water into
basins. On one side it flowed into an enclosed place in which were private halls
and bathing cisterns. This was the Jews' bathing place."

The Woman (Enue) With an Issue of Blood
169

A Woman (Lea) Cries Out in a Crowd

170

be distributed among the needy. Many of the devout Jews and the newly baptized followed this example of charity. They measured out corn and distributed linen, covers, mantles, and bread to the poor, for whom this was a gala day.

Lea, Sister-in-Law of Enue

ON Sunday, December 3, two days after Enue had touched the hem of Jesus's garment and been healed (Matt. 9:20), Jesus taught again in the house near the south gate of Capernaum and spoke of the beatitudes. Then approached the mother of Jesus accompanied by several women, namely, Martha, Susanna of Jerusalem, Dinah the Samaritan, and Susanna Alpheus, a daughter of Mary Cleophas and sister of the apostles. Among the hearers also was Lea, the sister-in-law of Enue.

Mary and her companions entered the court that led to the hall in which Jesus was teaching. He had been reproaching the Pharisees with their hypocrisy and impurity and, because he always interwove some of the beatitudes with his other teachings, he had just at that moment exclaimed: "Blessed are the pure of heart, for they shall see God!"

Lea, meanwhile, seeing Mary coming in, could no longer restrain herself and, as if intoxicated with joy, cried out from among the crowd: "More blessed" (these are the exact words that I heard) "more blessed the womb that bore thee and the breasts that gave thee suck!" To which I saw Jesus quietly replying: "And far more blessed are they that hear the word of God and keep it!" (Luke 11:27–28), and he went on with his discourse.

Lea went to Mary, saluted her, spoke of Enue's cure and of her own resolve to give her wealth to the community, and requested Mary to intercede with her son for her husband's conversion. He was a Pharisee of Paneas. Mary conversed with her in a low voice. She had not heard Lea's sudden exclamation nor Jesus's reply, and soon she withdrew with the women.

When Jesus later on addressed the people in Peter's house, Lea was among the other women present. Although her husband was a zealous opponent of Jesus, Lea herself was profoundly impressed by the instructions she had heard. I saw her at first, calm and sorrowful, often changing her place among the crowd, as if looking for someone, but I found out that she was in this way obeying the impulse that prompted her to proclaim aloud her reverence for Jesus.

Lais of Nain
(And Her Daughters Sabia and Athalia)

ON Wednesday, October 25, AD 30, Jesus was teaching on the preaching mountain in Meroz. Disputing with the Pharisees, he referred to the two commandments: love of God and love of neighbor (Matthew 22:36–40). Later in the day, while healing the sick, he was approached by a rich pagan widow from Nain, called Lais. She had come to implore his aid in behalf of her two daughters, Sabia and Athalia. They were in a fearful manner possessed by the devil, and were at home in Nain confined to their respective apartments. They were perfectly furious. They dashed themselves here and there, they bit their own flesh, and struck wildly around them; no one ventured to approach them. At other times their members were contracted by cramps and they fell to the ground pale and unconscious.

Their mother, accompanied by handmaids and menservants, had come to Jesus for help. She was waiting at a distance eagerly desirous of his approach, but to her disappointment she saw him always turning to others. The poor mother could not restrain her eagerness, but cried out from time to time as he drew near: "Ah, Lord, have mercy on me!" but Jesus appeared not to hear her. The women near her suggested that she should say: "Have mercy on my daughters!" since she herself was not a sufferer. She replied: "They are my own flesh. In having mercy on me, he will have mercy on them also!" and again she uttered the same cry. At last Jesus turned and addressed her: "It is proper that I should break bread to the children of my own household before attending to strangers." The mother replied: "Lord, you are right. I will wait or even come again, if you cannot help me today, for I am not worthy of thy assistance!"

Jesus had however finished his work of healing, and the cured, singing canticles of praise, were going off with their beds. Jesus had turned away from the disconsolate mother and appeared about to retire. Seeing this, the poor woman grew desperate. "Ah!" she thought, "He is not going to help me!" But as the words flashed through her mind, Jesus turned toward her and said: "Woman, what do you ask of me?" She cast herself veiled at his feet and answered: "Lord, help me! My two daughters at Nain are tormented by the devil. I know that you can help them if you will, for all things are possible to you." Jesus responded: "Return to your home! Your daughters are coming to meet you. But purify yourself! The sins of the parents are upon these children." These last words Jesus spoke to her privately. She replied: "Lord, I have already long wept my sin. What shall I do?" Then Jesus told her that she should get rid of her unjustly acquired goods, mortify her body, pray, fast, give alms, and comfort the sick. She promised with many tears to do all that he suggested, and then went away full of joy.

The two daughters were the fruit of an illicit connection. Lais had three sons born in lawful wedlock, but they lived apart from their mother, who still retained property belonging to them. She was very rich and, notwithstanding her repentance, lived, like most people of her class, a life of luxury. The daughters were confined in separate chambers. While Jesus was speaking with their mother, they fell unconscious, and satan went out of them in the form of a black vapor. Weeping vehemently and quite changed, they called their female attendants and informed them that they were cured. When they learned that their mother had gone to the prophet of Nazareth, they set out to meet her, accompanied by many of their acquaintances. They met her at about an hour's distance from Nain and related all that had happened to them. The mother then went on to the city, but the daughters with their maids and servants proceeded straight forward to Meroz. They wished to present themselves to Jesus who, they had heard, was going to teach there again the next morning.[1]

---

[1] "All three women later joined the circle of the helping women and accompanied the mother of Jesus when she went and taught among the pagan caravans in mid-November of the same year."

Next morning, Thursday, October 26, AD 30, before going again to the mountain, Jesus taught at the fountain in Meroz, and again reproached the Pharisees for the little care they took of the people. After that he ascended the mountain and delivered an instruction similar to that known as the sermon on the mount. When he went down the mountain he found some sick awaiting him. They were still able to walk. Jesus cured them. On the same spot upon which the pagan woman Lais of Nain had knelt yesterday at Jesus's feet praying for her sick daughters, were today those daughters, now both cured, awaiting the coming of Jesus. They were named Athalia and Sabia, and were accompanied by their maids and menservants. With all their attendants, they cast themselves down before Jesus, saying: "Lord, we esteemed ourselves unworthy to listen to thy instructions, therefore we waited here to thank thee for freeing us from the power of the evil one." Jesus commanded them to rise. He commended their mother's patience, humility, and faith, for as a stranger she had waited until he had broken bread to his own household. But now, he continued, she too belonged to his household, for she had recognized the God of Israel in his mercy. The heavenly Father had sent him to break bread to all that believed in his mission and brought forth fruits of penance. Then he ordered the disciples to bring food, which he gave to the maidens and all their attendants—to each a piece of bread and a piece of fish—delivering to them at the same time an instruction thereon full of deep significance. After that he went on with the disciples to the inn. One of the maidens was twenty, the other five and twenty years old. Their sickness and the confinement in which they lived had made them pale and wan.

On Saturday, November 11, AD 30, the Blessed Virgin with several of the women, among them Dinah, Mary, Lais, Athalia, Sabia, and Martha, went for a walk in the neighborhood of Bethsaida, a little beyond the lepers' asylum. A caravan of pagans was encamped thereabouts, and among them were several women from Upper Galilee. The Blessed Virgin consoled and instructed them. The women sat in a circle on a little eminence, and Mary sometimes sat, sometimes walked among them. They asked her questions which she answered clearly, and told them many things about the patriarchs, the prophets, and Jesus.

✝ ✝ ✝ ✝ ✝

AT *one time Anne Catherine counted all the holy women who were associated together till the death of Jesus to help the little community. There were seventy. At this time there were already thirty-seven who took part in this duty. Sabia and Athalia also, the daughters of Lais of Nain, were toward the last admitted among the female followers. At the time of St. Stephen, they were among the Christians who settled in Jerusalem.*

Lea the Widow

TO *the so-called five holy widows belong first and foremost the three mothers of the earliest disciples of Jesus: Lea and Seba of Nazareth, whose sons Kolaya and Eustachius, respectively, were received by Jesus on August 4, AD 29; and Sobe, daughter of the elder Sobe and cousin to the Blessed Virgin, who on many occasions lodged Jesus and his mother in Cana, and whose nephew was Nathaniel, the bridegroom at the wedding of Cana, who lived in Capernaum and, at about the same time as the other two, became a disciple of Jesus.*

The Essene youth Eustachius, and the son of the widow Lea, Kolaya, were received as disciples by Jesus in Bethsaida on Thursday, August 4, AD 29, along with Amandor. These three were the first disciples of Jesus.

✝ ✝ ✝ ✝

ON July 2 or July 3, AD 29, while journeying together, the tax collector Levi (the later apostle Matthew), and the son Kolaya of Lea the widow, and the Essene Eustachius (son of Seba of Nazareth) spoke with Jesus about John the Baptist.

A month later, on Thursday, August 4, AD 29, Jesus spoke with his mother at the house where she was staying and where the other holy women and friends were also gathered. Jesus ex-plained that, because of the hostility and rejection he had encountered in Nazareth, he would return to Capernaum and Bethsaida to teach. He left the house with Veronica's son Amandor, the Essene youth Eustachius, and the son of the widow Lea, Kolaya. Amandor, Eustachius, and Kolaya were his first three disciples.

Three weeks following, on Thursday, September 1, AD 29, a great feast was prepared in a public hall, down which stood three tables, side by side, and right and left burned lamps. Over the middle table, at which Jesus, some of the disciples, and the Pharisees sat, the aperture, customary in the roofs of that country, stood open. The followers of Jesus were seated at the side tables. In this city there must have been an ancient custom commanding the poor, of whom there were numbers dwelling in the greatest abandonment, to be invited; for as soon as Jesus sat down at table he turned to the Pharisees asking where were the poor, and whether it was not their right to take part in the feast. The Pharisees were embarrassed and they answered that the custom had long fallen into disuse. Then Jesus commanded his disciples Arastaria and Cocharia, the sons of Maraha, and Kolaya, the son of the widow Lea, to go gather together the poor of the city and bring them to the feast.

The following Tuesday, September 6, AD 29, the five disciples of Jesus went into Nazareth to visit their relatives and acquaintances, also the school. Jesus however stayed with Eliud, with whom he prayed and very confidentially conversed, for to that simplehearted, pious man many mysteries had been revealed. There were four women in Mary's house besides herself: her niece Mary Cleophas; Johanna Chusa, a cousin of Anna the prophetess; the relative of Simeon, Mary, mother of John Mark; and the widow Lea. Veronica was no longer there, nor was Peter's wife, whom I had lately seen at the place where the publicans lived.

Two weeks later, on the night of Wednesday, September 21, AD 29, when Jesus went to Lazarus's, I saw the Blessed Virgin, Johanna Chusa, Mary Cleophas, the widow Lea, and Mary Salome passing the night at an inn between the desert Gibea and the desert Ephron, about five hours from Bethany. They slept under a shed enclosed on all sides by light walls. It contained two apartments. The front one was divided off into two rows of alcoves, of which the holy women took possession; the back served as a kitchen. Before the inn was an open hut in which a fire was burning. Here the male attendants slept or kept watch. The innkeeper's dwelling was not far distant.

During the following morning, Thursday, September 22, AD 29, Jesus walked about in the courtyards and gardens of the castle, teaching those who were present. Then Martha took Jesus to visit her sister Mary, known as Silent Mary, who lived by herself like a hermit in part of the castle. Jesus was left alone to talk with Silent Mary, who lived in continuous vision of heavenly things. Normally silent in the presence of other people, Mary began to speak of the mysteries of Jesus's incarnation, passion, and death. After saying some prayers, Jesus returned to talk with Martha, who expressed her deep concern regarding her other sister, Mary Magdalene. At about half-past one, the holy Virgin Mary arrived, accompanied by Johanna Chusa, the widow Lea, Mary Salome, and Mary Cleophas. After a light meal, Jesus and his mother, Mary, retired to talk with one another.

During the summer two years later, on Monday, June 25, AD 31, Jesus went over the whole Lord's Prayer and gave the interpretation of the word Amen, as he had formerly done in Cyprus, saying that this word contains everything in itself, that it is the beginning and the end of prayer. Some other people and a couple of Pharisees from Bethsaida-Julias arrived while Jesus was speaking, and they too heard a part of his instruction. One of the latter invited him to dine at his house in Bethsaida-Julias, which invitation Jesus accepted. When he and the disciples started for Bethsaida, they directed their steps to the south of the Jordan bridge. On their way they came, this side of Bethsaida, to an inn where his mother, the widow of Nain, Lea, and two other women were waiting to take leave of him, because he was now going to teach on the other side of the Jordan.

Maraha of Sepphoris

MARAHA[1] *was the third child of the Essene couple Ismeria and Eliud. Her eldest sister was Sobe and her other sister was Anne, the mother of Mary. Thus she was Mary's aunt, and Jesus's great-aunt. Her two sons, Arastaria and Cocharia, were among the first disciples of Jesus. She is one of the "three widows" sometimes spoken of as friends of Mary.*

When in her fifth year Anne was taken to the Temple, as Mary was later. There she remained twelve years, returning home in her seven-

---

[1] Maraha was also the name of Abraham's nurse.

teenth year. Meantime, her mother had had a third daughter, whom she named Maraha, and Anne found also in the paternal house a little son of her eldest sister Sobe, who was called Eliud. Maraha afterward inherited the paternal property of Sepphoris and became the mother of the subsequent disciples Arastaria and Cocharia. The young Eliud was afterward the second husband of Maroni of Nain.

ON Sunday, August 14, AD 29, Jesus crossed a mountain with the three disciples and went to Sepphoris, four hours' distance from Nazareth. He stopped at his great-aunt's. She was Anne's youngest sister Maraha, and the mother of a daughter and two sons. These sons were clothed in long, white garments. They were named respectively Arastaria and Cocharia, and later on they joined the disciples. The Blessed Virgin, Mary Cleophas, and other women had also come hither. The feet of Jesus were washed, and a repast prepared in his honor. He passed the night in Maraha's house, which had been the home of Anne's parents. The following Thursday, August 18, AD 29, Jesus taught at the synagogue of the Sadducees in Sepphoris. Next to the synagogue was a madhouse, and inmates were obliged to attend the synagogue, accompanied by custodians. As Jesus taught, one or the other of the inmates began to speak out loud: "This is Jesus of Nazareth, born in Bethlehem, visited by wise men from the east." "His mother is with Maraha." "He is bringing a new teaching," and so on. Jesus spoke the words: "The spirit that speaks this is from below and should return there." At this, all the inmates became quiet and were healed. Afterward a great uproar broke out in Sepphoris, forcing Jesus to hide in a house. That night, he left the town, as did his three disciples and the two sons of Maraha (Arastaria and Cocharia). Later, the five met up with Jesus by some trees outside the town, on the way from Sepphoris to Bethulia. They then proceeded together to Bethulia.

About half a year later, on Thursday, March 2, AD 30, Mary and several holy women accompanied Jesus and a small group of disciples as far as the little place called Dothaim. Entering the town, they were welcomed by a group of men, some of them priests, who invited them to a meal. Jesus told the story of Joseph, who had been sold at a well nearby (Genesis 37:17–28). After the meal, Jesus took leave of his mother, who wept. Then Jesus went with his disciples and some people of Dothaim to Joseph's well and blessed it. Traveling further, Jesus and his disciples arrived toward evening at Sepphoris. Here he stayed with his great-aunt Maraha.

Mary of Hebron

THE *Essene couple Emerentia and Aphras bore three children: Elizabeth, the mother of John the Baptist; Rhoda; and Enue, who married Heli of Hebron, and the child of this marriage was Mary of Hebron, who was therefore cousin to John the Baptist. And as we read in the Visions, Johanna Chusa, together with Veronica and Mary of Hebron, a niece of Elizabeth, went to Herod's Castle at Machaerus to retrieve the head of Elizabeth's son, John the Baptist.*

Two Other Widows of Nain, One Named Mary

ANNE *Catherine said but little about these two widows of Nain (one named Mary), friends of the widow Maroni of Nain. At the latter's request—and with the help of his own mother Mary—Jesus healed Mary of Nain of possession from a distance, after which she also entered the circle of the holy women. He had earlier accepted the unnamed widow's offer of financial support for the community. Some further details follow.*

✝ ✝ ✝ ✝ ✝

ON Wednesday, August 2, AD 30, accompanied by three disciples, Jesus went to the town of Nain. The widow of Nain—Maroni— the sister of the wife of James the Greater, had been informed by Andrew and Nathaniel of Jesus's near approach and was awaiting his arrival. With another widow[1] she now went out to the inn to welcome him. They cast themselves veiled at his feet. Maroni begged Jesus to accept the offer of the other good widow (*not*

---

[1] To our knowledge, the name of this first widow is not given by Anne Catherine.

Mary of Nain), who wished to put all she possessed into the treasury of the holy women for the maintenance of the disciples and for the poor, whom she herself also wanted to serve. Jesus graciously accepted her offer, while he instructed and consoled her and her friend. They had brought some provisions for a repast, which along with a sum of money they handed over to the disciples. The latter was sent to the women at Capernaum for the common treasury.

Jesus took some rest here with the disciples, for he had on the preceding day taught in Engannim with indescribable effort and had cured the sick, after which he had journeyed to Nain, a distance of about seven hours. The widow, lately introduced to Jesus and accepted by him, told him of another woman, named Mary (whom I had never before seen), who likewise desired to give what she possessed for the support of the disciples. But Jesus replied that she should keep it till later when it would be more needed.

This woman was an adulteress, and had been, on account of her infidelity, repudiated by her husband, a rich Jew of Damascus. She had heard of Jesus's mercy to sinners, was very much touched, and had no other desire than to do penance and be restored to grace. She had visited Martha, with whose family she was distantly related, had confessed her transgression, and begged her to intercede for her with the mother of Jesus. She gave over to her also a part of her wealth, in the form of little gold bars.

Martha, Johanna Chusa, and Veronica, full of compassion for the sinner, interested themselves in her case and took her at once to Mary's dwelling at Capernaum. Mary looked at her gravely and allowed her to stand for a long time at a distance. But the woman supplicated with burning tears and vehement sorrow: "O mother of the prophet! Intercede for me with your Son, that I may find favor with God!" She was possessed by a dumb devil and had to be guarded, for in her paroxysms she could not cry for help and the devil drove her into fire or water. When she came again to herself, she would lie in a corner weeping piteously. Mary sent in behalf of the unhappy creature a messenger to Jesus, who replied that he would come in good time and heal her, adding that she would soon be freed even without his coming [see below]. And indeed I saw that this was so: While in Capernaum she sank to the earth as though dead, and the holy women brought her to bed, where she soon came back to herself and was entirely freed. It seemed to me that already earlier, during her pangs of possession, other devils had left her. And so the women carried her back to Martha at her house in Bethany, where she donated all she had to the community. She was in many ways like Magdalene, except of course that Magdalene had not been married. She was closely befriended also with the Samaritan woman (Dinah), who hailed from Damascus also.

Earlier, as was said, Mary had promised she would intercede for this woman [Mary of Nain], and Martha then took her back to Bethany and installed her in a building attached to her castle where lived a number of other women, all engaged in the preparation of articles of clothing for the disciples, and the poor more generally. Mary of Nain lived there quite at peace, busily engaged in her task. She was about thirty years of age.

In the German edition we find the additional entry: On Sunday, August 13, AD 30, Martha was in Cana, and there came to her a relative of the holy family, a widow about 30 years old, named Mary, who asked Martha if she could put in a request for her to Jesus. She was the widow who on August 2 in Nain had been recommended to Jesus by the woman ["the other widow"] with the widow of Nain [Maroni], but from whom Jesus had at that time turned away. I later experienced that this widow [Mary of Nain] was the daughter of a granddaughter of a sister of the holy mother Anne. On her father's side she was related to the mother of Lazarus, of Jerusalem. She was also related to Maroni, the widow of Nain [that is, she usually associated with this name], through Maroni's husband Eliud, a son of the sister (Sobe) of holy Anne. It was on this account that she was recommended to Jesus in Nain by the woman-friend of Maroni [the other, unnamed, widow of Nain].

Two days later, on Tuesday, August 15, AD 30, Jesus and the disciples traveled northward to the town of Gerasa, where they arrived that evening. Here Jesus received a message sent by the Holy Virgin on behalf of a widow of Nain [Mary of Nain] who was possessed. This widow was an acquaintance of Maroni,[1] whom Jesus had visited about two weeks earlier, on Wednesday, August 2. Receiving the message, Jesus healed the possessed woman from a distance [that is, as was said by Jesus above, "she would soon be freed even without his coming"].

Seba

SEBA *was one the so-called five holy widows, and mother to one of the earliest disciples of Jesus: Eustachius.*

Silent Mary

LAZARUS had three sisters: the eldest Martha, the youngest Mary Magdalene, and one between them also called Mary.[2] This last lived altogether secluded, her silence causing her to be looked upon as simple-minded. She went by no other name than

---

[1] Maroni is the one usually known under the appellation "widow of Nain," but for the sake of clarity in the context of this additional information from Anne Catherine regarding two other widows of Nain (that is, Mary of Nain, and the other, whose name Anne Catherine does not, to our knowledge, provide), we retain only the name Maroni here.

[2] Elsewhere Anne Catherine provides the following, related account of the family of Silent Mary: "The parents of Lazarus (Zarah, an Egyptian of noble descent, and Jezebel, a Jewess) had in all fifteen children, of whom six died young. Of the nine that survived, only four were living at the time of Christ's teaching. These four were: Lazarus; Martha, about two years younger; Mary, looked upon as simple-minded (whom we shall call Silent Mary), two years younger than Martha; and Mary Magdalene, five years younger than Silent Mary. The latter is not named in scripture, nor reckoned among the Lazarus family; but she is known to God. She was always put aside in her family, and lived altogether unknown. Magdalene, the youngest child, was very beautiful and even in her early years tall and well-developed like a girl of more advanced age. After the death of their father, lots were cast as to how the inheritance should be apportioned. The castle at Magdala and other properties in that area of the Sea of Galilee fell to Magdalene; the castle at Bethany, to Martha and Silent Mary; and the property on Mt. Zion, as well as a large number of properties in Southern Galilee and the castle near Herodium, fell to Lazarus."

Silent Mary. Jesus, speaking to Eliud the Essene[1] about Silent Mary, said, "She is possessed of great mind and understanding, but for the good of her soul they have been withdrawn from her. She is not for this world, therefore is she now altogether secluded from it. But she has never committed sin. If I should speak to her, she would perfectly comprehend the greatest mysteries. She will not live much longer."

Before others, Silent Mary never uttered a word; but when alone in her room or the garden she talked aloud to herself and to all the objects around her, as if they had life. It was only before others that she was perfectly mute and still; her eyes cast down, she looked like a statue. On being greeted, however, she inclined and was very polite in all her bearing. She was very pious, though she never appeared in any school. She prayed in her own chamber. She had visions and conversed with apparitions. Her love for her brother and sisters was beyond words, especially for Magdalene.

One day, accompanied by Lazarus, Jesus went to the abode of the women, and Martha took him to her silent sister Mary, with whom he wished to speak. A wall separated the large courtyard from a smaller one. They passed through a gate, and Jesus remained in a little garden there while Martha went to call her sister. The garden was highly ornamental. In the center stood a large date tree, and all around were aromatic herbs and shrubs. On one side was a kind of tiny lake with a stone seat in the center. Martha went to her and bade her come down into the garden, for there someone was waiting to speak to her. Silent Mary was very obedient. Without a word, she threw her veil around her and followed Martha into the garden. Then Martha retired.

Silent Mary was tall and very beautiful. She was about thirty years old. She generally kept her eyes fixed on heaven. If occasionally she glanced to one side where Jesus was, it was only a side glance and vaguely, as if she were gazing into the distance. Even when speaking of herself she never used the pronoun, "I," but always "you," as if she saw herself as a second person and spoke accordingly. She did not address Jesus nor cast herself at his feet.

[1] See "Eliud the Essene" in *People of the New Testament III*.

183

Jesus was the first to salute, and they walked together around the garden. Properly speaking, they did not converse together. Silent Mary kept her gaze fixed on high and recounted heavenly things, as if passing before her eyes. Jesus spoke in the same manner of his Father and to his Father. There was more a prayer, a song of praise, a contemplation, a revealing of mysteries, than a conversation. Silent Mary appeared as if unaware of her own existence. Her soul was in another world while her body lived on earth.

Glancing intuitively upon the Incarnation of Christ, they spoke as if gazing upon the Most Holy Trinity acting in that mystery. Silent Mary said, "The Father commissioned the Son to go down to humankind, among whom a Virgin should conceive Him." Then she described the rejoicings of the angels, and how Gabriel was sent to the Virgin. And so she ran through the nine angelic choirs, who all came down with the bearer of the glad tidings, just as a child would joyously describe a procession moving before its eyes, praising the devotion and zeal of all that composed it.

Then she seemed to glance into the chamber of the Virgin, to whom she spoke words expressive of her hope that she might receive the angel's message. She saw the angel arrive and an-nounce the coming of the Savior. She saw all and repeated all, as if uttering her thoughts aloud, gazing the while into the distance.

Suddenly she paused, her eyes fixed on the Virgin, who appeared to be recollecting herself before replying to the angel, and said very simply, "Then, you have made a vow of virginity? Ah, if you had refused to be the Lord's mother, what would have happened? Would there have been found another virgin?" Then, addressing her nation, she exclaimed: "Had the Virgin refused, long would you, O orphaned Israel, still have groaned!" And now, filled with joy by the Virgin's consent, she burst forth into words of praise and thanksgiving, rehearsed the wonders of Jesus's birth and, addressing the divine child, said, "Butter and honey shall you eat." She again repeated the prophecies, recalled those of Simeon and Anna, spoke with the different personages connected with them—and all this as if gazing upon those scenes, contemporary with them.

At last, descending to the present, she said, speaking as if alone: "Now you go on the painful, bitter way." Although she knew that

Jesus was at her side, yet she acted and spoke as if he were no nearer to her than all the other visions just recounted. Jesus interrupted her from time to time with prayer and thanksgiving, praising his Father and interceding for humankind.

Then Jesus left her. Relapsing into her usual silence and exterior quietude, she returned to the house. When Jesus went back to Lazarus and Martha, he said to them "She is not without understanding, but her soul is not of this world. She sees not this world, and this world comprehends her not. She is happy. She knows no sin."

Silent Mary had never before spoken in the presence of others as she had just done in that of Jesus. Before all others she kept silence, though not from pride or reserve. No, it was because she saw not those people as others do, saw not what they saw, but gazed upon redemption and the things of heaven alone. When at times accosted by a learned and pious friend of the family, she would indeed utter some words audibly, though without understanding a single word of what had been said to her. Not having reference to or connection with the vision upon which she was interiorly gazing at the time, she heard without hearing; consequently her reply, bearing upon what was then engrossing her own attention, mystified her hearers. It was for this reason that she was regarded by the family as simple-minded. Her state necessitated her dwelling alone, for her soul lived not in time. She cultivated her little garden and embroidered for the Temple. Martha brought her her work. She prayed most piously and devoutly and endured a kind of expiatory suffering for the sins of others, for her soul was often oppressed, as if the weight of the whole world was upon her. She died of grief at the immensity of Jesus's passion, which in spirit she foresaw.

On another occasion, in obedience to Jesus's direction, Lazarus brought his silent sister Mary and left her alone with the Master. Silent Mary's bearing toward Jesus now was somewhat different from that of the last interview, for she cast herself down before him and kissed his feet. Jesus made no attempt to prevent her, and raised her up by the hand. With her eyes turned heavenward, she, as before, uttered the most sublime and wonderful things, though in the most simple and natural manner.

She spoke of God, of his Son, and of his kingdom just as a peasant girl might talk of the father of the village lord and his inheritance. Her words were a prophecy, and the things of which she spoke she saw before her.

She recounted the grave faults and bad management of the wicked servants of the household. The Father had sent his Son to arrange affairs and pay off all debts, but they would receive him badly. He would have to die in great suffering, redeem his kingdom with his own blood, and efface the crimes of the servants, that they might again become the children of his Father.

She carried out the allegory in most beautiful language, and yet in as natural a manner as if she were recounting a scene enacted in her presence. At times she was light-hearted, at others sorrowful, calling herself a useless servant and grieving over the painful labors of the Son of the merciful Lord and Father. Another cause of sorrow to her was that the servants would not rightly understand the parable, although so simple and so true.

She spoke also of the resurrection. The Son, she said, would go to the servants in the subterranean prisons also. He would console them and set them free, because he had purchased their redemption. He would return with them to his Father. But at his second advent, when he would come again to judge, all those that had abused the satisfaction he had made and who would not turn from their evil ways, should be cast into the fire.

She then spoke of Lazarus's death and raising: "He goes forth from this world," she said, "and gazes upon the things of the other life. His friends weep around him as if he were never to return. But the Son calls him back to earth, and he labors in the vineyard."

Of Magdalene too she spoke: "The maiden is in the frightful desert where once were the children of Israel. She wanders in accursed places where all is dark, where never human foot has trod. But she will come forth, and in another desert make amends for the past."

Silent Mary spoke of herself as of a captive, for her body appeared to her a prison, and she longed to go home. She was so straitened on all sides; not one around her understood her, and they were, as it seemed to her, all blind. But, she said, she was

186

willing to wait, she would bear her captivity submissively, for she deserved nothing better.

Jesus spoke to her lovingly, consoling her and saying: "After the Passover, when I again come here, you shall indeed go home." Then as she knelt before him, he raised his hands over her and blessed her. When Jesus signified to her the time of her death, that is to say that she should, freed from captivity, at last go home, he anointed her for death. From this we may conclude that anointing is more necessary for the body than some people generally think. Jesus pitied Silent Mary who, as a reputed simpleton, would have received no embalming. Her holiness was hidden. Jesus dismissed her, and she returned to her abode.

Thereafter Magdalene occupied the little apartments of Silent Mary's dwelling when she was in Bethany. She often sat in a very narrow little room that appeared to be formed in a tower. It was a retired corner intended for penitential exercises. She still wept freely. True, she was no longer actually sick, but from contrition and penance she had become quite pale and reduced. She looked like one crushed by sorrow.

Toward the end of Jesus's forty-day fast, in late November, AD 29, I saw that the angels then ministering unto Jesus appeared under different forms and seemed to belong to different hierarchies. Those that, at the close of the spiritual banquet, bore away the cups of wine and morsels of bread, were clothed in priestly raiment. I saw at the instant of their disappearance all kinds of supernatural consolation descending upon the friends of Jesus, those of his own time and those of after ages. I saw Jesus appearing in vision to the Blessed Virgin—then at Cana—to comfort and strengthen her. I saw Lazarus and Martha wonderfully touched, while their hearts grew warm with the love of Jesus. I saw Silent Mary actually fed with the gifts from the table of the Lord. The angel stood by her while she, like a child, received the food. She had been a witness of all the temptations and sufferings of Jesus. Her whole life was one of vision and suffering through compassion, therefore such supernatural favors caused her no astonishment.

On Saturday, April 1, AD 30, after the sabbath, Jesus went to Bethany. I had not as yet seen him conversing with Silent Mary. Her end, I think, was near, for she appeared greatly changed. She was lying on the ground on a gray carpet, supported in the arms of her maids, and she was in a kind of swoon. She appeared to me to have drawn nearer to this world of ours, as if she had ever been absent in spirit, but now she appeared to have been brought back again to life. She was now to know that this Jesus here in Bethany, who lived in her own time and in her own vicinity, was he who had to suffer so cruelly. She was still alive in order to experience through compassion, in her own person, the sufferings of Jesus, after which she was soon to die.

That night Jesus visited her and conversed long with her. Part of the time she sat up on her couch, and part of the time walked around her chamber. She had now the perfect use of her senses. She distinguished between the present and the future, she recognized in Jesus the Savior and the Paschal lamb, and she knew that he was to suffer frightfully. All this made her inexpressibly sorrowful. The world appeared to her gloomy and an insupportable weight. But most of all was she grieved at man's ingratitude, which she foresaw. Jesus spoke long with her of the approach of the kingdom of God and his own passion, after which he gave her his blessing and left her. She was soon to die. She was tall and extraordinarily beautiful, white as snow and shining with light. Her hands were like ivory, her fingers long and tapering.

A week later, on Saturday, April 8, AD 30, Jesus kept the sabbath at Lazarus's, in Bethany, whither he had retired after the tumult occasioned by the cures wrought in the Temple. After the sabbath, the Pharisees went to the house of Mary Mark in Jerusalem, thinking to find Jesus there and to take him into custody. They did not find him, however, but only his mother and the other holy women whom, as the followers of Jesus, they commanded with harsh words to leave the city. The mother of Jesus and the other women became greatly troubled at hearing this, and in tears hurried to Martha in Bethany.

Mary, weeping, entered the room wherein Martha was with her sick sister, Silent Mary. The latter was again quite rapt in ecstasy. All that she had hitherto seen in spirit, she now beheld about to be fulfilled. She could no longer endure the pain it caused her, and so she died in the presence of Mary, Mary Cleophas, Martha, and the other women. For her part, as soon as she arrived in Bethany,

Magdalene went straight to the dwelling of her deceased sister, Silent Mary, by whom she had been very much beloved, and spent the whole night in tears. When Martha went to her in the morning, she found her weeping on the grave of her sister, her hair unbound and flowing around her.

Magdalene was pale and exhausted from weeping. She could not resist her desire to express her gratitude to Jesus, so she went over an hour's journey to meet him, threw herself at his feet, and bedewed them with repentant and grateful tears. Jesus extended his hand to her, raised her, and addressed to her words of kindness. He spoke of her deceased sister, Silent Mary. He said that she should tread in her footsteps and do penance as she had done, although she had never sinned.

Anne Catherine once reported that in vision she had been present the house of Lazarus in Bethany, on what occasion she could not recall. Lazarus had brought his sister Silent Mary some blankets, perhaps to be mended. Silent Mary was in spirit ever-present with Jesus. She beheld him always, and shared in his sufferings and fasts. That same evening she said, while close to sleep, that she was at that time together with Silent Mary in purgatory.

Sobe of Cana

TO *the so-called five holy widows belong first and foremost the three mothers of the earliest disciples of Jesus: Lea and Seba of Nazareth, whose sons Kolaya and Eustachius (along with Amandor, the son of Seraphia, who was later called Veronica) were received by Jesus on August 4, AD 29; and Sobe, daughter of the elder Sobe.[1] Sobe the elder was an aunt of Mary, and in the Visions is said to have had a daughter, who however is not then named, living in Cana. This unnamed daugh-*

---

[1] The elder Sobe was the first daughter of the Essenes Ismeria and Eliud, whose second daughter, Anne, was to be the mother of the Virgin Mary (a third daughter, Maraha, was later born to the Essence couple). Sobe married a man named Solomon, and became the mother of Mary Salome, who in turn married Zebedee and became the mother of the future apostles James the Greater and John. Apparently she had a second daughter at a later time, also called Mary, or Mary of Cana, as described earlier.

ter must be Sobe the younger (let us call her Sobe of Cana). This is confirmed by the entry for June 29, AD 29, where we read that the father of the bride at the wedding of Cana was a merchant called Israel. The bridegroom's name was Nathaniel (he was later given the name Amandor, derived from "Amen," but is not to be confused with Amandor the son of Seraphia mentioned above). In the entry for December 26, AD 29, Jesus stays with Sobe of Cana, as can be deduced from the text. Sobe of Cana is stated to be an aunt of Nathaniel the bridegroom, so of course he is Sobe of Cana's nephew. In this reading, Sobe of Cana (as she is being called) would be a direct cousin of Mary. On many occasions Sobe of Cana lodged Jesus and his mother when they passed through Cana. Some uncertainty remains with regard to both Mary of Cana and Sobe of Cana, sisters of Mary Salome, and daughters of Sobe the elder. Unfortunately, there are gaps and ambiguities to be found in the notes of the Visions, though there are relatively few, given the extraordinarily consistent detail prevailing for the greater part. Perhaps later research will shed light on this and other unresolved issues.

ON Wednesday, June 29, AD 29, Jesus was in Cana, where he visited his widowed cousin Mary,[1] the daughter of Sobe and the sister of Sobe of Cana and Mary Salome (see note below). Here in Cana Jesus taught. At this time he was not yet accompanied by any of his future disciples. It looked as if he were studying men, and building upon the foundation that John had laid. Sometimes a good man accompanied him from place to place.

On Sunday, December 18, AD 29, Lazarus brought Martha and Johanna Chusa to Mary then at Capernaum, whither she had come from Cana. They set off again for Tiberias, where they hoped to meet Jesus. Simeon's son was one of the escorts, and the bridegroom of Cana went also to meet the Lord. This bridegroom was the son of the daughter [Sobe of Cana] of Sobe, the elder sister of Anne. His name was Nathaniel. He did not belong to Cana, though he was married there.

---

[1] Or possibly second cousin, this point not being completely resolved yet from Brentano's notes.

A week later, on Monday, December 26, AD 29, Jesus spent much time walking and talking with those disciples who later became his apostles. When Jesus with his disciples arrived near Cana, he was most deferentially received by Mary, the bride's parents, the bridegroom, and others that had come out to meet him. Jesus with his familiar disciples, among them the future apostles, took up his abode in an isolated house belonging to the maternal aunt of the bridegroom. This aunt also was a daughter [Sobe of Cana] of Anne's sister Sobe. She held the mother's place to the bridegroom during the wedding ceremonies. The bride's father was named Israel and was a descendant of Ruth of Bethlehem.

The Syrophoenician Woman

ON Monday, February 12, AD 31, while going from house to house in Dan healing the sick, Jesus was perseveringly followed by an aged woman, a pagan, who was crippled on one side. She was from Ornithopolis. She remained humbly at some distance and, from time to time, implored help. But Jesus paid no attention to her; he even appeared to shun her, for he was now healing sick Jews only. A servant accompanied the woman, bearing her baggage. She was clothed in the garb of a foreigner. Her dress was of striped material, the arms and neck trimmed with lace. On her head she wore a high, pointed cap, over which was tied a colored kerchief, and lastly a veil. She had at home a daughter sick and possessed, and for a long time had been hoping for aid from Jesus. She had been in Dan at the time of the apostles' mission there, and they now more than once reminded Jesus of her. But he replied that it was not yet time, that he wanted to avoid giving offense, and that he would not then help the pagans before the Jews.

In the afternoon Jesus went with Peter, James, and John to the house of one of the Jewish elders of the city, a man very well disposed, a friend of Lazarus and Nicodemus, and in secret a follower of Jesus. He had contributed largely to the common fund of the holy women and to the support of the inns. He had two sons and three daughters, all of mature age, he himself being an old man far advanced in years. They were Nazarites. All were clothed in white. Jesus was very affable and treated the family with great confidence. But he did not remain long in the house, for the people, having found out his whereabouts, had gathered outside and in the forecourt.

Jesus went out through the court and into the garden where for several hours he taught and cured between the terraced walls that supported the gardens. The pagan woman had waited long at a distance.[1] Jesus never went near her, and she dared not approach him. From time to time, however, she repeated her cry: "Have mercy on me, O Lord, Son of David; my daughter is severely possessed by a demon." The disciples begged Jesus to help her, but he said: "I was sent only to the lost sheep of the house of Israel."

At last the woman drew nearer, ventured into the hall, cast herself down before Jesus, and cried: "Lord, help me." Jesus replied: "It is not fair to take the children's bread and to throw it to the dogs." But she continued to entreat: "Yes, Lord, yet even the dogs also eat the crumbs that fall from their master's table."

Then Jesus said: "O woman, great is your faith! On account of these words, help shall be given you!" Jesus asked her whether she herself did not want to be cured, for she was crippled on one side. But she replied that she was not worthy, and that she asked for her daughter's cure only. Then he laid one hand on her head, the other on her side, and said: "Straighten up! May it be done to you as you will! The devil has gone out of your daughter."

The woman stood upright. She was tall and thin. For some instants she uttered not a word, and then with uplifted hands cried out: "O Lord, I see my daughter lying in bed well and in peace!" She was out of herself with joy.

When on the following morning, Tuesday, February 13, AD 31, Jesus was healing and teaching under the market porticos, the pagan woman brought to Jesus one of her relatives who had come with her from Ornithopolis. He was paralyzed in the right arm, besides being deaf and mute. The woman begged Jesus to cure him and also to visit her home, that they might there thank him worthily. Jesus took the man aside from the crowd, laid his

---

[1] In Matthew (15:21–28) this individual is referred to as a Canaanite woman, whereas in Mark (7:24–29) she is referred to as a Syrophoenician Greek.

hand on the lame arm, prayed, and stretched out the arm, perfectly cured. Then he moistened his ears with a little spittle, told him to raise his cured hand to his tongue, glanced upward, and prayed. The man arose, spoke, and gave thanks.

Jesus stepped back with him to the pressing multitude, and the man began to speak wonderful and prophetic words. He cast himself at Jesus's feet and gave him thanks. Then, turning to the Jews and pagans, he said: "The food that you, the children of the house, reject, we outcasts shall gather up. We shall live upon it and give thanks. What you allow to go to waste of the bread of heaven will be to us the fruit of the crumbs that we gather up." There was a great power of inspiration in his words, and much agitation arose among the crowd. Immediately after this Jesus left the city and climbed with the apostles and disciples into the mountains to the west of Lesem.[1] They reached a solitary height, where they found a roomy cavern containing seats cut out of the rock.

Having resumed their route next morning, Wednesday, February 14, AD 31, they passed the great and very elevated city of Hammoth Dor, after which they climbed steep and toilsome heights until they reached a lofty ridge that commanded a view of the Mediterranean. They now descended the mountain for several hours, passed over a stream flowing into the sea through the north of Tyre, and put up at an inn on the roadside, between three and four hours from Ornithopolis. The Syrophoenician woman was a very distinguished lady in this, her native place. She had passed through these parts also on her way home, and had fitted up a comfortable inn for Jesus. The pagans came out most humbly to meet Jesus and his party, guided them to their destination, and showed them all kinds of attentions with an air at once timid and reverential. They looked upon Jesus as a great prophet.

Next day, Thursday, February 15, AD 31, Jesus and the disciples ascended a hill in the neighborhood of a little pagan city, and there found a teacher's chair. It had been in existence since the times of the early prophets, some of whom had often preached

---

[1] Lesem probably refers to Laish, the name of the city of Dan before it was conquered from the Sidonians by the tribe of Dan.

from it. The pagans had always held this place in high esteem, and today they had ornamented it by erecting a beautiful awning over the chair. There were numbers of sick assembled on the hill, but they remained shyly at a distance, until Jesus and the disciples approached and cured many of them.

The healing over, Jesus delivered an instruction on the vocation of the Gentiles. It was more than ordinarily impressive. He explained several passages from the prophets, and depicted the vanity of their idols. After that he went with the disciples three hours in a northwestwardly direction to Ornithopolis, which was distant from the sea three-quarters of an hour. This city, which was not very large, contained some beautiful buildings. On a height in the eastern environs stood a pagan temple. Jesus was received with more than ordinary affection. The Syrophoenician had prepared everything for the occasion in the most sumptuous and honorable manner, but in her humility she left to the few poor Jewish families living in the city the liberty of doing the honors of reception. The whole place resounded with the cure of her daughter, as well as with that of her own and her deaf and mute relative. The last-named, in recounting his cure, spoke of Jesus in words of inspiration.

The inhabitants were ranged outside the houses. The pagans stood back humbly and closed the procession that went with green branches to meet Jesus. The Jews, about twenty in number, among them some very aged men who had to be led, also the teachers with all the children, headed the procession. The mothers and daughters followed, veiled.

A house near the school had been prepared for Jesus and the disciples. It was fitted up by the lady with beautiful carpets, furniture, and lamps. There the Jews most humbly washed the feet of Jesus and his disciples and changed their sandals and clothes, until their own were shaken, brushed, and cleaned. Jesus then went with the elders to the school and taught.

After that, a magnificent entertainment was given in a public hall, at the expense of the Syrophoenician. One could see in all the preparations, in the dishes, the delicacies, and the table furniture generally, that it was a feast given by the pagans. There were three tables, much higher than those in use among the Jews, with couches correspondingly high. Some of the servings of food were very remarkable, being made up into figures representing animals, trees, mountains, and pyramids. Some others were quite deceptive, being in reality very different from what they appeared; for instance, there were all kinds of wonderful pastry, birds made out of fish, fish formed of flesh, and lambs made of spices, fruits, flour, and honey. There were also some real lambs.

At one table, Jesus ate with the apostles and the oldest among the Jews; at the two others, the disciples and the rest of the Jews. The women and children were seated at a table separated from the others by a screen. During the meal, the lady with her daughter and relatives entered to give thanks for the cures wrought among them, their servants following with presents in ornamented caskets, which they bore between them on tapestry. The daughter, veiled, stepped behind Jesus, broke a little vial of precious ointment over his head, and then modestly returned to her mother. The servants delivered the gifts (they were those of the daughter) to the disciples. Jesus returned thanks.

The lady bade him welcome to her native place, and declared how happy she should be if she could only show her good will and, in spite of her unworthiness, repair even the least of the many injuries he experienced so often from her fellow pagans. She spoke humbly and in few words, remaining all the while at a respectful distance. Jesus ordered the money that formed part of the gifts, as well as the food, to be distributed in her presence among the poor Jews.

The lady was a widow and very rich. Her husband had been dead five years. He possessed in his lifetime many large ships at sea and a great number of servants, besides much property. He owned whole villages. Not far from Ornithopolis there was a pagan settlement on a cape jutting out into the sea, all of which belonged to the lady, his widow. I think he had been a large-scale merchant. His widow was held in more than ordinary esteem in Ornithopolis, where the poor Jews lived almost entirely upon her bounty. She was both intelligent and beneficent, and not without a certain degree of illumination in her pagan piety. Her daughter was twenty-four years old, tall, and very beautiful. She dressed in colors and adorned her neck with chains, her arms with bracelets.

Her wealth brought around her numerous suitors, and she had become possessed of an evil spirit. She was afflicted with convulsions so violent that in her frenzy she would spring from her couch and try to run away; consequently she had to be guarded, and even bound. But when the paroxysm was over, she became again good and virtuous. Her state caused great affliction to herself and her mother, and to both it was a subject of deep humiliation. The poor girl was obliged to live retired, and she had now endured her sufferings for several years.

After the entertainment, when the mother neared her own home, she was met by her daughter, who had come out for that purpose as well as to tell her of her cure, which had taken place at the very instant in which Jesus had promised it. And, oh, her joy and wonder at seeing her once-crippled mother again a tall, graceful woman! And to hear herself distinctly and joyfully greeted by her paralyzed, deaf, and mute relative! She was filled with gratitude and reverence for Jesus, and helped prepare everything for his reception.

The gifts Jesus received consisted of trinkets belonging to the daughter. They had been given to her in her early years by her parents, principally by her father, whose business opened to him communications with distant lands, and whose only and well-beloved child she was. Some were jewels of ancient workmanship, objects wrought of precious metals, such as are ordinarily given to the children of the wealthy. Among them were some things that had formerly belonged to her parents' parents. There were many wonderful-looking little idols of pearls and precious stones set in gold, rare stones of great value, tiny vessels, golden animals, and figures about a finger long, the eyes and mouth formed of gems. There were also fragrant stones and amber and golden branches that looked like little live trees, laden with colored gems instead of fruit—and very, very many such things! It was a treasure indeed. Jesus said that he would distribute them to the poor and the needy, and that his Father in heaven would reward the donors.

Next day, Friday, February 16, AD 31, which was the sabbath, Jesus visited every one of the Jewish families, distributed alms, cured, and comforted. Many of these Jews were poor and abandoned. Jesus assembled them in the synagogue, where he spoke to them in terms at once deeply touching and consoling, for the poor creatures looked upon themselves as the outcast and unworthy children of Israel. He also prepared many of them for baptism. About twenty men were baptized in a bathing garden, among them the cured deaf and mute relative of the pagan lady.

Jesus then visited the Syrophoenician woman again, along with his disciples. She dwelt in a beautiful house surrounded by numerous courts and gardens, where he was received with great solemnity. The domestics in festal garments spread carpets under his feet. At the entrance of a beautiful summerhouse, which was supported on pillars, the widow and her daughter came forward veiled to meet him. They cast themselves at his feet and poured forth their thanks, in which they were joined by their cured relative, once deaf and mute.

In the summerhouse were set forth odd-looking figures in pastry and fruit of all kinds on costly dishes. The vessels were of glass, which looked as if made of many-colored threads that appeared to run together and cross one another, as if dissolving one into the other. Among rich Jews I have seen similar vessels, but only in small numbers. Here they seemed to be in abundance. Many such vessels were held in reserve behind curtains in the corners of the hall. They were arranged on shelves up high on the wall.

The dishes were set on little tables, some round, others with corners, that could be placed together to form one large table. Among the refreshments there were very fine dried grapes still hanging on the vine laid on those colored glass dishes, also another kind of dried fruit that arose from the branches as from a little tree. There were reeds with long, cordate leaves and fruit in form like the grape. They were perfectly white, perhaps sugared, and looked like the white part of the cauliflower. The guests snapped them off the stem, and found that they had a sweet, pleasant taste. They were raised not far from the sea, in a swampy place belonging to the Syrophoenician.

In a separate part of the hall, pagan maidens, friends of the daughter, were standing along with the domestics. Jesus went and spoke to them. The Syrophoenician woman earnestly entreated Jesus to visit and help the people of Sarepta, saying: "Sarepta, whose poor widow shared all she had with Elijah, is itself now a poor widow threatened with starvation. You, the greatest of prophets, have pity on her! Forgive me, a widow and once poor, to whom you have restored all, if I may be so bold as to plead also for Sarepta."[1] Jesus promised to do as she wished. She told him that she wanted to build a synagogue, and asked him to indicate where it should be. But I do not remember Jesus's reply.

The lady possessed large weaving and dyeing factories. In a little place near the sea and at some distance from her residence, there were great buildings on the top of which were platforms where gray and yellow stuffs were spread out. Among the gifts presented to Jesus were many little dishes and balls of amber, considered in those parts very precious.

Jesus celebrated the close of the sabbath in the Jewish school, which was very beautifully adorned. In order to console the poor Jews, he taught that the proverb "Our fathers have eaten sour grapes, and the teeth of the children are on edge" should no longer pass current in Israel. "Everyone that abides by the Word of God announced by me, that does penance and receives baptism, no longer bears the sins of his father." The people were extraordinarily rejoiced upon hearing these words.

On the afternoon of the following day, Saturday, February 17, AD 31, Jesus took leave of the lady who, in union with her daughter and cured relative, presented him with golden figures a hand in length, and provisions of bread, balsam, fruits, honey in reed baskets, and little flasks. These provisions were destined for his journey and for the poor of Sarepta. Jesus addressed words of advice to the whole family, recommended to them the poor Jews and their own salvation, and departed from the house amid the tears and reverential salutations of all. The lady had always been very enlightened and very earnest in seeking after perfection. Henceforth neither she nor her daughter went any more to the

---

[1] Sarepta (modern Sarafand, Lebanon) was a Phoenician city on the Mediterranean coast between Sidon and Tyre. The first book of Kings (17:8–24) describes the city as being subject to Sidon in the time of Ahab, and says that the prophet Elijah, after leaving the brook Kerith, multiplied the meal and oil of the widow of Zarephath (Sarepta) and raised her son from the dead there.

pagan temple. They observed the teachings of Jesus, joined the Jews, and sought by degrees to bring their people after them.

Some months later, Jesus was preparing for his trip to Cyprus, nearing Ornithopolis[1] with James the Less, Barnabas, Mnason, Azor, the two sons of Cyrinus, and a youth from Cyprus. On Wednesday, April 25, AD 31, Jesus went from the inn to a seaport about three hours distant from Tyre. Alongside of the port there stretched far out into the sea, like an island, a tongue of the mountain, whereon was built the pagan city of Ornithopolis. The few, but devout, Jews of the place, whom Jesus had earlier visited, seemed to live in dependence upon the pagans. I saw as many as thirty pagan temples scattered here and there. Sometimes it seems to me that the port belonged to Ornithopolis.

The Syrophoenician owned there so many buildings, factories for weaving and dyeing, so many ships, that I think the whole place must have been at one time subject to her deceased husband or his ancestors.[2] She dwelt now in Ornithopolis itself, though in a kind of suburb. Back of the city arose a high mountain, and behind that lay Sidon. A little river flowed between Ornithopolis

---

[1] As related in "Barnabas" in *People of the New Testament III* (but here repeated for ease of reference): "Ornithopolis was situated about three hours from the little place across the river where Jesus had spent the night, but from the settlement of the poor Jews it was one and a half hours. When Jesus went straight through this place to the port, Ornithopolis lay on his left. The Jewish settlement was toward Sarepta, which received the rays of the rising sun, for on that side the mountains rose in a gentle slope. On the north it was perfectly shady. The situation was very fine. Between Ornithopolis, the Jewish settlement, and the port, there lay so many solitary buildings, so many other little settlements, that looking down upon them from above, one might think that once upon a time they were all united. Jesus had with him now only James the Less, Barnabas, Mnason, Azor, Cyrinus's two sons, and a Cypriote youth whom those last-named had brought to Jesus. All the other apostles and disciples were scattered throughout the country on missions."

[2] "The property of the Syrophoenician, with its numerous buildings, courts, and gardens, looked like an immense estate. Its factories and plantations were full of workmen and slaves, whose families had their homes there. But just at present, things had come to a standstill; the former activity was not yet re-sumed. The lady was about to free herself from all such ties, and wished her people to choose a superior from among themselves."

and its port. The shore between Tyre and Sidon was, with the exception of the port, but little accessible, being rough and wild. The seaport to which I have alluded was the largest between Sidon and Tyre, and the number of ships crowding its waters made it almost like a little city itself.

Jesus went with his companions to the home of the Syrophoenician who, by her cured relatives, had sent him an invitation to an entertainment. A number of persons were assembled to meet him, also the poor and the crippled. Of the latter, Jesus cured many. The dwelling of the Syrophoenician with its gardens, courts, and buildings of all kinds was probably as large as Dülmen.[1] Pieces of stuff, yellow, purple, red, and sky blue, were extended on the galleries of many of the buildings. These galleries were broad enough to permit a person's walking on them. The yellow dye was extracted from a plant cultivated in the neighborhood. For red and purple, they employed sea snails.

Jesus was received with solemnity. As he was reclining at table, the widow's daughter poured a flask of fragrant ointment over his head. The mother presented him with pieces of stuff, girdles, and three-cornered golden coins; the daughter, pieces of the same precious metal chained together. He did not tarry with them long, but went with his companions to the seaport, where he was solemnly received by the Jewish inhabitants and by the Cypriote Jews, who were gathered there on their way back from the Passover feast. Jesus taught in the synagogue, around which a great many pagans stood listening from without. It was by starlight that Jesus, accompanied by all the travelers, went down to the harbor and embarked for Cyprus. The night was clear, and the stars looked larger than they do to us. There was quite a little fleet ready to receive the travelers.

On Monday, April 30, AD 31, by which time Jesus had arrived in Cyprus and was staying in the home of the father of the disciple Jonas, who was an Essene, Jesus spoke of another pagan woman, Mercuria,[2] saying that she would soon join the Syrophoenician,

---

[1] The town where Anne Catherine lived at the time.

[2] See "Lady Mercuria, Pagan Priestess of Cyprus" in *People of the New Testament V.*

who was likewise making preparations to leave Ornithopolis. They would first go to Gessur and thence proceed further. Already many people had left Cyprus, and a certain number would soon land at Joppa.

Some weeks later, on Wednesday, June 13, AD 31, not long after Jesus's return from Cyprus to Capernaum, there were gathered around him almost thirty disciples. Some were come from Judea with the news of the arrival at Joppa of ships bringing two hundred Cypriote Jews, who were there to be received by Barnabas, Mnason, and his brother. John, who was still at Hebron with the relatives of Zechariah, was charged with providing suitable quarters for these emigrants. The Essenes also occupied themselves with the same cares. For a time the Cypriotes were lodged in the grottoes until proper destinations could be assigned them. Lazarus and the Syrophoenician woman provided settlements near Ramoth-Gilead for the Jewish emigrants from the region of Ornithopolis.

The Syrophoenician Woman and Her Daughter

Minor Women
Disciples and Others

Abigail, Repudiated
Wife of Philip the Tetrarch

ON Thursday, September 14, AD 30, after healing the sick of Ephron, Jesus and the disciples made their way toward Betharamphtha. From Ephron, Jesus went with his disciples and several of
the Rechabites about five hours to the north to Betharamphtha-
Julias, a beautiful city situated on a height. On the way he gave an
instruction near a mine from which was obtained the copper that
was wrought in Ephron. There were some Rechabites in Betharamphtha, and among them priests. Those of Ephron appeared to
me to be under their jurisdiction. On the following day the company came to the city of Betharamphtha, which was large and
extended far around a mountain. The western part was inhabited
by Jews, the eastern and a portion of the heights by idolaters. The
two quarters were separated by a walled-in road and a pleasure
garden full of shady walks. High on the mountain arose a beautiful castle with its towers, its gardens, and trees. It was occupied by
a divorced wife of the tetrarch Philip, who had settled upon her all
the revenues of this part of his territory. She was descended from
the kings of Gessur, and had with her five daughters already well
grown. She was named Abigail and, although tolerably advanced
in years, was still active and beautiful. Her disposition was full of
goodness and benevolence.

Philip was older than Herod of Pera and Galilee. He was a
pagan of peaceable inclinations, but a lover of pleasure. He was
half-brother of the other Herod, born of a different mother, and
had first married a widow with one daughter. When Abigail's husband was dispatched by Philip to a war or to Rome, I know not
which, he left his wife behind. She meanwhile was seduced by

203

Philip, who married her, whereupon her husband died of grief. When after some years Philip's first wife, whom he had repudiated for the sake of Abigail, was about to die, she begged him on her deathbed to have pity at least on her daughter. Philip, who had by this time grown tired of Abigail, married his stepdaughter, and banished Abigail and her five daughters to Betharamphtha, called also Julias in honor of a Roman empress. Here she occupied herself in doing good. She was favorably disposed toward the Jews, and cherished a great desire after truth and salvation. She was, however, under the watchful guardianship of some of Philip's officers, who had to render an account of her. Philip had one son, and his present wife was much younger than himself. Jesus was received cordially and hospitably in Betharamphtha.

Next morning, Saturday, September 16, AD 30, was the first day of the month of Tisri, when the New Year was celebrated, which fact was announced from the roof of the synagogue by all kinds of musical instruments, among them harps and a number of large trumpets with several mouthpieces. I saw again one of those wonderful instruments I had formerly seen on the synagogue of Capernaum. It was filled with wind by means of a bellows.

All the houses and public buildings were adorned on this feast day with flowers and fruit. The different classes of people had different customs. Mutual gifts were interchanged, the poor being largely remembered. They commenced by giving them a good entertainment, and on a long rampart were deposited numerous gifts for them, consisting of food, raiment, and covers. Every one that received presents from his friends bestowed a part of them upon the poor. The Rechabites present superintended and directed all things. They saw what each one gave to the poor and how it was distributed. They kept three lists, in which they secretly recorded the generosity of the donors. One of these lists was called the book of life; another, the middle way; and the third, the book of death. It was customary for the Rechabites to exercise all such offices, while in the temple they were gatekeepers, treasurers, and above all, chanters. This last office they fulfilled on today's feast. Jesus also received presents in Betharamphtha of clothing, covers, and money, all of which he caused to be distributed among the poor.

The festival celebrating the start of the civil year continued the next day, Sunday, September 17, AD 30, during which Jesus went to visit the pagans. Abigail had pressed him earnestly to come to see her, and the Jews themselves, upon whom she bestowed many benefits, had begged him to have an interview with her. I saw Jesus with some of his disciples crossing the Jewish quarter of the city to that of the pagans. He reached the public pleasure grounds, pleasant and shady, that lay between the two quarters, and where the Jews and pagans usually met when necessary. Abigail was already there with her suite, her five grown daughters, many other pagan maidens, and some pagan followers.

Abigail was a tall, vigorous woman of about fifty years, almost the same age as Philip. She wore an expression of sadness and anxious yearning. She sighed after instruction and conversion to a better life, but she knew not how to set about its attainment, for she was not allowed to act freely and was jealously watched by her wardens. She cast herself at Jesus's feet. He raised her up and, walking up and down, instructed her and her companions. He spoke of the fulfillment of the prophecies, of the vocation of the Gentiles, and of baptism.

Jesus received from Abigail the customary marks of honor. She had appointed Jewish servants to wash his feet and to offer him the refreshments usually extended to strangers as tokens of welcome. She very humbly begged his pardon for desiring an interview with him, but, as she said, she had so long sighed after his instructions. She begged him to take part in an entertainment she had prepared in his honor. Jesus was very courteous toward all, but especially toward Abigail herself. His every word and glance made a strong impression on her soul. She was full of anxiety, and was not without some glimmering of the truth. This instruction to the pagans lasted till nearly afternoon.

Then at Abigail's invitation Jesus passed to the east side of the city not far from the pagan temple. There were many baths in the vicinity and a kind of public feast going on, for the pagans also celebrated the new moon today with special magnificence. In coming hither Jesus took the road that separated the two quarters of the city, the Jewish from the pagan. In the abodes formed in the walls were many poor, sick pagans lying in chests full of straw and chaff. The destitute among the pagans were numerous. As yet, Jesus cured none of their sick. On the pleasure grounds of the pagans, where the entertainment was prepared, Jesus taught for a long time, sometimes walking around, and again during the meal. He made use of all kinds of parables relating to animals, in order to illustrate to them their own vain and fruitless lives. He spoke of the unwearied and often useless labor of the spider, of the active industry of the ant and wasp, and placed before them as a contrast the beautifully ordered work of the bee. The food offerings of the entertainment, at which Abigail assisted in person, reclining at the table, were for the most part distributed at Jesus's request to the poor.

There were also on this day great solemnities in the pagan temple, a very magnificent building with large open porticos on five sides through which was afforded a view into the interior. It was capped by a high cupola. There were many idols in the different halls of the temple, the principal one being named Dagon. The upper part of its body was like a human being, the lower part like a fish. There were others in the form of animals, but none so beautiful as the idols of the Greeks and Romans. I saw young maidens hanging wreaths on and around the idols, then singing and dancing before them, while the pagan priests burnt incense on a little three-legged table. On the cupola was a very wonderful and ingenious piece of mechanism that revolved the whole night. It was a brilliant globe covered with stars. As it slowly revolved, it could be seen from the interior of the temple as well as from without. It represented something connected with the course of the stars and the new moon, or the new year. When in its slow revolution it had reached one of the extreme points in its orbit, the songs and rejoicings in the temple ceased on the opposite side, to be taken up on that to which the globe had turned.

Not far from the festive scene where Jesus had been entertained was a large pleasure garden, and in it were the young girls amusing themselves at various games. Their robes were slightly raised and their lower limbs strapped with bands. They were armed with bows, arrows, and little spears wreathed with flowers. A kind of race course had been ingeniously formed of branches, flowers, and decorations of all kinds, along which the girls ran, shooting their arrows at the same time after the birds that were fastened here and there for that purpose, and darting their spears at the different animals, the kids and little asses, that were fenced in around the course. On this festal race course was a horrible idol with broad, open jaws like a beast, and hands hanging before it like a human being. It was hollow, and under it blazed a fire. The animals killed by the girls were placed in its jaws, where they were consumed, their ashes falling into the fire below. Those that had escaped the darts of the young huntresses were set aside and regarded as sacred. The priests laid upon them the sins of the people and set them free. It was something like the Jewish scapegoat. Were it not for the torture of the animals, so painful to behold, and the horrible idol, the fleetness and skill of the young girls would have been a very pleasing sight.

The feast lasted till evening and, when the moon rose, animals were offered in sacrifice. When night closed, the whole temple and Abigail's castle were ablaze with torches.

Jesus taught again after the repast. Many of the pagans were converted and went to Ainon for baptism. That evening Jesus went up the mountain by torchlight and had an interview with Abigail in the portico of her castle. Near her were some of Philip's officers, who watched her constantly. Her every action was on that account one of constraint, and she gave the Lord to understand her embarrassing position by the look she cast upon those men. Jesus, however, knew her whole interior and the bonds that held her captive. He had compassion upon her. She asked whether she might hope for pardon from God. One thing in particular constantly harassed her, namely, her infidelity to her lawful husband and his death. Jesus comforted her, saying that her sins would be forgiven her, she should continue her good works, persevere, and pray. She was of the race of Jebusites. These pagans were accustomed to allow their deformed children to perish and were very superstitious about the signs that accompanied their birth.

Anna of the Temple

THE prophecies of Anna and Simeon were known to the family of Zarah,[1] who were waiting for the messiah. And even in Jesus's youth they were acquainted with the holy family, just as pious, noble people are wont to be with their humble, devout neighbors.

At the time of the immaculate conception of Mary, Joachim was conducted by the priests to the entrance of the subterranean passage that ran under the Temple and under the golden gate. This was a passage set aside for special purposes. Under certain circumstances, penitents were conducted by it for purification, reconciliation, and absolution. The priests parted from Joachim at the entrance, and he went alone into the narrow, gradually widening, and almost imperceptibly descending passage. In it stood pillars twined with foliage. They looked like trees and vines, and the green and gold decorations of the walls sparkled in the rosy light that fell from above. Joachim had accomplished a third part of the way when Anne met him in the center of the passage directly under the golden gate, where stood a pillar like a palm tree with hanging leaves and fruit. Anne had been conducted into the subterranean passage through an entrance at the opposite end by the priest to whom she and her maid had brought the offering of doves in baskets, and to whom also she had told what the angel had revealed to her. She was also accompanied by some women, among them the prophetess Anna.[2]

At time of birth of Mary I saw Anna, the prophetess, and another one of Mary's future teachers in the Temple aroused and instructed in vision upon the birth of the child. They told each other what had happened. I think they knew of Anne.

Upon Mary's entrance to the Temple, the priests, among whom Zechariah was one of those standing on the lower steps, led Mary down by the hand. One of them took the light from her and the

---

[1] Father of Lazarus, Martha, Silent Mary, and Magdalene.

[2] Johanna Chusa, whose son was acquainted with the twelve-year-old Jesus when the latter remained behind in Jerusalem, was a niece of the prophetess Anna, who was in the Temple when Simeon blessed the child Jesus (Luke 2:36–38).

little garlands off her arms, and handed them to the other girls. Mary was then led through a door into another hall where six other temple virgins, their mistress Naomi (who was the sister of Lazarus's mother), Anna, and another female met them and scattered flowers before her. To them the priest delivered the child.

Far back in the Temple were numerous chambers built in the wall and connected with the dwellings of the women. Mary's cell was one of the most distant, one nearest the holy of holies. From the passage that led to it, one raised a curtain and stepped into an apartment, a sort of antechamber separated from the cell by a light, semicircular, movable screen. Here in the corners, right and left, were shelves for clothing and other things. Opposite the door in the screen that led into the cell was an opening hung with gauze and tapestry, and looking down into the Temple. A small round table like a stool stood in the room, and on it I saw Anna setting a dish of fruit the size of beans, and a little jug. I often saw the child Mary seized with holy longing for the messiah and saying to Anna: "Oh, will the promised child be born soon? Oh, if I could only see that child! Oh, if only I am living when he is born!" Then Anna would give this reply: "Think how old I am and how long I have waited for that child! And you, you are still so young!" And Mary would shed tears of longing for the promised Savior.

Mary entered the Temple in her fourth year, and in all things was she distinguished and remarkable. Naomi, the sister of Lazarus's mother, was her teacher and nurse. Her whole manner of acting was so remarkable, so marvelous, that I have seen great rolls written by aged priests about her. I think they still lie hidden with other writings. Then came the wonderful manifestations at Joseph's espousals and the blossoming of his rod, the accounts of the three kings and of the shepherds, the presentation of Jesus, Anna's and Simeon's testimony, and the teaching of Jesus at the age of twelve in the Temple. But all this the priests and Pharisees noticed not. Their mind was preoccupied by business and court affairs. Because the holy family lived in voluntary retirement and poverty, they were forgotten in the crowd. The more enlightened, however, such as Simeon, Anna, and others, knew of them.

At the time of the birth of Jesus I saw that Anne at Nazareth, Elizabeth in Jutta, Naomi, Anna, and Simeon in the Temple—all had on this night visions from which they learned the birth of the Savior. When the time came for Mary's purification, the apparition of an angel appeared before Simeon, telling him to notice particularly the first child that would, early the next morning, be brought for presentation, for that it was the messiah whom he had now awaited so long. Anna in her temple cell was also rapt in prayer; and she too had a vision.

Mary was led by the woman to a porch in that part of the Temple in which the ceremony of presentation was to take place. Anna and another woman (Naomi, Mary's former directress) received her. Simeon came out to the porch and conducted Mary with the child in her arms into the hall to the right of the women's porch. It was in this porch that the treasure box stood by which Jesus was sitting when the widow cast in her mite. Old Anna, to whom Joseph had handed over the basket of fruit and doves, followed with Naomi, and Joseph retired to the standing place of the men.

Simeon conducted Mary through the altar rail and up to the table of sacrifice. When the child had been placed in the cradle, Simeon led Mary out again to the standing place of the women. And now one of them went behind, one before, and two on either side of the table, and prayed over the child, while Anna approached Mary, gave her the doves and fruit in two little baskets, one on top of the other, and went with her to the altar rail. Anna remained there while Mary, led again by Simeon, passed on through the railing and up to the altar.

After that Simeon again led Mary to the railing, whence Anna accompanied her to the place set apart for the women. In the meantime, about twenty mothers with their firstborn had arrived. Joseph and several others were standing back in the place assigned to the men.

Then two priests at the altar proper began a religious service accompanied by incense and prayers, while those in the rows of seats swayed to and fro a little, but not like the Jews of the present day. When these ceremonies were ended, Simeon went to where Mary was standing, took the child into his arms and, entranced with joy, spoke long and loud. When he ceased, Anna, also filled with the Spirit, spoke a long time. All were deeply impressed, and regarded Mary and the child with great reverence. Mary shone like a rose. Her public offerings were indeed the poorest; but Joseph in private gave to Simeon and to Anna many little, yellow, triangular pieces to be employed for the use of the Temple, and chiefly for the maidens belonging to it who were too poor to meet their own expenses. It was not everyone that could have his children reared in the Temple. Once I saw a boy in Anna's care. I think he was the son of a prince, or king, but I have forgotten his name. Mary was now led back into the court by Anna and Naomi. Here she took leave of them and was joined by Joseph and the old people with whom she and Joseph had lodged.

At the time of the flight into Egypt, when Herod saw that the kings did not return, he thought they had failed to find Jesus, and the whole affair seemed to be dying out. But after Mary's return to Nazareth, Herod heard of Simeon's and Anna's prophecies at the presentation of the child in the Temple and his fears were reawakened. I saw him in as great disquietude as at the time of the kings' stay in Jerusalem.

ON Wednesday, September 7, AD 29, Eliud the Essene's confident communications with Jesus were to me singularly touching.[1] He knew of and believed in his mission and supernatural advent, still without appearing to have a suspicion that he was God himself. He told Jesus quite naturally, as they walked together, many things connected with his youth, what the prophetess Anna had related to him, also what she had heard from Mary after the Return from Egypt, for Mary had sometimes visited her in Jerusalem. While Eliud was relating what Anna had heard from Mary and told to him, I saw all in pictures. I rejoiced to find them exactly similar to what I had long before seen and partly forgotten.

Two weeks later, on Wednesday, September 21, AD 29, Lazarus was with Nicodemus, John Mark, the only son of Simeon, and an old man named Obed, a brother or brother's son of the prophet-

---

[1] See "Eliud the Essene" in *People of the New Testament III*.

ess Anna. All were, in secret, friends of Jesus, partly through John the Baptist, partly through the holy family, and again through the prophecies of Simeon and Anna in the Temple.[1]

On Holy Saturday, April 4, AD 33, the Blessed Virgin and her companions reverently visited many parts of the Temple. She showed them where, as a little girl, she had first entered the sacred edifice, and where on the south side she had been educated until her espousals with Joseph. She pointed out to them the scene of her marriage, that of Jesus's presentation, and that of Simeon's and Anna's prophecies. At this point she wept bitterly, for the prophecy had been fulfilled, the sword had pierced her soul.

Years later I saw Mary in Ephesus, and her holy way of the cross. She was with five other women making the holy way, along which she went first. She was perfectly white and transparent, indescribably touching to look upon. It seemed to me that she was now making the devotion for the last time. Among the holy women who were praying with her, there were several that had become acquainted with her in the first year of Jesus's teaching. One was a relative of the prophetess Anna, and another was the granddaughter of a maternal aunt of Elizabeth. I saw two of the women making the way of the cross by turns every morning and evening.

Enue the Elder,
Widowed Sister of Elizabeth

SEVERAL days previous to the birth of Mary, Anne informed Joachim that the time of her delivery was at hand. She sent messengers to her sister Maraha, at Sepphoris, also to the widow Enue, Elizabeth's sister, in the valley of Zebulon, and to her sister

---

[1] "Regarding Claudia Proculus, the wife of Pilate, I remember that she saw the annunciation to Mary, the birth of Christ, the adoration of the shepherds and the kings, the prophecies of Simeon and Anna, the flight into Egypt, the massacre of the holy innocents, the temptation in the desert, and other scenes from the holy life of Jesus. She saw him always environed with light, while the malice and wickedness of his enemies appeared under the most terrible pictures."

Sobe's daughter Salome, the wife of Zebedee, of Bethsaida. The sons of Sobe and Zebedee, James the Greater and John, were not yet born. Anne sent for these three women to come to her. Later, after Mary's birth, Enue, Elizabeth's sister, brought the infant, swathed in red and transparent white, and gave her to Joachim.

Lysia

LYSIA was the apostle Thomas's half-sister. She converted to the faith around the time of the stoning of Stephen. She was a rich widow and donated all she possessed to the community of holy women in Jerusalem. Her two sons later became disciples.

A Third Mary
(Daughter of Anne)

TODAY Zechariah went away again, but Anne came back to visit the holy family with her eldest daughter, her second husband, and the maidservant. Anne's eldest daughter is bigger than her mother and really looks older than Anne. Anne's second husband is taller and older than Joachim was. His name is Eliud, and he had a post at the Temple connected with the supervision of the sacrificial animals. Anne had a daughter by him, also called Mary. At Jesus's birth she must have been six or eight years old. This Eliud died soon after this, and it was God's will that Anne should marry for the third time. Of this marriage there was a son, who was called one of Jesus's brethren.[1]

The maidservant brought by Anne from Nazareth a week ago is still with the Blessed Virgin. While the Blessed Virgin was living in the cave of the nativity, this maidservant lived in the little cave at the side; but now, as Mary is in the cave at the side, the maidser-

---

[1] On another occasion, when Brentano asked Anne Catherine what was the name of Anne's second husband, she thought a moment and said "'Eli' [a later note reads, 'not Eli, but Eliud']. He was active in the Temple, having something to do with the sacrificial animals. Anne had a daughter by him, who was also called Mary. She must have been between six and eight years old when Jesus was born. By her third husband Anne had a son who was sometimes

vant sleeps under a shelter put up for her by Joseph in front of the cave. Anne and her companions sleep in the cave of the nativity. The holy family is now deeply joyful. Anne is blissfully happy. Mary often lays the infant Jesus in her arms for her to nurse.

I did not see her do that with anyone else. I saw, to my great wonderment, that the infant's hair, which is yellow and curly, ends in little fine rays of light intersecting each other. I think they make his hair curly, for I see them rubbing his head after washing it. They put a little cloak round him the while. I always see in the holy family the most touching and devout honor being paid to the infant Jesus, but it is all quite simple and human, as it always is with holy and elect ones. The child turns to his mother with love such as I have never seen in one so young.

Mary told her mother all about the visit of the three holy kings, and Anne was greatly moved on hearing that the Lord God had summoned them from so far to acknowledge the child of the promise. She was shown the gifts of the kings, which were hidden in a wicker basket in a covered niche in the wall. She recognized them as tokens of homage and gazed at them with deep humility. She helped to give away some of them and to arrange and pack up the rest.

All is now quiet in the neighborhood; all the paths except the one through the gate of the town have been closed by the authorities. Joseph no longer goes to Bethlehem for what he wants; the shepherds bring him everything needful. The kinswoman with whom Anne stayed in Benjamin is Mara, the daughter of Elizabeth's sister Rhoda. She is poor, and later had several sons, who

---

called the brother of the Christ. There was a mystery bound up with the multiple marriages of Anne, a divine command that she obeyed. The grace that made her fruitful with [the Virgin] Mary was not exhausted—it was as though this Blessing had to be fully expended." Anne Catherine could not say with confidence, however, whether the Mystery Joachim had received from the Ark of the Covenant was passed on to Anne's later husbands. [To summarize: Joachim (Heli), the first husband of Anne, was the father of Mary Heli and the Virgin Mary. Anne's second husband, Eliud, was the natural father of yet another, third, child named Mary, a half-sister to the other two Marys. With her third (unnamed, as far as has yet been determined), Anne had a son, known only by the name "brother of Christ (Jesus)."]

became disciples. One of them was called Nathaniel and was later the bridegroom at Cana. This Mara was present at the Blessed Virgin's death at Ephesus...

Today Anne sent away her husband Eliud with a loaded donkey and the maidservant, her relation, with two big packs. She carried one on her back and one in front. These contain part of the kings' gifts, stuffs of various kinds and golden vessels, which in later years were used at the first Christian religious services. They are sending everything away in secret, for some sort of investigation is always going on about here. It seems as though they are only taking these things to some place on the way to Nazareth whence they will be fetched by servants, for in earlier visions I saw Eliud back in Bethlehem at Anne's departure thence, which will soon take place. Anne was now alone with Mary in the side-cave. I saw that they were working together, plaiting and knitting a coarse blanket. The cave of the nativity is now completely cleared out. Joseph's donkey is hidden behind wicker screens.

Mary Alpheus (2)

ANNE *Catherine reports that on an occasion when she saw in vision the apostle Simon the Zealot with his mother Mary Cleophas, she saw for the first time that the latter's first husband, Alpheus, brought not only a son (Levi, latter called Matthew) into their marriage, but also a daughter named Mary [Mary Alpheus]. This Mary married a minor customs official in Chorazin, who after receiving the baptism of John immediately resigned his post to take employment at Peter's fishery. He was one of those working on the ships when Jesus came to the fishery.*

On another occasion Anne Catherine learned that from her husband Alpheus, Mary Cleophas had, first of all, Judas Thaddeus (who was slightly older than Jesus), Simon, and then also a daughter named Mary (not the step-daughter of the same name):[1]

The Mary Alpheus born of Mary Cleophas's marriage with Alpheus married a twenty-four-year old temple servant named

---

[1] The matter is rather confusing. From Brentano's notes it appears that at a certain point Anne Catherine came to understand that when Mary Cleophas married Alpheus, the latter brought into the marriage not only his son Levi

David, from the line of Levi, whose task was to purify the vessels used in the blood sacrifices. They lived together in Jerusalem in a house attached to the Temple. David was only permitted to be together with his wife for stretches of eight days, at certain times, during which his duties were taken over by another servant. And before he returned to his service, he had to submit to purifications. He was a very pious Jew, but withal a strict observer of the law. He was somewhat provoked by the disorderliness of the travels of Jesus and his disciples. He was acquainted with Nicodemus, who in due course placated David's reservations and convinced him to join the community, a step that his wife Mary had taken already. I had seen this Mary, and her stepsister Mary [Matthew's sister], often among the women, but only on this occasion did I finally understand who they were. The Mary who was the wife of David I saw often in service to Blessed Virgin during the time of her tribulations.

Mary of Cana

THE *elder Sobe was the first daughter of the Essenes Ismeria and Eliud, whose second daughter, Anne, was to be the mother of the Virgin Mary (a third daughter, Maraha, was later born to the Essene couple). Sobe married a man named Solomon, or Salomo, and became the mother of Mary Salome, who in turn married Zebedee and became the mother of the future apostles James the Greater and John. Apparently Sobe had a second daughter at a later time, also called Mary, or Mary of Cana, referred to below:*[1]

(the later apostle Matthew), but also a daughter Mary, who is thus called Mary Alpheus. However, according to other notes we learn that from the marriage of Mary Cleophas and Alpheus, among the other children born to them (the later apostles Judas Thaddeus, Simon the Zealot, and James the Less, as well as Susanna Alpheus) was another Mary, who would also be called Mary Alpheus, after her father, so that in the combined family there were now stepsister both with the same name (at least, as we come to know them in the context of Anne Catherine's visions).

[1] In fact, there is some evidence in Brentano's notes that Sobe the elder had yet another daughter, whom we shall call Sobe the younger. See separate reference under that heading.

On Wednesday, June 29, AD 29, Jesus was in Cana, where he visited his widowed cousin Mary, the daughter of Sobe and the sister of Mary Salome. Mary Salome was married to Zebedee—their children James and John afterward became apostles—whereas Mary of Cana was also the aunt of the bridegroom Nathaniel who, six months hence, married the daughter of the wealthy Israel of Cana.

Lady Mercuria,
Pagan Princess of Cyprus

MERCURIA *was another pagan woman—like the Syrophoenician woman—who was converted by Jesus, and whom Anne Catherine described in considerable detail. The entry on the Syrophoenician woman ends on Monday, April 30, AD 31, at which time Jesus was in Cyprus:*

Jesus had just passed through Salamis and was staying at the home of the Essene father of the disciple Jonas. On that day Jesus spoke of Mercuria, saying that she would soon join the Syrophoenician woman, who was likewise making preparations to leave Ornithopolis. Mercuria was tall, and about twenty-five years old. She was enveloped in a white mantle, long and flowing in the back but rather shorter in front, which formed a cap around the head. Her other garments also were white, though with colored borders. The fabrics in which the pagan women dressed were so soft and clung so closely to the form that the latter could readily be traced by the eye.

The previous day, Sunday, April 29, AD 31, after healing some people who were then baptized by the disciples, Jesus taught on a hill, where a large crowd had gathered to hear him. The Roman commandant of Salamis sent an invitation to Jesus, which Jesus accepted. At the commandant's palace Jesus answered questions that were put to him. Around two in the afternoon Jesus then arrived at the home of the father of his disciple Jonas. From this place, Jesus went with the disciples to a newly-constructed baptismal well, where he prepared many Jews for baptism by a discourse in which he exhorted them to penance and blessed the baptismal water. I saw Barnabas, James, and Azor baptizing.

The next morning Jesus taught close to the place of baptism. Then, in the afternoon, he visited some private homes, where he healed the sick. That evening he dined with the rabbis as their guest of honor. Later, when he and the disciples had returned to their inn, a pagan came to Jesus and begged him to go with him to a certain garden a few steps distant, where a person in distress was waiting to implore his assistance.

Jesus went with the disciples to the place indicated. There he saw standing, between the walls on the road, the pagan lady Mercuria, who inclined low before him. He ordered the disciples to fall back a little and then questioned the woman as to what she wanted. She was a very remarkable person, perfectly destitute of instruction, quite sunk in paganism, and wholly given up to its abominable service. One glance from Jesus had cast her into disquiet and roused in her the feeling that she was in error, but she was without simple faith and had a very confused manner of accusing herself. She told Jesus that she had heard of his having helped Magdalene, as also the woman afflicted with the issue of blood, who she had been told had merely touched the hem of his garment to effect her cure. She begged Jesus to cure and instruct her, but then again, she said, perhaps he could not cure her as she was not, like the woman with the issue of blood, physically sick.[1] Jesus told her that the faith of that afflicted woman was simple; that, in the firm belief that if she could touch only the hem of his garment she would be cured, she had approached him stealthily and her faith had saved her.

Mercuria asked Jesus how he could have known that Enue touched him and how he healed her. She did not comprehend

---

[1] On the preceding day Mercuria had watched Jesus from a window and seen a halo of light around his head, which sight very powerfully impressed her. She at first thought that her emotion sprang from love for Jesus, and the idea caused her anguish so intense that she fell to the ground unconscious. When returned to herself, her whole life, her whole interior, had passed before her in so frightful a manner that she entirely lost her peace of mind. It was then that she had made inquiries about Jesus and learned from some Jewish women of Magdalene's cure, as also that of Enue of Caesarea-Philippi, the woman afflicted with the issue of blood. Thus it was that she now implored Jesus to heal her if he possibly could.

Jesus or his power, although she heartily longed for his assistance. She confessed also that she was married and had three children, but that one, unbeknownst to her husband, had been begotten in adultery. She had had intercourse also with the Roman commandant. Jesus rebuked her, commanded her to renounce her shameful life, and told her of God the Almighty and of his commandment: "Thou shalt not commit adultery." He placed before her all the abominations of the debauchery (against which her nature itself revolted) practiced in the impure service of her gods; but he met her with words so earnest and so full of mercy that she retired weeping and penetrated with sorrow.

Some days later, on Wednesday, May 2, AD 31, Jesus traveled with Jonas and another disciple one half-hour westward from Salamis to a rich, fertile region, instructing the workers as he went. On that day at Salamis I saw Mercuria the sinner walking up and down her apartments, a prey to deep sadness and disquietude. She wept, wrung her hands, and, enveloped in her veil, often threw herself on the floor in a corner. Her husband, who appeared to me not very bright, thought, like her maids, that she had lost her mind. But Mercuria was torn by remorse for her sins; her only thought, her constant dream, was how she could break loose from her bonds and join the holy women in Palestine.

Mercuria had two daughters, of eight and nine years, and a boy of fifteen. Her home, near to the great temple, was large, with massive walls and surrounded by servants' dwellings, pillars, terraces, and gardens.[1] They called upon her to attend the temple, but she declined on the plea of sickness. This temple was an extraordinary building full of columns, chambers, abodes for the

---

[1] Mercuria's house became subsequently the dwelling of Costa, the father of St. Catherine. Catherine was born and reared in it. Her father was descended from a princely race of Mesopotamia. For certain services he was rewarded with large possessions in Cyprus. He married in Salamis a daughter of the same pagan priestly family to which Mercuria belonged. Even in her childhood, Catherine was full of wisdom, and had interior visions, by which she was guided. She could not endure the pagan idols, and thrust them out of sight wherever she could. As a punishment for this, her father once put her in confinement. See following section: "Mercuria Considered in the Life of Her Later Relative, St. Catherine."

pagan priests, and vaults. In it stood a gigantic statue of a goddess, which shone like gold. The body was that of a fish and the head was horned like a cow. Before it was another figure of lesser stature upon whose shoulders the goddess rested her short arms, or claws. The figures stood upon a high pedestal, in which were cavities for the burning of incense and other offerings. The sacrifices in honor of the goddess consisted even of children, especially cripples.

After nearly a month of further travels, Jesus and the disciples arrived back in Salamis around two in the afternoon on Tuesday, May 29, AD 31. Here Jesus met again with the Roman commandant of the town, who decided to convert. Mercuria also sent to beg Jesus to grant her an interview in the garden near the aqueduct. Jesus assented and followed the servant that had delivered the message to the place designated. Mercuria came forward veiled, holding her two singularly-dressed little girls by the hand. They wore only a short tunic down to the knee, the rest of their covering consisting of some kind of fine, transparent material upon which were wreaths of woolen, or feather flowers. Their arms were bare, their feet enveloped in little bands, and their hair loose. They were dressed almost like the angels we make for representations of the crib.

Jesus spoke long and graciously with Mercuria. She wept bitterly and was very much troubled at the thought of having to leave her son behind her, also because her parents lived at a distance from her younger sister, who would thus remain in the blindness of paganism. She wept also over her own sins. Jesus consoled her and assured her again of pardon. The two little girls looked at their mother in surprise and they too began to cry and to cling to her. Jesus blessed the little ones.

Several days later, on Friday June 1, AD 31, as Jesus and his disciples—newly returned from Cyprus—made their way northward, crossed the river Belus, and then headed eastward to the town of Misael, the Syrophoenician woman from Ornithopolis sent hither by some of the disciples little golden bars and plates of the same metal chained together. She was desirous to send one of her ships to Cyprus in order to facilitate Mercuria's flight from the island.

The Jews that had emigrated from Cyprus to Palestine had lived at first in caves, but by degrees their settlement became a city, which received the name of Eleutheropolis. It was situated west of Hebron and not far from the well of Samson. More than once the Jews sought to destroy the little colony,[1] but after every attack the inhabitants again returned. The caves lay under the city, so that in times of persecution the inhabitants could take refuge in them. It was in the first attack—which was made at the time of the stoning of Stephen, when the colony between Ophel and Bethany was destroyed—that Mercuria lost her life.[2]

Mercuria and Her
Later Relative, St. Catherine

ELSEWHERE in Brentano's notes, in the context of Anne Catherine's visions regarding St. Catherine,[3] further light is shed on the pagan princess Mercuria, as follows.

Catherine's father was named Costa. He belonged to a royal race and was a descendant of Hazael, whom Elijah by God's command anointed king of Syria. I saw the prophet with the box of ointment crossing the Jordan and anointing Hazael, with whom after that all went well. Costa's immediate ancestors emigrated to Cyprus with the Persians or Medes and there obtained possessions. They were, like Costa himself, star- and fire-worshippers, and held also to the Syrophoenician worship of idols. Catherine, on her mother's side, was descended from the family of the pagan princess Mercuria, who had been converted by Jesus at Salamis. Mercuria had after her conversion emigrated to the holy land,

---

[1] The people of this colony often went to the cenacle and to the church at the pool of Bethesda, to carry thither their offerings and contributions, and at the destruction of Ophel they fled to Eleutheropolis. Joseph Barsabbas, son of Mary Cleophas and her second husband Sabbas, became the first bishop of that city, and there during a persecution he was crucified on a tree.

[2] Ophel and Bethany, established under the deacons. Mercuria contributed largely toward the buildings and the support of the brethren. I saw also that in an insurrection against the Christians (Saul not yet being converted) Mercuria was murdered.

[3] For more on St. Catherine see *Scenes from the Lives of the Saints*.

received in baptism the name Famula, and in the persecution that broke out after the stoning of Stephen had gained the martyr's crown.

There had long existed in Mercuria's family the oft-told prediction that a great prophet would come from Judea to change all things, to overturn the idols, to announce the true God, and that he would come in contact with this family. When Mercuria fled to Palestine with her two daughters she left behind in Cyprus an illegitimate son whose father was then the Roman consul. He had been baptized as early as the time of Jesus and afterward left the island with Paul and Barnabas. This son married his mother's youngest sister, from which union was born Catherine's mother.

Catherine was Costa's only daughter. Like her mother, she had yellow hair, was very sprightly and fearless, and had always to suffer and to struggle. She possessed in a high degree the prophetic spirit of her maternal ancestors and the prediction of the great prophet was shown her in vision when she was scarcely six years old. At the midday repast she related it to her parents, to whom Mercuria's history was not unknown. But her father, a very cold, stern man, shut her up, as a punishment, in a dark vault. There I saw her, a bright light shining around her and the mice and other little creatures playing tamely by her.

Naomi of Dabrath

THERE was a rich woman in Dabrath named Naomi. She had been unfaithful to her husband, and he had died of grief. For a long time she had promised to marry the agent that attended to her business, but he too was being deceived by her. Naomi had heard Jesus's instructions in Dothan and had been in consequence very much changed. She was full of repentance and desired only to beg of him pardon and penance. She attended Jesus's teaching in Dabrath on Friday, November 3, AD 30, was present at the cures he wrought, and tried by every means to approach him, but he always turned away from her. She was a person of distinction and well-known in the city, and as her disorders were not public she had not fallen into general disesteem. While she was trying to approach Jesus she encountered the Pharisees, who asked her whether she was not ashamed of herself and bade her return to her home. Their words, however, did not restrain her; she was as if out of herself in her eager desire for pardon. At last she succeeded in breaking through the crowd. She threw herself down on the ground before Jesus, crying out: "Lord, is there grace, is there pardon still for me? Lord, I can no longer live so! I sinned grievously against my husband, and I have deceived the man that now has charge of my affairs!" And thus she confessed her sins before all.

All, however, did not hear her, for Jesus had stepped aside, and the Pharisees pressing forward had made a great uproar. Jesus said to Naomi: "Arise! Your sins are forgiven you!" She obeyed, begging at the same time for a penance, but Jesus put her off till another time. Then she divested herself of her rich ornaments: the strings of pearls around her headdress, her rings, her bracelets, and the golden cords around her arms and neck. She handed them all over to the Pharisees with the request that they should be given to the poor, and then she drew her veil closely around her.

Jesus now went into the synagogue, for the sabbath had begun. The infuriated Pharisees and Sadducees followed him. The reading for the day was about Jacob and Esau. Jesus applied the details connected with the birth of the two brothers to his own time. Esau and Jacob struggled in their mother's womb, thus did the synagogue struggle against the piously disposed. The law was harsh and severe (the firstborn, like Esau), but it had sold its birthright to Jacob for a mess of pottage (for the redolent odors arising from all kinds of unimportant usages and exterior ceremonies). Jacob, who had now received the Blessing, would become a great nation whom Esau would have to serve. The whole explanation was very beautiful and the Pharisees could bring nothing forward against it, although they disputed long with Jesus. They reproached him upon several heads: that he attached to himself followers, that he established private inns throughout the country, employing for the same the money and property of rich widows that should have been given for the use of the synagogue and the doctors. And so, they said, would it now be with Naomi; besides, how could he forgive her her sins?

Naomi of the Temple, Aunt of Lazarus

AT the time of Mary's entrance to the Temple, the priests, among whom Zechariah was one of those standing on the lower steps, led Mary down by the hand. One of them took the light from her and the little garlands off her arms and handed them to the other girls. Mary was then led through a door into another hall where six other temple virgins, their mistress Naomi (the sister of Lazarus's mother), Anna, and another female met them and scattered flowers before her. To them the priest delivered the child.

I saw also a feast among the temple children. They had a meal at which Mary had to question first the mistresses and then the maidens separately as to whether they were willing to have her among them. This was the custom. Then the girls had a dance among themselves. In the evening, Naomi took Mary to her cell, from which she could see down into the Temple. Here Mary mentioned to Naomi her desire to get up more frequently in the night to pray, but Naomi refused her request for the present.

At the time of the birth of the child Jesus I saw that Anne at Nazareth, Elizabeth in Jutta, Naomi, Anna, and Simeon in the Temple—all had on this night visions from which they learned of the birth of the Savior. The child John was unspeakably joyful. But only Anne knew where the newborn child was; the others, and even Elizabeth, knew indeed of Mary and saw her in vision, but they knew nothing of Bethlehem.

At the time of Mary's purification, she was led to a porch in that part of the Temple in which the ceremony of presentation was to take place. Anna and another woman (Naomi, Mary's former directress) received her. Simeon came out to the porch and conducted Mary, with the child in her arms, into the hall to the right of the women's porch. It was in this porch that the treasure box stood by which Jesus was sitting when the widow cast in her mite. Old Anna, to whom Joseph had handed over a basket of fruit and doves, followed with Naomi, and Joseph retired to the standing place of the men.

I did not witness the purification ceremonies of the other mothers; but I had an interior conviction that all the children offered on that day would receive special grace, and that some of the martyred innocents were among them. When the most holy child Jesus was laid upon the altar in the basket cradle an indescribable light filled the Temple. I saw that God was in that light, and I saw the heavens open up as far as the Most Holy Trinity. Mary was now led back into the court by Anna and Naomi. Here she took leave of them and was joined by Joseph and the old people with whom she and Joseph had lodged. They went with the ass straight out of Jerusalem, and the good, old people accompanied them a part of the way.

On Wednesday, September 7, AD 29, Eliud the Essene, who had been discoursing with Jesus upon the mysteries of the Old Testament and the incarnation, related also many things connected with the virtues of Mary in the Temple. As he spoke, I saw it all in vision. I saw that her teacher Naomi was one of Lazarus's relatives. She was about fifty years old and, like all the other women who served in the Temple, an Essene. I saw that Mary learned from her how to knit. Even as a child she used to go with Naomi when the latter went to cleanse the different vessels and utensils that had been soiled with the blood of sacrifice. Certain parts of the animal sacrificed were received by them, then cut up and prepared as food for the priests and others who served in the Temple, for they depended in part upon that for support. I saw the Blessed Virgin at a later period helping in these duties. Two days later, on Saturday, September 10, AD 29, I understood again from the continuing conversation that Naomi, Mary's teacher in the Temple, was the aunt of Lazarus, his mother's sister. I was shown also that Lazarus's father was the son of a Syrian king who had, for services in war, received some property as a reward.

Pagan Priestess of Gadara
(Also, Regarding Moloch and Beelzebub)

ON the morning of Saturday, September 23, AD 30, as Jesus was curing numbers of sick outside the city of Gadara,[1] the priests approached to salute him. "Why," said he addressing them, "why

---

[1] Gadara was a stronghold. The pagan quarter was tolerably large and somewhat sheltered by the highest peak of the mountain, at whose northern base were warm baths and beautiful buildings.

were ye so disturbed last night over my teaching of yesterday? Why should ye tremble before an army, since God protects the just? Fulfill the *Law* and the *Prophets*! Why then should ye fear?" Jesus again taught in the synagogue as on the preceding day.

Toward noon a pagan woman timidly approached the disciples and implored them to bring Jesus to her house that he might cure her child. Jesus went with several of his disciples into the pagan quarter. The woman's husband met him at the gate and led him into the house. The wife cast herself at Jesus's feet, saying: "Master, I have heard of thy wonders and that thou canst perform greater prodigies than Elijah. Behold, my only boy is dying, and our wise lady cannot help him. Do thou have pity on us!" The boy, about three years old, lay in a little crib in the corner. The evening before, the father had taken the child into the vineyard and he had eaten a few grapes. Soon after, the boy became sick and the father had to take him back home whimpering loudly. The mother had held him all night in her arms, vainly trying to relieve him. He already wore the appearance of death, indeed he looked as if he might really be dead.

At this point the mother had hastened to the Jewish quarter to implore Jesus's aid, for the pagans had heard of the cures wrought by him on the day before. Jesus said to her: "Leave me alone with the child and send to me two of my disciples!" Then came Judas Barsabbas and Nathaniel the bridegroom. Jesus took the boy from his crib into his arms, laid him on his breast, breast to breast, pressed him to himself, bowed his face upon the face of the child, and breathed upon him. The child opened his eyes and rose up. Then Jesus held him out in his arms and commanded the two disciples to lay their hands upon the child's head and to bless him. They obeyed, and the child was cured. Jesus then took him to the anxiously waiting parents, who, embracing the child, cast themselves down at Jesus's feet. The mother cried out: "Great is the God of Israel! He is far above all the gods! My husband has already told me that, and henceforth I will serve no other god!" A crowd soon gathered and several other children were brought to the Lord, whom he cured in various ways.

The pagan mothers complained of the frequent illness of their children and of the little assistance they derived from their priestess in such trials. Jesus commanded the priestess to be summoned before him. She obeyed reluctantly, for she did not want to enter Jesus's presence. She was closely enveloped in veils. Jesus ordered her to draw near. But she would not look at him, she turned her face away and behaved exactly like the possessed. She was irresistibly forced to turn away from the glance of Jesus, though at his command she approached. Jesus, addressing the pagan men and women before him, said: "I will show you now what wisdom you reverence in this woman and what is her skill," and he commanded the spirits to leave her. Thereupon a black vapor issued from her and all kinds of figures—noxious insects, snakes, toads, rats, dragons—withdrew from her like shadows. It was a horrible sight. Jesus exclaimed: "Behold what doctrine you follow!" The woman fell upon her knees weeping and sobbing.

She was now quite changed, quite tractable, and Jesus ordered her to disclose by what means she had tried to cure the children. With many tears and half-reluctantly she obeyed. She told that she had been taught to make the children sick by charms and witchcraft, that she might afterward cure them for the honor of the gods. Jesus then commanded her to accompany him and the disciples to where the god Moloch was kept, and he directed several of the pagan priests to be called. A crowd had gathered, for the news of the child's cure was soon spread. The place to which Jesus now went was not a temple, but a hill surrounded by tombs. The god was in a subterranean vault in the midst of them. The vault was closed on top by a cover. Jesus told the pagan priests to call forth their god. When by means of machinery they had caused the idol to rise into sight, Jesus expressed to them his regret that they had a god that was unable to help himself.

Then turning to the priestess, he commanded her to rehearse the praises of her god, tell how she served him, and what reward he gave her. Like Balaam the prophet, the woman began to repeat aloud before all the people the horrors of Moloch's worship and the wonders of the God of Israel. Jesus then directed the disciples to upset the idol and to shake it violently. They did as commanded. Jesus said to the pagans: "Behold the god that you serve! Behold the spirits that you adore!" and in the sight of all present there appeared all kinds of diabolical figures issuing from the idol.

They trembled convulsively, crept around for awhile, and vanished into the earth among the tombs.

The idolaters gazed at the scene in affright and confusion. Jesus said: "If we cast your god down again into his den, he will surely go to pieces." The priests implored Jesus not to destroy their idol, whereupon he allowed them to raise it as before and lower it into its place. Most of the idolaters were deeply touched and ashamed, especially the priests, although some were very indignant. The people were, however, on Jesus's side. He gave them a beautiful instruction and many were converted.

Moloch was seated like an ox on his hind legs, his forepaws stretched out like the arms of one who is going to receive something upon them, but by means of machinery he could be made to draw them in. His gaping mouth disclosed an enormous throat, and on his forehead was one crooked horn. He was seated in a large basin. Around the body were several projections like outside pockets. On festival days long straps were hung around his neck. In the basin under him fire was made when sacrifices were to be offered. Around the rim of the basin numbers of lamps were kept constantly burning before the god. Once upon a time it was customary to sacrifice children to him, but now they dared no longer do so, and animals of all kinds were offered in their stead. They were consumed in the openings of his body or cast into his yawning jaws. The sacrifice most agreeable to him was an Angora goat. There was also a machine by which the priests and others could descend to the idol in the subterranean vault among the tombs. The worship of Moloch was, however, no longer in great repute. He was invoked chiefly for purposes of sorcery and especially by the mothers of sick children. Each pocket around his person was consecrated to special sacrifices. Children used to be laid on his arms and consumed by the fire under him and in him, for he was hollow. He drew his arms in when the victim was deposited upon them and pressed it tightly that its screams might not be heard. There was machinery in the hind legs by which he could be made to rise. He was surrounded with rays.

The pagans whose children Jesus had cured asked him whither they should remove, for they were determined to renounce idolatry. Jesus spoke to them of baptism, exhorting them in the meantime to remain tranquil and persevere in their good resolutions. He spoke to them of God as of a father to whom we must sacrifice our evil inclinations and who asks no other offering from us than that of our own heart. When addressing the pagans Jesus always said to them, more plainly than he did to the Jews, that God has no need of our offerings. He exhorted them to contrition and penance, to thanksgiving for benefits received, and to compassion toward the suffering. Returned to the Jewish quarter, he terminated the exercises of the sabbath and took a repast, after which began a fast in atonement for the adoration of the golden calf.

After further teaching and healing in Gadara the morning of the following day, Sunday, September 24, AD 30, Jesus left the city in the afternoon. The pagans whose children he had cured thanked him again outside their own quarter. He blessed them, and with twelve disciples went down through the valley to the south of Gadara. He crossed a mountain and reached a little stream flowing from the range below Betharamphtha-Julias where the mines were. It was three hours from Gadara to the inn near the stream at which Jesus and the disciples put up. The Jews dwelling around that part of the country were engaged in gathering in the fruits. Jesus instructed them.

There was also a band of pagans near the stream busy gathering white flowers from a blooming hedge, but it was not the flowers alone that they gathered, but also great, ugly beetles and other insects. When Jesus approached them, they drew back as if in fear. It was shown me that these insects were intended for the idol Beelzebub at Dion. I saw the idol outside the gate of the city, sitting under a large willow. It had a figure something like a monkey with short arms and slender legs, and it was seated like a human being. Its head was pointed and furnished with two little horns bent like a crescent, and the face with its extremely long nose was horrible. The chin was short but projecting, the mouth large and like that of a beast, the body lank, the legs long and thin with clawed toes. It wore an apron. In one hand it grasped a vessel by the stem, and in the other held a butterfly just escaping the larva cocoon. The butterfly, which was something like a bird and something like a disgusting insect, shone with variegated colors. Around the head of the idol and just above the forehead was a wreath of loathsome beetles and flying vermin, forming as it were a compact mass, one appearing to hold the other fast. Above the forehead and in the center of the pointed head between the horns sat one of those disgusting things larger and more hideous than the others. They were glittering and they radiated all the colors, but they were horrible, venomous things with long bodies, horns, feelers, and stings. When Jesus drew near to the pagans that were seeking these insects for the idol, the whole crown flew asunder like a dark swarm and hid in the holes and corners around the country, while all kinds of frightful black spirits crept with them, frightened, into the holes. They were the wicked spirits that were honored in Beelzebub with those beetles.

Petronella

AFTER the death of his wife, Jonah, the owner of a fishery near Capernaum at the northwest end of the Sea of Galilee, handed it over to his younger son, Simon. Simon, referred to as Simon Bar-Jonas (bar signifying "son"), was later named Peter by Jesus. After three years Simon-Peter married a widow whose husband had been a fisherman from Bethsaida, near Capernaum, on the Sea of Galilee. The widow was older than Simon-Peter, and from her previous marriage had two sons and a daughter. The daughter was later martyred, and as the stepdaughter of Peter came to be known as Petronella.

Rhoda

TO the north of Mount Tabor was situated the city of Tabor, whence the mountain derived its name, and about an hour westward in the direction of Sepphoris was another fortified place. Casaloth was in the valley on the south side of the mountain, northward from Nain, and in the direction of Apheke. The tribe of Zebulon extends farthest to the north on this side. I have heard a more modern name given to this place and I saw that relatives of Jesus once dwelt there, namely a sister of Elizabeth, who, like the maidservant of Mary Mark, bore the name of Rhoda. She had three daughters and two sons. One of the daughters was one of the three widows, friends of Mary, and her two sons were among

Raising of Salome, the Daughter of Jairus of Capernaum

Salome, Daughter of Herodias, Dancing

232

the disciples. One of Rhoda's sons married Maroni, and died without issue. His widow, in obedience to the law, entered into a second marriage with one of her first husband's family named Eliud, a nephew of Mother Anne. She lived at Nain and by her second husband had one son, who was called Martialis. She was now a widow for the second time, and she is the so-called widow of Nain whose son Martialis was raised from the dead by the Lord.

Salome, Daughter of Jairus of Capernaum

SALOME, *the daughter of Jairus, leader of the synagogue at Capernaum, was raised twice from the dead (not to be confused with the daughter of Jairus the Essene, of Phasael, whose daughter Jesus also raised from the dead).*

Salome, Daughter of Herodias—Her Death

AT the time Salome's parents were in misery and met their death in a swampy place [they died in exile in France], I saw Salome dancing at a great festival. Among the instruments the musicians played were pipes, curved horns, kettle-drums, and barrels over which strings had been stretched. The musicians were positioned around the hall and their music was rather primitive. Salome danced as one out of her senses. Anxious and fearful, her thoughts dwelling on John [the Baptist], she hurried over to a window to get some air. But then blood broke forth from her throat, and in a fit of dizziness she plummeted into an inaccessible ditch, breaking the nape of her neck, leaving her tongue hanging out of her throat. This place must have been at some distance from Jerusalem, for it seemed to me that she fell onto ice below; it was as though the ice knocked off her throat. It was not possible to reach her, and so an opening was broken in the wall, so that her body could be retrieved.[1]

---

[1] For more on this account, and Salome generally, see "King Herod Antipas" in the section "Opponents of Jesus" in *People of the New Testament IV.*

Sobe the Elder

THE elder Sobe was the first daughter of the Essenes Ismeria and Eliud, whose second daughter, Anne, was to be the mother of the Virgin Mary (a third daughter, Maraha, was later born to the Essene couple). Sobe married a man named Solomon (or Salomo) and became the mother of Mary Salome, who in turn married Zebedee and became the mother of the future apostles James the Greater and John. Apparently, the elder Sobe had a second daughter at a later time, also called Mary, or Mary of Cana, referred to in the entry for Wednesday, June 29, AD 29.[1]

The eminent chastity and mortification of Stolanus and Emorun had descended to Ismeria and Eliud. When at Sobe's birth the sign of the Promise was not found on her, her parents were much troubled. They journeyed to the prophet on Mount Horeb. He exhorted them to prayer and sacrifice and promised them consolation. For about eighteen years they were without children, and then Anne was born. Both father and mother had the same vision one night upon their couch. Ismeria saw an angel near her, writing on the wall. On awakening she told her husband, who had had the same vision, and both still saw the written character on the wall. It was the letter M. At her birth Anne brought with her into the world the same sign upon the region of the stomach.

When in her fifth year, Anne was taken to the Temple, as Mary was later. There she remained twelve years, returning home in her seventeenth year. Meantime, her mother had had a third daughter, whom she named Maraha, and Anne found also in the paternal house a little son of her eldest sister Sobe, who was called Eliud. Maraha afterward inherited the paternal property of Sepphoris and became the mother of the subsequent disciples, Arastaria and Cocharia. The young Eliud was afterward the second husband of Maroni, of Nain.

Several days before the birth of Mary, Anne informed Joachim that the time of her delivery was at hand. She sent messengers to

---

[1] In fact there is some evidence in Brentano's notes that Sobe the elder had yet another daughter, whom we shall call Sobe the younger. See separate reference under that heading.

her sister Maraha at Sepphoris, also to the widow Enue, Elizabeth's sister, in the valley of Zebulon, and to her sister Sobe's
daughter [Mary] Salome, the wife of Zebedee, of Bethsaida. The
sons of Mary Salome and Zebedee, James the Greater and John,
were not yet born. Anne sent for these three women to come to
her. I saw them on their journey. Two of them were accompanied by their husbands, who returned, however, when they had
reached the neighborhood of Nazareth. Joachim had sent the
menservants off to the herds, and had otherwise disposed of the
domestics not absolutely needed in the house. Mary Heli, Anne's
eldest daughter, now the wife of Cleophas, took charge of the
household affairs.

ON Wednesday, June 29, AD 29, Jesus was in Cana, where he visited his widowed cousin Mary, the daughter of Sobe and the sister
of Mary Salome. (Mary Salome was married to Zebedee—their
children, James and John, afterward became apostles—whereas
Mary of Cana was also the aunt of the bridegroom Nathaniel
who, six months hence, married the daughter of the wealthy
Israel of Cana). Here in Cana Jesus taught. At this time he was not
yet accompanied by any of his future disciples. It looked as if he
were studying men, and building upon the foundation that John
had laid. Sometimes a good man accompanied him from place to
place.

Lazarus had brought Martha and Johanna Chusa to Mary, then
at Capernaum, whither she had come from Cana. They set off
again for Tiberias where they hoped to meet Jesus. Simeon's son
was one of the escorts, and the bridegroom of Cana went also to
meet Jesus. This bridegroom was the son of the daughter of Sobe,
the sister of Anne. His name was Nathaniel. He did not belong to
Cana, though he was married there.

Half a year later, on Monday, December 26, AD 29, Jesus stayed
in Cana at a house belonging to one of Mary's cousins. This
cousin was the daughter of Anne's sister Sobe and was also an
aunt of Nathaniel the bridegroom. Today Jesus spent much time
walking and talking with those disciples who later became his
apostles. When Jesus with his disciples arrived near Cana he was

most deferentially received by Mary, the bride's parents, the bride-groom, and others who had come out to meet him.

Jesus with his familiar disciples, among them the future apos-tles, took up his abode in an isolated house belonging to the maternal aunt of the bridegroom. This aunt also was a daughter of Anne's sister Sobe. She held the mother's place to the bride-groom during the wedding ceremonies. The bride's father was named Israel and was a descendant of Ruth of Bethlehem. He was an opulent merchant, who carried on a large freighting business. He owned warehouses and great inns and storing places along the highroads for supplying caravans with fodder. His employees were numerous, for most of the inhabitants of Cana earned their living by working for him; in fact, all business transactions were wholly in the hands of himself and a few others. The bride's mother was a little lame; she limped on one side and had to be led.

Susanna Alpheus

MARY Cleophas was the daughter of Mary Heli and Cleophas. Because of the age difference between Mary Heli and the Virgin Mary (the second daughter of Anne and Joachim), Mary Cleo-phas, although a niece of Mary, was about four years older than her. She was the playmate of the young Mary.

In the course of her life, Mary Cleophas had three husbands. Her first husband was called Alpheus, who had been married before and already had a son, who thus became the stepson of Mary Cleophas and who grew up in their home.[1] This son was Levi (later called Matthew), who later became one of the twelve apostles. She bore one daughter, Susanna Alpheus (but see foot-note), and three sons to Alpheus: Judas Thaddeus, Simon, and

---

[1] However, a passage discovered in Brentano's notes mentions a daughter that Alpheus also brought into the marriage, named Mary, or Mary Alpheus. This is further complicated by the fact that in the notes Anne Catherine also mentions a daughter *born* to Mary Cleophas and Alpheus, *also* named Mary (or, again, Mary Alpheus). Unfortunately, such ambiguities remain in the volu-minous notes, and on such points it seems some uncertainty must remain. See "Mary Alpheus (2)" in this volume.

James the Less, all of whom went on to become part of the circle of the twelve apostles of Jesus.

In AD 30, Susanna Alpheus, a daughter of Mary Cleophas and sister of the apostles, was about thirty years old and had grown children. Her husband lived in Nazareth, and it was there that she had joined the holy women.

An Unnamed Girl Raised

ON Thursday, June 12, AD 32, not far from the village were ten lepers in a tent. Jesus healed them, but only one ran after Jesus to thank him (Luke 17:11–19). The leper who ran after Jesus later became a disciple. Shortly afterward, as they passed along, a man came out of a shepherd settlement and begged Jesus to come because his daughter had just died. Jesus, accompanied by Peter, James, and John, went with the shepherd to his house. His daughter, who was about seven years old, lay dead. Looking up to heaven, Jesus placed one hand on her head and the other on her breast and prayed. The child then rose up, alive. Jesus told the apostles that—in his name—they should do as he did.

The Journey to the Kings, to Ur, and to Heliopolis
August 7, AD 32–January, AD 33

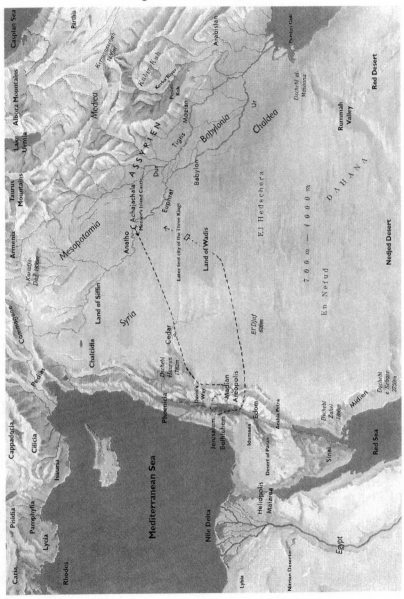

Women Mentioned
During Jesus's Journey East

Prefatory Note

THE *journey east here referred to is described more fully in* People of the New Testament IV, *and even more so in* The Visions of Anne Catherine Emmerich, Book II. *In order to provide context for this present section, a portion of the introductory material in the former text will be repeated immediately below.*

When Anne Catherine communicated in 1821 her primary visions of the journey of the three holy kings, she had already related the whole of Jesus's earthly ministry, and had among other things seen how, after the raising of Lazarus, he withdrew beyond the Jordan. During his sixteen weeks' absence there, he visited the three kings, who on their return from their journey to Bethlehem had settled all together, with their attendants, nearer to the promised land.[1] Only Mensor and Theokeno were alive then. The dark-skinned Sair was in his grave when Jesus came there. It seems necessary to inform the reader about these events (which were thirty-two years later in date, but described earlier *by Anne Catherine) in order that certain references to them in what follows may be understandable.*

On the journey to the three kings, according to Anne Catherine, Jesus gave instruction to the pagans and made it clear that he had come not only for the Jews but for them also. Now, for the people of Israel, who were the pagans? The people of Egypt and Chaldea were the closest and most important ones. The father of Israel, Abraham, had been born in Ur in Chaldea, and the Jewish people had lived in Chaldea at the time of the Babylonian captivity. Chaldea was therefore of great significance to the people of Israel. Similarly, from the time of the patriarch Jacob, whose son Joseph had been sold as a slave and carried off to Egypt, the Jewish nation had lived in Egypt until the Exodus led by Moses. Jesus himself as a child had been obliged to flee Israel with his parents because of Herod the Great, and the

---

[1] No such visit of Jesus to the abode of the three kings in Arabia is recorded in the gospels.

holy family had then lived for a time at Heliopolis in Egypt. So Egypt also represented an important station on the path of the people of Israel.

The journey made by Jesus to Chaldea and Egypt retraced the path of the people of Israel—a path retraced immediately prior to the last three months of the life of the messiah in Israel, leading up to the Mystery of Golgotha. This journey by the Son of God was therefore a brief recapitulation of the steps made by God's chosen people just before the sacrifice on Golgotha, which represented the culmination of the history of Israel.

Cuppes • Serena

ON the evening of Saturday, September 27, AD 32, at the close of the sabbath, Jesus went into the pagan temple, where there was an idol of a dragon. Before the priest began his instruction, a woman, attended by many others, went in front of the dragon, cast herself down and kissed the earth. She performed this action with marked enthusiasm and devotion. At this moment Jesus stepped into the middle of the circle and asked why she did that. She answered that the dragon awoke her every morning before day, and that when she arose she turned toward the quarter in which the image stood, prostrated before her couch, and adored it. Jesus next asked: "Why dost thou cast thyself down before satan? Thy faith has been taken possession of by satan. It is true indeed that thou wilt be awakened, but not by satan. It is an angel that will awake thee. Behold whom thou adorest!" At the same moment, there stood by the woman and in sight of all present a spirit in the form of a figure lank and reddish, with a sharp, hideous countenance. The woman shrank back in fright. Jesus, pointing to the spirit, said: "This is he that has been accustomed to awake thee, but every human being has also a good angel. Prostrate before him and follow his advice!" At these words of Jesus, all perceived a beautiful luminous figure hovering near the woman. Tremblingly she prostrated before him. So long as satan stood beside the woman, the good angel remained behind her, but when he disappeared, the angel came forward. The woman, deeply affected, now returned to her place. She was called Cuppes. She was afterward baptized Serena by Thomas, under which name she was later martyred and venerated as a saint.

240

The husband of Cuppes was a son of Mensor's brother. He had, when a youth, accompanied his uncle to Bethlehem. He and Cuppes were of a yellowish-brown complexion, and both were descendants of Job.

Jesus left the city by the side upon which stood the temple and passed the magnificent tent of the converted Cuppes, who ran forward with her children to meet him. He drew the children to himself and spoke to the mother, who cast herself prostrate at his feet in tears.

Mira, Mother of Deodatus

WHEN Jesus commenced his remarkable journey to the land of the three kings, to Ur, and to Heliopolis (extending from August 7, AD 32 to January 7, AD 33), he took with him three shepherd youths (Eliud, Silas, and Eremenzear). Later he added Caisar as a fourth, and later still Deodatus as a fifth (by the end of this journey, there were sixteen such young disciples in all).

On Sunday, January 4, AD 33, when Jesus, escorted by many of the inhabitants, left Heliopolis, he took with him a young man belonging to the city, and who he now made his fifth disciple. His name was Deodatus, and that of his mother was Mira. She was that tall old lady who had, on the first evening of Jesus's arrival, been among those that welcomed him under the portico. During Mary's sojourn in Heliopolis, Mira was childless; but on the prayer of the Blessed Virgin, this son was afterward given her.[1] He was tall and slender and appeared to be about eighteen years old. When his escort had returned to the city, I saw Jesus journeying through the desert with his five disciples. He took a direction more to the east than that taken by the holy family on their flight into Egypt.

The Wife of Azarius, and Ratimiris (Emily)

THE story of Ratimiris and the wife of Azarius takes place in Atom, just after Jesus has left the tent city of the kings, commenc-

---

[1] The name means "given by God."

ing on Friday, October 3, AD 32. On this evening, while Jesus was celebrating the sabbath with the disciples in the open hut in which he had passed the night, I saw the sick wife of Azarias seeking her cure before an idol. The lady had many children, and I saw in her apartments several other women, maidservants perhaps. Back from the fireplace and in a corner between the apartments stood a slab, or table, supported on columns. On it was a beautiful pedestal pierced on all sides with holes and covered with a little ornamental roof of leaves and foliage. The pedestal supported an idol in the form of a sitting dog with a thick, flat head. It was resting upon some written pages that were fastened together with cords in the form of a book, one of its forepaws raised over it as if drawing attention to it. Above this idol arose another, a scandalous-looking figure with many arms. I saw priests bringing in fire from the pan near the temple and pouring it under the hollow figure of the sitting dog, whose eyes began to sparkle, and from his mouth and nose immediately issued fire and smoke.

Two women conducted Azarias's wife (who was afflicted with an issue of blood) up to the idol and placed her upon cushions and rugs before it. Azarias himself was present. The priests prayed, burnt incense, and offered sacrifice before the idol, but all to no purpose. Flames shot forth from it and in the dense black smoke issued horrible dog-like figures that disappeared in the air. The sick woman became perfectly miserable. She sank down faint and exhausted like one in a dying state, saying "These idols cannot help me! They are wicked spirits! They cannot longer remain here, they are fleeing from the prophet, the king of the Jews, who is among us. We have seen his star and have followed him! The prophet alone can help me!" After uttering these words, she fell back immovable and, to all appearances, lifeless.

The bystanders were filled with terror. They had been under the impression that Jesus was only an envoy of the king of the Jews. They went immediately to the retired hut in which he and the disciples were celebrating the sabbath and respectfully begged him to go to the sick woman. They told him that she had cried out that he alone could help her, and they informed him likewise of the impotence of their idols.

Jesus was still in his sabbatic robes, the disciples also, when they went to the sick woman, who was lying like one at the point of death. In earnest, vehement words, Jesus inveighed against idols and their worship. They were, he said, the servants of satan, and all in them was bad. He reproached Azarias for this, that after his return from Bethlehem, whither as a youth he had accompanied the kings, he had again sunk so deep into the abominations of idolatry. He concluded by saying that if they would believe in his doctrine, would obey the commandments of God, and would allow themselves to be baptized, he would in three years send his apostle to them, and he would now help the lady. Then he questioned the latter, and she answered: "Yes, I do believe in thee!" All the bystanders gave him the same assurance.

The screens had been removed from around the tent and a crowd of people were standing by. Jesus asked for a basin of water, but bade them not to bring it from their sacred fountain. He wanted only ordinary water, nor would he use their holy water sprinkler. They had to bring him a fresh branch with fine, narrow leaves. They had likewise to cover their idols, which they did with fine, white tapestry embroidered in gold. Jesus placed the water on the altar. The three disciples stood around him, one at either side, right and left, and the third behind him. One of them handed him a metal box from the wallet that they always carried with them. Several such boxes of oil and cotton were placed one above the other.

In that which the disciple handed to Jesus there was a fine, white powder, which appeared to me to be salt. Jesus sprinkled some of it on the water and bent low over it. He prayed, blessed it with his hand, dipped the branch into it, sprinkled the water over all around him, and extended his hand to the woman with the command to arise. She obeyed instantly and rose up cured. She threw herself on her knees and wanted to embrace his feet, but he would not suffer her to touch him.

This cure effected, Jesus proclaimed to the crowd that there was another lady present who was much more indisposed than the first and who, notwithstanding, did not ask his help. She adored not an idol, but a man. This lady, by name Ratimiris, was married. Her malady consisted in this, that at the sight, the name, or even the thought of a certain youth, she fell into a sort of fever

243

and became ill unto death. The youth, meanwhile, was perfectly ignorant of her state.[1]

Ratimiris, at the call of Jesus, stepped forward greatly confused. Jesus took her aside and laid before her all the circumstances both of her sickness and her sins, all which she freely acknowledged. The youth was one of the temple servers, and whenever she brought her offerings, which he was charged to receive, she fell into that sad state.

After Jesus had spoken awhile with her alone he led her again before the people and asked her whether she believed in him and whether she would be baptized when he would send his apostle hither. When she, deeply repentant, answered that she did believe and that she would be baptized, Jesus drove the devil out of her. The evil one departed in the form of a spiral column of black vapor.

The following day Jesus and the four youths[2] spent the day in prayer. At the close of the sabbath they went to the temple. Jesus taught the people and then gave instruction to the priests concerning the communion of bread and wine. He consecrated the bread and wine and blessed the priests. When the sabbath was over, Jesus called all together again and instructed them.

Azarias later on became a priest and martyr. The two women also whom Jesus cured here were afterward martyred, like Cuppes. The Lord spoke against a multiplicity of wives and gave instructions on the married state. The wife of Azarias, as well as Ratimiris, wanted Jesus to baptize them right away. He replied that he could indeed do so, but that it would be inopportune. He must first return to the Father and send the consoler, after which his apostles would come and baptize them. They should, he said, live in the desire of baptism and submission to his will, and such dispositions would, to those that might die in the interim, serve as baptism.

---

[1] The youth's name was Caisar, and more can be read of him (as also of the other youths who accompanied Jesus on his journey to the East) in *People of the New Testament IV.*

[2] That is, the three shepherd youths, who accompanied Jesus on this journey, and the youth Caisar.

Ratimiris was in fact baptized under the name of Emily by Thomas when, three years after Christ's Ascension, he visited this country accompanied by Thaddeus and Caisar. They came in a direction more from the south than did Jesus, and it was then that the kings and their people were baptized.

87686027R00168

Made in the USA
San Bernardino, CA
06 September 2018